The Essential
CHÖGYAM TRUNGPA

The Essential
CHÖGYAM TRUNGPA

Edited by Carolyn Rose Gimian

SHAMBHALA
Boston & London
1999

SHAMBHALA PUBLICATIONS, INC.
Horticultural Hall
300 Massachusetts Avenue
Boston, Massachusetts 02115
www.shambhala.com

9   8   7   6   5   4   3   2

Printed in the United States of America
⊚ This edition is printed on acid-free paper that meets
the American National Standards Institute z39.48 Standard.
Distributed in the United States by Random House, Inc.,
and in Canada by Random House of Canada Ltd

Library of Congress Cataloging-in-Publication Data
Trungpa, Chogyam, 1939–
     The essential Chögyam Trungpa/edited by Carolyn Rose Gimian.—
  1st ed.
        p.   cm.
     Includes index.
     ISBN 1-57062-466-6 (alk. paper)
        1. Spiritual life—Buddhism.   2. Spiritual life—Tantric Buddhism.
  3. Tantric Buddhism—Doctrines.   I. Gimian, Carolyn Rose.
  II. Title.
  BQ4302.T782   1999   99-13945
  294.3'923—dc21   CIP

CONTENTS

EDITOR'S PREFACE

CHÖGYAM TRUNGPA was among the very first Tibetan Buddhist lamas to present the Buddhist teachings in English to Westerners and to publish those teachings in the English language. In 1966, Chögyam Trungpa published his account of his upbringing as a high lama in Tibet and recounted his daring escape over the Himalayas. Aptly enough, he entitled his first book *Born in Tibet*.

In the early 1970s, having spent a number of years in England (talks from these years were gathered together and published in *Meditation in Action*) and then having moved to North America, Chögyam Trungpa published the first collection of his talks in America. *Cutting through Spiritual Materialism* quickly garnered a substantial reputation on the American spiritual scene. It remains a classic today. Several other titles, including the popular *Myth of Freedom*, followed in the 1970s.

Then, in 1984, Trungpa Rinpoche published another title that broke new ground and captured the attention of a large readership. *Shambhala: The Sacred Path of the Warrior* presented meditation as the path to what Trungpa Rinpoche referred to as "secular enlightenment." The last book published before his death in 1987, it is available today not only in English but in nine foreign editions. Altogether, between his arrival in England in 1963 and his death in Canada in 1987, thirteen books of his were published in trade editions. In addition to his dharma teachings, two books of poetry were published as well as a translation of *The Tibetan Book of the Dead* with Francesca Fremantle and several other translations from the Tibetan, joint efforts of Trungpa Rinpoche and the Nalanda Translation Committee.

Remarkably, since his passing, two of his senior editors, Judith Lief and Sherab Chödzin, have edited almost a dozen additional books of Trungpa Rinpoche's Buddhist teachings. Among these, Ms. Lief has also edited two books that show us Chögyam Trungpa as artist: *The Art of Calligraphy: Joining Heaven and Earth* and *Dharma Art*. Trungpa Rinpoche's poetry has also been newly selected and presented in *Timely Rain*, edited by David I. Rome. And in addition to these trade editions, Vajradhatu Publications (the publishing arm of Chögyam Trungpa's meditation centers) continues to publish limited editions of edited transcripts and special-interest titles. All of this may be just the beginning of the literary legacy that he leaves us, for there remain several thousand dharma talks that could be transcribed, edited, and published.

The Essential Chögyam Trungpa is drawn from his two dozen books published by Shambhala Publications over the last thirty years. A complete listing of these titles can be found at the back of this volume. While I reread and considered all of these books, not all are represented here. *The Essential Chögyam Trungpa* includes thirty-eight selections drawn from fifteen published sources, one unpublished poem, and a chapter from the forthcoming *Great Eastern Sun: The Wisdom of Shambhala*. The present volume includes material on both the Buddhist and the Shambhala teachings. It includes a sprinkling of Chögyam Trungpa's poems and several chapters on the theme of art but does not attempt to treat these aspects of his teaching comprehensively. The Shambhala teachings are presented first in this volume, although they were the later teachings given by Trungpa Rinpoche. Their accessibility and heartfelt nature made them seem the best introductory material for this book.

Although drawn from the diverse archive of Trungpa Rinpoche's published work, this volume has been structured to be read as a coherent whole. Rather than picking a page here and a page there, I generally have chosen complete chapters from his books, to allow the flavor and flow of his teaching style to come through. The reader will no doubt notice differences in tone, language, and style from one chapter to the next. Nevertheless, there is a unifying thread that runs through the material and connects it, one hopes, in a compelling fashion.

That thread is the essence of the teachings. Chögyam Trungpa was a master in presenting that essential quality, free from the trappings of exotic culture. The word *essence* comes to us from the Latin *esse,* "to be." If one were to summarize Trungpa Rinpoche's teachings in a single word or phrase, surely *being* and *how to be* might be terms one would choose. It was his passion, and one might even say his mission, to present the essence of nowness, the essence of being, as it manifests in all activities of life. Thus, it seems singularly appropriate to speak of the essential Chögyam Trungpa and to give that title to this book.

Trungpa Rinpoche presented the essence of the Shambhala path as basic goodness: the human nature of genuine tenderness and bravery. Within the Buddhist path, he often taught in terms of a journey through the three *yanas—hinayana, mahayana,* and *vajrayana—*the three great vehicles or schools of Buddhism. That three-yana structure has been incorporated into this book. The essence of the hinayana, or the narrow path, is the realization of egolessness through the practice of meditation. In the mahayana, the open path, the inherent quality of human wakefulness, or one's buddha nature, is an essential element. And on the diamond path of vajrayana, the essence is *vajra* nature: the indestructibility of sanity and wisdom. Whatever the subject, Chögyam Trungpa spoke from the heart and addressed the heart of the matter. His teaching was multifaceted and multidimensional. He spoke at once to both beginning practitioners and seasoned meditators.

In reviewing his published work to make selections for this volume, I was particularly struck by the inclusive, or nondualistic, nature of his teaching. Whatever the experience of the practitioner, whatever human strengths and weaknesses one possesses, Trungpa Rinpoche always encouraged us to start with the raw materials and not to reject any part of ourselves. In that sense as well, he spoke to what is essential in human beings and pointed out how it can be found throughout our experience, throughout our lives, good and bad, happy and sad.

One cannot adequately introduce *The Essential Chögyam Trungpa* without noting the author's remarkable grasp of English. Chögyam Trungpa loved the English language. He studied it; he played with it; and in the 1970s, he employed it to pioneer the language of Buddhism in America. By this, I mean that he sought and found English words and phrases that would aptly convey the essence of the Tibetan Buddhist teachings in their new home: in the West and specifically in North America. He was a major force in the creation of a lexicon for the presentation of Buddhism in America, one that is used by virtually every teacher today. For example, while he certainly did not invent the word *ego*, he popularized the use of this term for the concept of *atman*, the self or the soul. And he used the term *egolessness* to apply to *anatman*, or the insubstantiality of self. "Cutting through spiritual materialism"; "buddhadharma without credentials"; "one taste"; "crazy wisdom"; "back to square one"; "first thought-best thought"; "cool boredom"; "basic goodness"—these are but a few of the colorful phrases he employed to describe the noble path of the Buddha and the warrior's sacred journey toward enlightened society.

I hope that the reader will enjoy the feast of teachings in this book and enjoy the words that Chögyam Trungpa used to serve up this feast. It has been daunting but rewarding to select the courses from the myriad ingredients that might have been used. Although this book seeks to present the essential Chögyam Trungpa, it is far from exhaustive. Some may find this a complete meal, but for many it will merely whet their appetite, like an hors d'oeuvre of *nowness*. For those readers, there are more than seventeen of his books still in print from which to choose.

May this book serve to introduce you to the work of this extraordinary dharma master. May it proclaim genuine dharma in all directions.

Carolyn Rose Gimian
Halifax, Nova Scotia
October 1998

EDITOR'S NOTE

IN A VERY FEW PLACES in *The Essential Chögyam Trungpa,* I have made editorial changes. To create continuity from one chapter to the next, I have sometimes changed or reordered the opening sentences of a chapter. In several chapters, gender references have been modernized, and in some places, I have omitted material so specific to the original book that it would not be appropriate in its new context. Spelling, punctuation, and capitalization have been somewhat standardized, but some differences from one source to another remain.

C.R.G.

The Essential
CHÖGYAM TRUNGPA

The Dohā of Confidence
Sad Song of the Four Remembrances

As I look constantly to the Great Eastern Sun,
Remembering the only father guru,
Overwhelming devotion blazes like a bonfire—
I, Chökyi Gyatso, remain alone.

Having been abandoned by my heart friends,
Though my feverish mind feels great longing,
It is joyful that I am sustained by this great confidence
Of the only father guru and the Great Eastern Sun.

Having seen the beauty of a mist covering the mountain,
The pines moving gently in the wind,
The firm power of rock-hard earth,
I am constantly reminded of the splendor and beauty
Of the only father guru and the Great Eastern Sun.

Wildflowers extend everywhere
On mountain meadows filled with the sweet smell of fragrant herbs.
Seeing the gentle deer frolicking from place to place,
I constantly remember the compassion and gentleness
Of the only father guru and the Great Eastern Sun.

Fighting enemies in the chasm of love and hate,
Having sharpened the weapon's point of joy and sorrow, hope and fear,
Seeing again and again these cowardly hordes,
I take refuge in the sole confidence
Of the only father guru and the Great Eastern Sun.

Fatherless, always dwelling in foreign lands,
Motherless, not hearing the speech of my own country,
Friendless, tears not quenching my thirst,
Remembering the warriors of the father and mother lineages,
I live alone in the sole blessing
Of the only father guru and the Great Eastern Sun.

The Rain of Wisdom, Page 289

Part I
THE SACRED PATH
OF THE WARRIOR

The Shambhala teachings are founded on the premise that there is basic human wisdom that can help solve the world's problems. This wisdom does not belong to any one culture or religion, nor does it come only from the West or the East. Rather, it is a tradition of human warriorship that has existed in many cultures at many times throughout history.

Creating an
Enlightened Society

IN TIBET, as well as many other Asian countries, there are stories about a legendary kingdom that was a source of learning and culture for present-day Asian societies. According to the legends, this was a place of peace and prosperity, governed by wise and compassionate rulers. The citizens were equally kind and learned, so that, in general, the kingdom was a model society. This place was called Shambhala.

It is said that Buddhism played an important role in the development of the Shambhala society. The legends tell us that Shakyamuni Buddha gave advanced tantric teachings to the first king of Shambhala, Dawa Sangpo. These teachings, which are preserved as the *Kalacakra Tantra,* are considered to be among the most profound wisdom of Tibetan Buddhism. After the king had received this instruction, the stories say that all of the people of Shambhala began to practice meditation and to follow the Buddhist path of loving kindness and concern for all beings. In this way, not just the rulers but all of the subjects of the kingdom became highly developed people.

Among the Tibetan people, there is a popular belief that the kingdom of Shambhala can still be found, hidden in a remote valley somewhere in the Himalayas. There are, as well, a number of Buddhist texts that give detailed but obscure directions for reaching Shambhala, but there are mixed opinions as to whether these should be taken literally or metaphorically. There are also many texts that give us elaborate descriptions of the kingdom. For example, according to the *Great Commentary on the Kalacakra* by the renowned nineteenth-century Buddhist teacher Mipham, the land of Shambhala is north of the river Sita, and the country is divided by eight mountain ranges. The palace of the Rigdens, or the imperial rulers of Shambhala, is built on top of a circular mountain in the center of the country. This mountain, Mipham tells us, is named Kailasa. The palace, which is called the palace of Kalapa, comprises many square miles. In front of it to the south is a beautiful park known as Malaya, and in the middle of the park is a temple devoted to Kalacakra that was built by Dawa Sangpo.

Other legends say that the kingdom of Shambhala disappeared from the earth many centuries ago. At a certain point, the entire society had become enlightened, and the kingdom vanished into another more celestial realm. According to these stories, the Rigden kings of Shambhala continue to watch over human affairs and will one day return to earth to save humanity from destruction. Many Tibetans believe that the great Tibetan warrior king Gesar of Ling was inspired and guided by the Ringdens and the Shambhala wisdom. This reflects the belief in the celestial existence of the kingdom. Gesar is thought not to have traveled to Shambhala, so his link to the kingdom was a spiritual one. He lived in approximately the eleventh century and ruled the provincial kingdom of Ling, which is located in the province of Kham, east Tibet. Following Gesar's reign, stories about his accomplishments as a warrior and ruler sprang up throughout Tibet, eventually becoming the greatest epic of Tibetan literature. Some legends say that Gesar will reappear from Shambhala, leading an army to conquer the forces of darkness in the world.

In recent years, some Western scholars have suggested that the kingdom of Shambhala may actually have been one of the historically documented kingdoms of early times, such as the Zhang-Zhung kingdom of Central Asia. Many scholars, however, believe that the stories of Shambhala are completely mythical. While it is easy enough to dismiss the kingdom of Shambhala as pure fiction, it is also possible to see in this legend the expression of a deeply rooted and very real human desire for a good and fulfilling life. In fact, among many Tibetan Buddhist teachers, there has long been a tradition that regards the kingdom of Shambhala, not as an external place, but as the ground or root of wakefulness and sanity that exists as a potential within every human being. From that point of view, it is not important to determine whether the kingdom of Shambhala is fact or fiction. Instead, we should appreciate and emulate the ideal of an enlightened society that it represents.

I have presented a series of "Shambhala teachings" that use the image of the Shambhala kingdom to represent the ideal of secular enlightenment—that is, the possibility of uplifting our personal existence and that of others without the help of any religious outlook. For although the Shambhala tradition is founded on the sanity and gentleness of the Buddhist tradition, at the same time, it has its own independent basis, which is directly cultivating who and what we are as human beings. With the great problems now facing human society, it seems increasingly important to find simple and nonsectarian ways to work with ourselves and to share our understanding with others. The Shambhala teachings or "Shambhala vision," as this approach is more broadly called, is one such attempt to encourage a wholesome existence for ourselves and others.

The current state of world affairs is a source of concern to all of us: the threat of nuclear war, widespread poverty and economic instability, social and political chaos, and psychological upheavals of many kinds. The world is in absolute turmoil. The Shambhala teachings are founded on the premise that there *is* basic human wisdom that can help to solve the world's problems. This wisdom does not belong to any one culture or religion, nor does it come only from the West or the East. Rather, it is a tradition of human warriorship that has existed in many cultures at many times throughout history.

Warriorship here does not refer to making war on others. Aggression is the source of our problems, not the solution. Here the word *warrior* is taken from the Tibetan *pawo,* which literally means "one who is brave." Warriorship in this context is the tradition of human bravery, or the tradition of fearlessness. The North American Indians had such a tradition, and it also existed in South American Indian societies. The Japanese ideal of the samurai also represented a warrior tradition of wisdom, and there have been principles of enlightened warriorship in Western Christian societies as well. King Arthur is a legendary example of warriorship in the Western tradition, and great rulers in the Bible, such as King

David, are examples of warriors common to both the Jewish and Christian traditions. On our planet Earth, there have been many fine examples of warriorship.

The key to warriorship and the first principle of Shambhala vision is not being afraid of who you are. Ultimately, that is the definition of bravery: not being afraid of yourself. Shambhala vision teaches that in the face of the world's great problems, we can be heroic and kind at the same time. Shambhala vision is the opposite of selfishness. When we are afraid of ourselves and afraid of the seeming threat the world presents, then we become extremely selfish. We want to build our own little nests, our own cocoons, so that we can live by ourselves in a secure way.

But we can be much more brave than that. We must try to think beyond our homes, beyond the fire burning in the fireplace, beyond sending our children to school or getting to work in the morning. We must try to think how we can help this world. If we don't help, nobody will. It is our turn to help the world. At the same time, helping others does not mean abandoning our individual lives. You don't have to rush out to become the mayor of your city or the president of the United States in order to help others, but you can begin with your relatives and friends and the people around you. In fact, you can start with yourself. The important point is to realize that you are never off duty. You can never just relax, because the whole world needs help.

While everyone has a responsibility to help the world, we can create additional chaos if we try to impose our ideas or our help upon others. Many people have theories about what the world needs. Some people think that the world needs communism; some people think that the world needs democracy; some people think that technology will save the world; some people think that technology will destroy the world. The Shambhala teachings are not based on converting the world to another theory. The premise of Shambhala vision is that in order to establish an enlightened society for others, we need to discover what inherently we have to offer the world. So to begin with, we should make an effort to examine our own experience, in order to see what it contains that is of value in helping ourselves and others to uplift their existence.

If we are willing to take an unbiased look, we will find that in spite of all our problems and confusion, all our emotional and psychological ups and downs, there is something basically good about our existence as human beings. Unless we can discover that ground of goodness in our own lives, we cannot hope to improve the lives of others. If we are simply miserable and wretched beings, how can we possibly imagine, let alone realize, an enlightened society?

Discovering real goodness comes from appreciating very simple experiences. We are not talking about how good it feels to make a million dollars or finally graduate from college or buy a new house, but we are speaking here of the basic goodness of being alive—which does not depend on our accomplishments or fulfilling our desires. We experience glimpses of goodness all the time, but we often fail to acknowledge them. When we see a bright color, we are witnessing our own inherent goodness. When we hear a beautiful sound, we are hearing our own basic goodness. When we step out of the shower, we feel fresh and clean, and when we walk out of a stuffy room, we appreciate the sudden whiff of fresh air. These events may take a fraction of a second, but they are real experiences of goodness. They happen to us all the time, but usually we ignore them as mundane or purely coincidental. According to the Shambhala principles, however, it is worthwhile to recognize and take advantage of those moments, because they are revealing basic nonaggression and freshness in our lives—basic goodness.

Every human being has a basic nature of goodness, which is undiluted and unconfused. That goodness contains tremendous gentleness and appreciation. As human beings, we can make love. We can stroke someone with a gentle touch; we can kiss someone with gentle understanding. We can appreciate beauty. We can appreciate the best of this world. We can appreciate its vividness: the yellowness of yellow, the redness of red, the greenness of green, the purpleness of purple. Our experience is real. When yellow is yellow, can we say it is red if we don't like the yellowness of it? That would be contradicting reality. When we have sunshine, can we reject it and say that the sunshine is terrible? Can we really say that? When we have brilliant sunshine or wonderful snowfall, we appreciate it. And when we appreciate reality, it can actually work on us. We may have to get up in the morning after only a few hours' sleep, but if we look out the window and see the sun shining, it can cheer us up. We can actually cure ourselves of depression if we recognize that the world we have is good.

It is not just an arbitrary idea that the world is good, but it is good because we can *experience* its goodness. We can experience our world as healthy and straightforward, direct and real, because our basic nature is to go along with the goodness of situations. The human potential for intelligence and dignity is attuned to experiencing the brilliance of the bright blue sky, the freshness of green fields, and the beauty of the trees and mountains. We have an actual connection to reality that can wake us up and make us feel basically, fundamentally good. Shambhala vision is tuning in to our ability to wake ourselves up and recognize that goodness can happen to us. In fact, it is happening already.

But then, there is still a question. You might have made a genuine connection to your world: catching a glimpse of sunshine, seeing bright colors, hearing good music, eating good food, or whatever it may be. But how does a glimpse of goodness relate with ongoing experience? On the one hand, you might feel: "I want to get that goodness that is in me and in the phenomenal world." So you rush around trying to find a way to possess it. Or on an even cruder level, you might say: "How much does it cost to get that? That experience was so beautiful. I want to own it." The basic problem with that approach is that you never feel satisfied even if you get what you want, because you still *want* so badly. If you take a walk on Fifth Avenue, you see that kind of desperation. You might say that the people shopping on Fifth Avenue have good taste and that therefore they have possibilities of realizing human dignity. But on the other hand, it is as though they were covered with thorns. They want to grasp more and more and more.

Then, there is the approach of surrendering or humbling yourself to get in touch with goodness. Someone tells you that he can make you happy if you will just give your life to his cause. If you believe that he has the goodness that you want, you may be willing to shave your hair or wear robes or crawl on the floor or eat with your hands to get in touch with goodness. You are willing to trade in your dignity and become a slave.

Both of those situations are attempts to retrieve something good, something real. If you are rich, you are willing to spend thousands of dollars on it. If you are poor, you are willing to commit your life to it. But there is something wrong with both of those approaches.

The problem is that when we begin to realize the potential goodness in ourselves, we often take our discovery much too seriously. We might kill for goodness or die for goodness; we want it so badly. What is lacking is a sense of humor. Humor here does not mean telling jokes or being comical or criticizing others and laughing at them. A genuine sense of humor is having a light touch: not beating reality into the ground but appreciating reality with a light touch. The basis of Shambhala vision is rediscovering that perfect and real sense of humor, that light touch of appreciation.

If you look at yourself, if you look at your mind, if you look at your activities, you can repossess the humor that you have lost in the course of your life. To begin with, you have to look at your ordinary domestic reality: your knives, your forks, your plates, your telephone, your dishwasher, and your towels—ordinary things. There is nothing mystical or extraordinary about them, but if there is no connection with ordinary everyday situations, if you don't examine your mundane life, then you will never find any humor or dignity or, ultimately, any reality.

The way you comb your hair, the way you dress, the way you wash your dishes—all of those activities are an extension of sanity; they are a way of connecting with reality. A fork is a fork, of course. It is a simple implement of eating. But at the same time, the extension of your sanity and your dignity may depend on how you use your fork. Very simply, Shambhala vision is trying to provoke you to understand how you live, your relationship with ordinary life.

As human beings, we are basically awake and we *can* understand reality. We are not enslaved by our lives; we are free. Being free, in this case, means simply that we have a body and a mind, and we can uplift ourselves in order to work with reality in a dignified and humorous way. If we begin to perk up, we will find that the whole universe—including the seasons, the snowfall, the ice, and the mud—is also powerfully working with us. Life is a humorous situation, but it is not mocking us. We find that, after all, we can handle our world; we can handle our universe properly and fully in an uplifted fashion.

The discovery of basic goodness is not a religious experience, particularly. Rather, it is the realization that we can directly experience and work with reality, the real world that we are in. Experiencing the basic goodness of our lives makes us feel that we are intelligent and decent people and that the world is not a threat. When we feel that our lives are genuine and good, we do not have to deceive ourselves or other people. We can see our shortcomings without feeling guilty or inadequate, and at the same time, we can see our potential for extending goodness to others. We can tell the truth straightforwardly and be absolutely open, but steadfast at the same time.

The essence of warriorship, or the essence of human bravery, is refusing to give up on anyone or anything. We can never say that we are simply falling to pieces or that anyone else is, and we can never say that about the world either. Within our lifetime, there will be great problems in the world, but let us make sure that, within our lifetime, no disasters happen. We can prevent them. It is up to us. We can save the world from destruction, to begin with. That is why Shambhala vision exists. It is a centuries-old idea: by serving this world, we can save it. But saving the world is not enough. We have to work to build an enlightened human society as well.

Shambhala: The Sacred Path of the Warrior, Pages 25–34

Discovering
Basic Goodness

A GREAT DEAL OF chaos in the world occurs because people don't appreciate themselves. Having never developed sympathy or gentleness toward themselves, they cannot experience harmony or peace within themselves, and therefore, what they project to others is also inharmonious and confused. Instead of appreciating our lives, we often take our existence for granted or we find it depressing and burdensome. People threaten to commit suicide because they aren't getting what they think they deserve out of life. They blackmail others with the threat of suicide, saying that they will kill themselves if certain things don't change. Certainly we should take our lives seriously, but that doesn't mean driving ourselves to the brink of disaster by complaining about our problems or holding a grudge against the world. We have to accept personal responsibility for uplifting our lives.

When you don't punish or condemn yourself, when you relax more and appreciate your body and mind, you begin to contact the fundamental notion of basic goodness in yourself. So it is extremely important to be willing to open yourself to yourself. Developing tenderness toward yourself allows you to see both your problems and your potential accurately. You don't feel that you have to ignore your problems or exaggerate your potential. That kind of gentleness toward yourself and appreciation of yourself is very necessary. It provides the ground for helping yourself and others.

As human beings, we have a working basis within ourselves that allows us to uplift our state of existence and cheer up fully. That working basis is always available to us. We have a mind and a body, which are very precious to us. Because we have a mind and body, we can comprehend this world. Existence is wonderful and precious. We don't know how long we will live, so while we have our life, why not make use of it? Before we even make use of it, why don't we appreciate it?

How do we discover this kind of appreciation? Wishful thinking or simply talking about it does not help. In the Shambhala tradition, the discipline for developing both gentleness toward ourselves and appreciation of our world is the sitting practice of meditation. The practice of meditation was taught by the Lord Buddha over twenty-five hundred years ago, and it has been part of the Shambhala tradition since that time. It is based on an oral tradition: from the time of the Buddha, this practice has been transmitted from one human being to another. In this way, it has remained a living tradition, so that, although it is an ancient practice, it is still up to date. In this chapter, we are going to discuss the technique of meditation in some detail, but it is important to remember that if you want to fully understand this practice, you need direct, personal instruction.

By *meditation* here, we mean something very basic and simple that is not tied to any one culture. We are talking about a very basic act: sitting on the ground, assuming a good posture, and developing a sense of our spot, our place on this earth. This is the means of rediscovering ourselves and our basic goodness, the means to tune ourselves in to genuine reality, without any expectations or preconceptions.

The word *meditation* is sometimes used to mean contemplating a particular theme or object: meditating *on* such and such a thing. By meditating on a question or problem, we can find the solution to it. Sometimes meditation also is connected with achieving a higher state of mind by entering into a trance or absorption state of some kind. But here we are talking about a completely different concept of meditation: unconditional meditation, without any object or idea in mind. In the Shambhala tradition, meditation is simply training our state of being so that our mind and body can be synchronized. Through the practice of meditation, we can learn to be without deception, to be fully genuine and alive.

Our life is an endless journey; it is like a broad highway that extends infintely into the distance. The practice of meditation provides a vehicle to travel on that road. Our journey consists of constant ups and downs, hope and fear, but it is a good journey. The practice of meditation allows us to experience all the textures of the roadway, which is what the journey is all about. Through the practice of meditation, we begin to find that, within ourselves, there is no fundamental complaint about anything or anyone at all.

Meditation practice begins by sitting down and assuming your seat cross-legged on the ground. You begin to feel that, by simply being on the spot, your life can become workable and even wonderful. You realize that you are capable of sitting like a king or queen on a throne. The regalness of that situation shows you the dignity that comes from being still and simple.

In the practice of meditation, an upright posture is extremely important. Having an upright back is not an artificial posture. It is natural to the human body. When you slouch, that is unusual. You can't breathe properly when you slouch, and slouching also is a sign of giving in to neurosis. So when you sit erect, you are proclaiming to yourself and to the rest of the world that you are going to be a warrior, a fully human being.

To have a straight back you do not have to strain yourself by pulling up your shoulders; the uprightness comes naturally from sitting simply but proudly on the ground or on your meditation cushion. Then, because your back is upright, you feel no trace of shyness or embarrassment, so you do not hold your head down. You are not bending to anything. Because of that, your shoulders become straight automatically, so you develop a good sense of head and shoulders. Then you can allow your legs to rest naturally in a cross-legged position; your knees do not have to touch the ground. You complete your posture by placing your hands lightly, palms down, on your thighs. This provides a further sense of assuming your spot properly.

In that posture, you don't just gaze randomly around. You have a sense that you are *there* properly; therefore, your eyes are open, but your gaze is directed slightly downward, maybe six feet in front of you. In that way, your vision does not wander here and

I-Chou Lohan. This statue shows one of the disciples of the Buddha in the posture of meditation. *Courtesy Robert Newman. Photograph by Betty Morris. From the collection of the British Museum.*

there, but you have a further sense of deliberateness and definiteness. You can see this royal pose in some Egyptian and South American sculptures, as well as in Oriental statues. It is a universal posture, not limited to one culture or time.

In your daily life, you should also be aware of your posture, your head and shoulders, how you walk, and how you look at people. Even when you are not meditating, you can maintain a dignified state of existence. You can transcend your embarrassment and take pride in being a human being. Such pride is acceptable and good.

Then, in meditation practice, as you sit with a good posture, you pay attention to your breath. When you breathe, you are utterly there, properly there. You go out with the outbreath, your breath dissolves, and then the inbreath happens naturally. Then you go out again. So there is a constant going out with the outbreath. As you breathe out, you dissolve, you diffuse. Then your inbreath occurs naturally; you don't have to follow it in. You simply come back to your posture, and you are ready for another outbreath. Go out and dissolve: *tshoo;* then come back to your posture; then *tshoo,* and come back to your posture.

Then there will be an inevitable *bing!*—thought. At that point, you say, "thinking." You don't say it out loud; you say it mentally: "thinking." Labeling your thoughts gives you tremendous leverage to come back to your breath. When one thought takes you away completely from what you are actually doing—when you do not even realize that you are on the cushion, but in your mind you are in San Francisco or New York City—you say "thinking," and you bring yourself back to the breath.

It doesn't really matter what thoughts you have. In the sitting practice of meditation, whether you have monstrous thoughts or benevolent thoughts, all of them are regarded purely as thinking. They are neither virtuous nor sinful. You might have a thought of assassinating your father, or you might want to make lemonade and eat cookies. Please don't be shocked by your thoughts: any thought is just thinking. No thought deserves a gold medal or a reprimand. Just label your thoughts "thinking," then go back to your breath. "Thinking," back to the breath; "thinking," back to the breath.

The practice of meditation is very precise. It has to be on the dot, right on the dot. It is quite hard work, but if you remember the importance of your posture, that will allow you to synchronize your mind and body. If you don't have good posture, your practice will be like a lame horse trying to pull a cart. It will never work. So first you sit down and assume your posture, then you work with your breath; *tshoo*, go out, come back to your posture; *tshoo*, come back to your posture; *tshoo*. When thoughts arise, you label them "thinking" and come back to your posture, back to your breath. You have mind working with breath, but you always maintain body as a reference point. You are not working with your mind alone. You are working with your mind and your body, and when the two work together, you never leave reality.

The ideal state of tranquillity comes from experiencing body and mind being synchronized. If body and mind are unsynchronized, then your body will slump—and your mind will be somewhere else. It is like a badly made drum: the skin doesn't fit the frame of the drum, so either the frame breaks or the skin breaks, and there is no constant tautness. When mind and body are synchronized, then, because of your good posture, your breathing happens naturally; and because your breathing and your posture work together, your mind has a reference point to check back to. Therefore, your mind will go out naturally with the breath.

This method of synchronizing your mind and body is training you to be very simple and to feel that you are not special, but ordinary, extra-ordinary. You sit simply, as a warrior, and out of that, a sense of individual dignity arises. You are sitting on the earth, and you realize that this earth deserves you and you deserve this earth. You are there—fully, personally, genuinely. So meditation practice in the Shambhala tradition is designed to educate people to be honest and genuine, true to themselves.

In some sense, we should regard ourselves as being burdened: we have the burden of helping this world. We cannot forget this responsibility to others. But if we take our burden as a delight, we can actually liberate this world. The way to begin is with ourselves. From being open and honest with ourselves, we can also learn to be open with others. So we can work with the rest of the world, on the basis of the goodness we discover in ourselves. Therefore, meditation practice is regarded as a good, and in fact excellent, way to overcome warfare in the world: our own warfare as well as greater warfare.

Shambhala: The Sacred Path of the Warrior, Pages 35–41

The Genuine Heart
of Sadness

IMAGINE THAT YOU are sitting naked on the ground, with your bare bottom touching the earth. Since you are not wearing a scarf or hat, you are also exposed to heaven above. You are sandwiched between heaven and earth: a naked man or woman, sitting between heaven and earth.

Earth is always earth. The earth will let anyone sit on it, and earth never gives way. It never lets you go—you don't drop off this earth and go flying through outer space. Likewise, sky is always sky; heaven is always heaven above you. Whether it is snowing or raining or the sun is shining, whether it is daytime or nighttime, the sky is always there. In that sense, we know that heaven and earth are trustworthy.

The logic of basic goodness is very similar. When we speak of basic goodness, we are not talking about having allegiance to good and rejecting bad. Basic goodness is good because it is unconditional, or fundamental. It is there already, in the same way that heaven and earth are there already. We don't reject our atmosphere. We don't reject the sun and the moon, the clouds and the sky. We accept them. We accept that the sky is blue; we accept the landscape and the sea. We accept highways and buildings and cities. Basic goodness is that basic, that unconditional. It is not a "for" or "against" view, in the same way that sunlight is not "for" or "against."

The natural law and order of this world is not "for" or "against." Fundamentally, there is nothing that either threatens us or promotes our point of view. The four seasons occur free from anyone's demand or vote. Hope and fear cannot alter the seasons.

There is day; there is night. There is darkness at night and light during the day, and no one has to turn a switch on and off. There is a natural law and order that allows us to survive, and that is basically good, good in that it is there and it works and it is efficient.

We often take for granted this basic law and order in the universe, but we should think twice. We should appreciate what we have. Without it, we would be in a total predicament. If we didn't have sunlight, we wouldn't have any vegetation, we wouldn't have any crops, and we couldn't cook a meal. So basic goodness is good *because* it is so basic, so fundamental. It is natural and it works, and therefore, it is good, rather than being good as opposed to bad.

The same principle applies to our makeup as human beings. We have passion, aggression, and ignorance. That is, we cultivate our friends and we ward off our enemies and we are occasionally indifferent. Those tendencies are not regarded as shortcomings. They are part of the natural elegance and equipment of human beings. We are equipped with nails and teeth to defend ourselves against attack, we are equipped with a mouth and genitals to relate with others, and we are lucky enough to have complete digestive and respiratory systems so that we can process what we take in and flush it out. Human existence is a natural situation, and like the law and order of the world, it is workable and efficient. In fact, it is wonderful, it is ideal.

Some people might say this world is the work of a divine principle, but the Shambhala teachings are not concerned with divine origins. The point of warriorship is to work personally with our situation now, as it is. From the Shambhala point of view, when we say that human beings are basically good, we mean that they have every faculty they need, so that they don't have to fight with their world. Our being is good because it is not a fundamental source of aggression or complaint. We cannot complain that we have eyes, ears, a nose, and a mouth. We cannot redesign our physiological system, and for that matter, we cannot redesign our state of mind. Basic goodness is what we have, what we are provided with. It is the natural situation that we have inherited from birth onward.

We should feel that it is wonderful to be in this world. How wonderful it is to see red and yellow, blue and green, purple and black! All of these colors are provided for us. We feel hot and cold; we taste sweet and sour. We have these sensations, and we deserve them. They are good.

So the first step in realizing basic goodness is to appreciate what we have. But then we should look further and more precisely at what we are, where we are, who we are, when we are, and how we are as human beings, so that we can take possession of our basic goodness. It is not really a possession, but nonetheless, we deserve it.

Basic goodness is very closely connected to the idea of *bodhicitta* in the Buddhist tradition. *Bodhi* means "awake" or "wakeful," and *citta* means "heart," so *bodhicitta* is "awakened heart." Such awakened heart comes from being willing to face your state of mind. That may seem like a great demand, but it is necessary. You should examine yourself and ask how many times you have tried to connect with your heart, fully and truly. How often have you turned away, because you feared you might discover something terrible about yourself? How often have you been willing to look at your face in the mirror, without being embarrassed? How many times have you tried to shield yourself by reading the newspaper, watching television, or just spacing out? That is the sixty-four-thousand–dollar question: how much have you connected with yourself at all in your whole life?

The sitting practice of meditation, as we discussed in the last chapter, is the means to rediscover basic goodness, and beyond that, it is the means to awaken this genuine heart within yourself. When you sit in the posture of meditation, you are exactly the naked man or woman whom we described earlier, sitting between heaven and earth. When you slouch, you are trying to hide your heart, trying to protect it by slumping over. But when you sit upright but relaxed in the posture of meditation, your heart is naked. Your entire being is exposed—to yourself, first of all, but to others as well. So through the practice of sitting still and following your breath as it goes out and dissolves, you are connecting with your heart. By simply letting yourself be, as you are, you develop genuine sympathy toward yourself.

When you awaken your heart in this way, you find, to your surprise, that your heart is empty. You find that you are looking into outer space. What are you, who are you, where is your heart? If you really look, you won't find anything tangible and solid. Of course, you might find something *very* solid if you have a grudge against someone or you have fallen possessively in love. But that is not awakened heart. If you search for awakened heart, if you put your hand through your rib cage and feel for it, there is nothing there except for tenderness. You feel sore and soft, and if you open your eyes to the rest of the world, you feel tremendous sadness. This kind of sadness doesn't come from being mistreated. You don't feel sad because someone has insulted you or because you feel impoverished. Rather, this experience of sadness is unconditioned. It occurs because your heart is completely exposed. There is no skin or tissue covering it; it is pure raw meat. Even if a tiny mosquito lands on it, you feel so touched. Your experience is raw and tender and so personal.

The genuine heart of sadness comes from feeling that your nonexistent heart is full. You would like to spill your heart's blood, give your heart to others. For the warrior, this experience of sad and tender heart is what gives birth to fearlessness. Conventionally, being fearless means that you are not afraid or that, if someone hits you, you will hit him back. However, we are not talking about that street-fighter level of fearlessness. Real fearlessness is the product of tenderness. It comes from letting the world tickle your heart, your raw and beautiful heart. You are willing to open up, without resistance or shyness, and face the world. You are willing to share your heart with others.

Shambhala: The Sacred Path of the Warrior, Pages 42–46

Discovering Magic

IN TWENTIETH-CENTURY SOCIETY, the appreciation of simplicity has almost been lost. From London to Tokyo, there are problems with trying to create pleasure and comfort out of speed. The world is mechanized to such an extent that you don't even have to think. You just push a button and a computer gives you the answer. You don't have to learn to count. You press a button, and a machine counts for you. Casualness has become increasingly popular, because people think in terms of efficiency rather than appreciation. Why bother to wear a tie if the purpose of wearing clothes is just to cover your body? If the reason for eating food is only to fill your stomach and provide nutrition, why bother to look for the best meat, the best butter, the best vegetables?

But the reality of the world is something more than the lifestyle that the twentieth-century world has embraced. Pleasure has been cheapened, joy has been reduced, happiness has been computerized. The goal of warriorship is to reconnect to the nowness of reality, so that you can go forward without destroying simplicity, without destroying your connection to this earth. Nowness is a way of joining together the wisdom of the past with the challenge of the present. In this chapter, we are going to discuss how to discover the ground of nowness. In order to rediscover nowness, you have to look back, back to where you came from, back to the original state. In this case, looking back is not looking back in time, going back several thousand years. It is looking back into your own mind, to before history began, before thinking began, before thought ever occurred. When you are in contact with this original ground, then you are never confused by the illusions of past and future. You are able to rest continuously in nowness.

This original state of being can be likened to a primordial, or cosmic, mirror. By *primordial,* we mean unconditioned, not caused by any circumstances. Something primordial is not a reaction for or against any situation. All conditionality comes from unconditionality. Anything that is made has to come from what was unmade, to begin with. If something is conditioned, it has been created or formed. In the English language, we speak of formulating ideas or plans, or we may say, "How should we *form* our organization?" or we may talk about the formation of a cloud. In contrast to that, the unconditioned is free from being formed, free from creation. This unconditioned state is likened to a primordial *mirror* because, like a mirror, it is willing to reflect anything, from the gross level up to the refined level, and it still remains as it is. The basic frame of reference of the cosmic mirror is quite vast, and it is free from any bias: kill or cure, hope or fear.

The way to look back and experience the state of being of the cosmic mirror is simply to relax. In this case, relaxation is quite different from the setting-sun idea of flopping or taking time off, entertaining yourself with a good vacation. Relaxation here refers to relaxing the mind, letting go of the anxiety and concepts and depression that normally bind you. The way to relax, or rest the mind in nowness, is through the practice of meditation. The practice of meditation is connected to renouncing small-mindedness and personal territory. In meditation, you are neither "for" nor "against" your experience. That is, you don't praise some thoughts and condemn others, but you take an unbiased approach. You let things be as they are, without judgment, and in that way you yourself learn to be, to express your existence directly, nonconceptually. That is the ideal state of relaxation, which allows you to experience the nowness of the cosmic mirror. In fact, it is *already* the experience of the cosmic mirror.

If you are able to relax—relax to a cloud by looking at it, relax to a drop of rain and experience its genuineness—you can see the unconditionality of reality, which remains very simply in things as they are, very simply. When you are able to look at things without saying, "This is for me or against me," "I can go along with this," or "I cannot go along with this," then you are experiencing the state of being of the cosmic mirror, the wisdom of the cosmic mirror. You may see a fly buzzing; you may see a snowflake; you may see ripples of water; you may see a black widow spider. You may see anything, but you can actually look at all of those things with simple and ordinary, but appreciative, perception.

You experience a vast realm of perceptions unfolding. There is unlimited sound, unlimited sight, unlimited taste, unlimited feeling, and so on. The realm of perception is limitless, so limitless that perception itself is primordial, unthinkable, beyond thought. There are so many perceptions that they are beyond imagination. There are a vast number of sounds. There are sounds that you have never heard. There are sights and colors that you have never seen. There are feelings that you have never experienced before. There are endless fields of perception.

Perception here is not just what you perceive but the whole act of perceiving—the interaction between consciousness, the sense organs, and the sense fields, or the objects of perception. In some religious traditions, sense perceptions are regarded as problematic, because they arouse worldly desires. However, in the Shambhala tradition, which is a secular tradition rather than a religious one, sense perceptions are regarded as sacred. They are regarded as basically good. They are a natural gift, a natural ability that human beings have. They are a source of wisdom. If you don't see sights, if you don't hear sounds, if you don't taste food, you have no way to communicate with the phenomenal world at all. But because of the extraordinary vastness of perception, you have possibilities of communicating with the depth of the world—the world of sight, the world of sound—the greater world.

In other words, your sense faculties give you access to possibilities of deeper perception. Beyond ordinary perception, there is super-sound, super-smell, and super-feeling existing in your state of being. These can be experienced only by training yourself in the depth of meditation practice, which clarifies any confusion or cloudiness and brings out the precision, sharpness, and wisdom of perception—the nowness of your world. In meditation, you experience the precision of breath going in and out. You feel your breath: it is *so* good. You breathe out, breath dissolves: it is so sharp and good, it is so extraordinary that ordinary preoccupations become superfluous. So meditation practice brings out the supernatural, if I may use that word. You do not see ghosts or become telepathic, but your perceptions become super-natural, simply super-natural.

Normally, we limit the meaning of perceptions. Food reminds us of eating; dirt reminds us to clean the house; snow reminds us that we have to clean off the car to get to work; a face reminds us of our love or hate. In other words, we fit what we see into a comfortable or familiar scheme. We shut any vastness or possibilities of deeper perception out of our hearts by fixating on our own interpretation of phenomena. But it is possible to go beyond personal interpretation, to let vastness into our hearts through the medium of perception. We always have a choice: we can limit our perception so that we close off vastness, or we can allow vastness to touch us.

When we draw down the power and depth of vastness into a single perception, then we are discovering and invoking magic. By magic, we do not mean unnatural power over the phenomenal world but rather the discovery of innate or primordial wisdom in the world as it is. The wisdom we are discovering is wisdom without beginning, something naturally wise, the wisdom of the cosmic mirror. In Tibetan, this magical quality of existence, or natural wisdom, is called *drala*. *Dra* means "enemy" or "opponent," and *la* means "above." So *drala* literally means "above the enemy," "beyond the enemy." Drala is the unconditioned wisdom and power of the world that are beyond any dualism; therefore, drala is above any enemy or conflict. It is wisdom beyond aggression. It is the self-existing wisdom and power of the cosmic mirror that are reflected both in us and in our world of perception.

One of the key points in discovering drala principle is realizing that your own wisdom as a human being is not separate from the power of things as they are. They are both reflections of the unconditioned wisdom of the cosmic mirror. Therefore, there is no fundamental separation or duality between you and your world. When you can experience those two things together, as one, so to speak, then you have access to tremendous vision and power in the world—you find that they are inherently connected to your own vision, your own being. That is discovering magic. We are not talking here about an intellectual revelation; we are speaking of actual experience. We are talking about how we actually perceive reality. The discovery of drala may come as an extraordinary smell, a fantastic sound, a vivid color, an unusual taste. Any perception can connect us to reality properly and fully. What we see doesn't have to be pretty, particularly; we can appreciate anything that exists. There is some principle of magic in everything, some living quality. Something living, something real, is taking place in everything.

When we see things as they are, they make sense to us: the way leaves move when they are blown by the wind, the way rocks get wet when there are snowflakes sitting on them. We see how things display their harmony and their chaos at the same time. So we are never limited by beauty alone, but we appreciate all sides of reality properly.

Many stories and poems written for children describe the experience of invoking the magic of a simple perception. One example is "Waiting at the Window" from *Now We Are Six*, by A. A. Milne. It is a poem about spending several hours on a rainy day looking out the window, watching drops of water come down and make patterns on the glass. Reading this poem, you see the window, the rainy day, and the child with his face pressed to the glass watching the raindrops, and you feel the child's sense of delight and wonder. The poems of Robert Louis Stevenson in *A Child's Garden of Verses* have a similar quality of using very ordinary experiences to communicate the depth of perception. The poems "My Shadow," "My Kingdom," and "Armies in the Fire" exemplify this. The fundamental vastness of the world cannot be expressed directly in words, but in children's literature, very often it is possible to express that vastness in simplicity.

The Little Prince by Antoine de Saint Exupéry is another wonderful example of literature that evokes the sense of ordinary, or elemental, magic. At one point in this story, the little prince meets a fox. The prince is very lonely and wants the fox to play with him, but the fox says that he cannot play unless he is tamed. The little prince asks the meaning of the word *tame*. The fox explains that it means "to establish ties" in such a way that the fox will become unique to the little prince and the prince unique to the fox. Later, after the fox has been tamed and the little prince must leave him, the fox also tells the prince what he calls "my secret, a very simple secret," which is, "it is only with the heart that one can see rightly; what is essential is invisible to the eye."

Saint Exupéry has a different vocabulary here for describing the discovery of magic, or drala, but the experience is basically the same. Discovering drala is indeed to establish ties to your world, so that each perception becomes unique. It is to see with the heart, so that what is invisible to the eye becomes visible as the living magic of reality. There may be thousands or billions of perceptions, but they are still one. If you see one candle, you know exactly what all the candles in the whole world look like. They are all made out of fire, flame. Seeing one drop of water can be seeing all water.

Drala could almost be called an entity. It is not quite on the level of a god or gods, but it is an individual strength that does exist. Therefore, we not only speak of drala principle, but we speak of meeting the "dralas." The dralas are the elements of reality— water of water, fire of fire, earth of earth—anything that connects you with the elemental quality of reality, anything that reminds you of the depth of perception. There are dralas in the rocks or the trees or the mountains or a snowflake or a clod of dirt. Whatever is there, whatever you come across in your life, those are the dralas of reality. When you make that connection with the elemental quality of the world, you are meeting dralas on the spot; at that point, you are meeting them. That is the basic existence of which all human beings are capable. We always have possibilities of discovering magic. Whether it is medieval times or the twentieth century, the possibility of magic is always there.

A particular example of meeting drala, in my personal experience, is flower arranging. Whatever branches you find, none of them is rejected as ugly. They can always be included. You have to learn to see their place in the situation; that is the key point. So you never reject anything. That is how to make a connection with the dralas of reality.

Drala energy is like the sun. If you look in the sky, the sun is there. By looking at it, you don't produce a new sun. You may feel that you created or made today's sun by looking at it, but the sun is eternally there. When you discover the sun in the sky, you begin to communicate with it. Your eyes begin to relate with the light of the sun. In the same way, drala principle is always there. Whether you care to communicate with it or not, the magical strength and wisdom of reality are always there. That wisdom abides in the cosmic mirror. By relaxing the mind, you can reconnect with that primordial, original ground, which is completely pure and simple. Out of that, through the medium of your perceptions, you can discover magic, or drala. You actually can connect your own intrinsic wisdom with a sense of greater wisdom or vision beyond you.

You might think that something extraordinary will happen to you when you discover magic. Something extra-ordinary does happen. You simply find yourself in the realm of utter reality, complete and thorough reality.

Shambhala: The Sacred Path of the Warrior, Pages 99–106

The Art of the
Great Eastern Sun

GREAT EASTERN SUN terminology is used quite a lot in the Shambhala tradition, which is very ancient, and it is also applicable to the present. It also applies to involving ourselves with visual *dharma*, or dharma art. A work of art brings out the goodness and dignity of a situation. That seems to be the main purpose of art altogether.

The three principles of *Great, East,* and *Sun* have specific meanings. *Great* means having some kind of strength, energy, and power. That is, we are not fearful or regretful in presenting our expressions or our works of art—or for that matter, in our way of being. That power is absolutely fearless. If we were cowardly, we would have a problem in trying to handle an object, or even thinking of touching it or arranging it, much less in arranging our life or our world. We would be afraid to do any of that. So the absence of that fear is fearlessness, which develops out of delight. We are so delighted that we spontaneously develop that kind of strength and energy. Then we can move freely around our world without trying to change it particularly, but just expressing what needs to be expressed or uncovering what needs to be uncovered by means of our art.

East is the concept of wakefulness. The direction in which we are going, or the direction we are facing, is unmistakable. In this case, the word *East* is not necessarily the geographical direction. Here, it means simply the place you see when you can open your eyes and look fearlessly ahead of you. Since this East is unconditional, it does not depend on south, west, or north. It is just unconditional East as basic wakefulness.

Then we have the third category, or Sun. *Sun* has a sense of all-pervasive brilliance, which does not discriminate in the slightest. It is the goodness that exists in a situation, in oneself, and in one's world, which is expressed without doubt, hesitation, or regret. The Sun represents the idea of no laziness, and the Sun principle also includes the notion of blessings descending upon us and creating sacred world. The Sun also represents clarity, without doubt.

Those three categories are the nature of Great Eastern Sun. We could say that they are trying to bring us out and to uncover the cosmic elegance that exists in our lives and in our art. In contrast, the notion of *setting sun* is that of wanting to go to sleep. Obviously, when the sun sets, you go to sleep. You want to go back to your mother's womb, to regress, appreciating that you can hide behind dark clouds. That is to say, there is no bravery; it is complete cowardice. At the same time, there is struggle: you do not want to step out of this world completely; you are still trying to survive, still trying to prevent death. So the setting-sun world is based on a psychological attitude of fear. There is constant fear, and at the same time it is deliberately suicidal.

We have a lot of examples of setting-sun art. Some of them are based on the principle of entertainment. Since you feel so uncheerful and solemn, you try to create artificial humor, manufactured wit. But that tends to bring a tremendous sense of depression, actually. There might be a comic relief effect for a few seconds, but apart from that there is a constant black cloud, the black air of tormenting depression. As a consequence, if you are rich, you try to spend more money to cheer yourself up—but you find that the more you do, the less it helps. There is no respect for life in the setting-sun world. The only respect you can find there is in the brotherhood of human beings who are trying to combat death with the wrong end of the stick. I'm afraid at this point I have to be biased; there's nothing positive I can say about setting sun at all. But that actually helps, in that we can see black and white clearly and properly, so there is no doubt whatsoever.

Obviously, Great Eastern Sun vision does not mean that the good people have to win all the time in plays or films. It is not all that simpleminded. For instance, in the Buddhist tradition, there's a series of stories about the Great Bodhisattva being eaten and recycled, so there is no problem there. That seems to be OK. And the same thing could be said about the Bible, which contains the Crucifixion and Resurrection but still continues that vision. So the question of Great Eastern Sun versus setting sun is not so much whether somebody physically wins a victory but whether psychologically that sense of vision is continued.

The three categories—Great, East, and Sun—are categories of awaking or arising. But I should mention that there is a difference between rising sun and Great Eastern Sun. Rising sun is like a baby; there is potential. The Great Eastern Sun is fully developed, a fully matured sun, whereas the rising sun is an infant sun. So the idea of Great Eastern Sun is to be fully confident and fully developed, full speed ahead. The Buddhist analogy is that buddha nature exists in you, fully developed. You don't have to try to bring buddha nature into you, but you are already fully awake, on the spot.

The Great Eastern Sun principle has three additional categories or attributes. The first is a quality of *peace*. It is permeated with confidence and dignity—that is, nonaggression. The essence of a good work of art is absence of aggression. Sometimes you might find the elegance and dignity so overwhelming that it's threatening, but that has nothing to do with any aggression that exists in that work of art. It is just that you are so cowardly that you get frightened. So you shouldn't regard such an overwhelmingly splendid presentation as aggression.

The second category of the Great Eastern Sun principle is known as *showing the path*. That is, the artist begins to develop some sense of discriminating awareness wisdom in picking and choosing between wholesome and unwholesome situations. We are not just being naive and accepting everything, but some discrimination takes place, which shows the path from the point of view of Great Eastern Sun vision. This showing of the path could be regarded as first thought–best thought. First thought–best thought is not necessarily a chronological event. Quite possibly, the first thought might be the worst thought, chronologically speaking. In this case, first thought refers to that thought which is fresh and free.

In the beginning, there is some kind of gap. After the gap, there is an expression of that gap, which is first thought. It is not particularly vague; rather, it is very definite, extremely definite. And it has discriminating capabilities. For instance, when you have your paper and ink and brush, and you project your Great Eastern Sun vision, at first nothing might come into your mind. You might think that you are running out of inspiration. You wait for the good moment—the infamous first thought—but nothing happens. There is a thought of giving up the whole thing or else trying to crank something up artificially. But neither of those things works. Then you sort of become distracted by something else—and when you come back, there it is! The whole thing exists there. That little flicker of gap brings you to first thought. Then you have the confidence and dignity to execute your brushstroke, your calligraphy, or your painting. And the same thing could apply to musicians or photographers, or to any artist. So showing the path is a guideline of how to see these situations on the spot, on the first thought–best thought level.

The third category is *victory over the three worlds*. That is somewhat mysterious sounding, but we have to look at the concept of victory. Usually, victory seems to mean being able to beat somebody, becoming the best by either sheer pressure, sheer one-upmanship, or sheer knowledge. But from the Great Eastern Sun point of view, the concept of victory is a natural sense of existence that provides no need for challenge, so no enemies exist. Since there is no regret and no laziness, you begin to appreciate the sacredness of the world. Everything is complete and extremely wholesome, so there is no problem. The threefold world is the world of heaven, the world of earth, and the world that joins heaven and earth together, which is your physical body, your speech, and your psychological state of mind. So there is victory over the neuroses of all those realms.

To summarize, the concept of Great Eastern Sun vision is threefold. First is having a sense of goodness in yourself. Second, having some sense of decency in yourself already, you can project that to your audience, your clientele, or the world in general. In that way, a tremendous trust is established: goodness, decency, and trust. Third, because all of that has been established, therefore you can create what's known as *enlightened society*—by works of art, by basic sanity, and also by artists' beginning to practice sitting meditation. Needless to say, we have to slip that in somewhere.

In the early days of the Western world, Great Eastern Sun artwork was happening constantly. Great Eastern Sun vision appeared not only in a lot of art but in the lifestyle as well. Then people began to lose the sense of Great Eastern Sun vision, because their dignity was being questioned. Dignity was regarded as purely something to be cultivated, something belonging to the rich and above the heads of the peasants. The noble families had more food to eat than the peasants, and that kind of economic situation led to the industrial revolution. Then, of course, the notion of democracy came along, saying that all men are equal. This meant that no hierarchy could take place.

Nowadays, on the whole, I think that some modern artists are good and sane and have a tremendous sense of Great Eastern Sun vision, but they are extremely rare. There are only a few of them—very few. It is up to you to figure out who. Otherwise, we will be discriminating between good and bad, happy and sad. I think there is a definite trend of Great Eastern Sun vision; it is beginning to pick up. It did pick up in the sixties, though in the early seventies nothing happened at all. Everybody leaned toward setting-sun drama. But now people are beginning to come around and to pick up on it. During the twenties in America, a lot of interesting things began to happen. People didn't know what they were doing, but there were good feelings and real things took place: people actually knew how to conduct their lives and how to produce works of art. Unfortunately, art has now become an economic investment, which is a great obstacle to the artist. It doesn't leave us with very much to work on.

There is also a lot of setting-sun vision in the Japanese tradition. The flower-arranging school I came from is very much a setting-sun school, which I somewhat regret and respect at the same time. You see, the whole point is that we have to develop ourselves first, before we engage in anything else. We can't do very much other than that. We have to develop some understanding of Great Eastern Sun vision first, and then we can go out and study with teachers according to that particular principle. That seems to be the only way. We can't find any holy land of flower arrangers or another art form we want to do. We have to find it within ourselves.

In developing Great Eastern Sun vision, I think we have to emphasize the Western tradition as well as the Eastern. In order to inspire American students, I've been working with them in all kinds of ways. I've been telling them how to buy a good tie, a good suit, cuff links, shoes, how to say "Yes, sir" and "Please, may I." I've been training them to behave as good human beings. And it's the same with art. We have to have some understanding of Buddhist Oriental composure, but at the same time, we should also have the vision of the Western world, which in itself is quite remarkable. Tremendous things have happened here, but lately everybody has been trying to ignore that and make an amusement piece out of the whole tradition, to cut it down and make it all into a Coca-Cola world. When we do that, we run into problems. But as long as we don't give up our Occidental vision and dignity, I don't think there's any problem. And actually, there is such a thing as the Occidental Great Eastern Sun. That is a linguistic contradiction, like saying that the sun rises in the west, which is a silly thing to say. But the West is west, and therefore the sun also rises in the West, something like that. I myself have been inspired by great artists, painters, and musicians of the West. Therefore, I'm here: I'm living in the Western world, and I appreciate my world tremendously.

Dharma Art, Pages 8–13

The Universal Monarch

WE DISCUSSED THE possibility of discovering magic, or drala. That discovery can allow us to transform our existence into an expression of sacred world. Although, in some respects, all of these Shambhala teachings are based on very simple and ordinary experiences, at the same time, you might feel somewhat overwhelmed by this perspective, as though you were surrounded by monumental wisdom. You still might have questions about how to go about actualizing the vision of warriorship.

Is it simply your personal willpower and exertion that bring about the courage to follow the path of the Shambhala warriors? Or do you just imagine that you are seeing the Great Eastern Sun and hope for the best—that what you have seen is "it"? Neither of these will work. We have seen in the past that some people try to become warriors with an intense push. But the result is further confusion, and the person uncovers layer upon layer of cowardice and incompetence. If there is no sense of rejoicing and magical practice, you find yourself simply driving into the high wall of insanity.

The way of the warrior, how to be a warrior, is not a matter of making amateurish attempts, hoping that one day you will be a professional. There is a difference between imitating and emulating. In emulating warriorship, the student of warriorship goes through stages of disciplined training and constantly looks back and reexamines his own footprints or handiwork. Sometimes you find signs of development, and sometimes you find signs that you missed the point. Nevertheless, this is the only way to actualize the path of the warrior.

The fruition of the warrior's path is the experience of primordial goodness, or the complete, unconditional nature of basic goodness. This experience is the same as the complete realization of egolessness, or the truth of non–reference point. The discovery of non–reference point, however, comes only from working with the reference points that exist in your life. By reference points here, we simply mean all of the conditions and situations that are part of your journey through life: washing your clothes; eating breakfast, lunch, and dinner; paying bills. Your week starts with Monday, and then you have Tuesday, Wednesday, Thursday, Friday, Saturday, and Sunday. You get up at six AM, and then the morning passes, and you have noon, afternoon, evening, and night. You know what time to get up, what time to take a shower, what time to go to work, what time to eat dinner, and what time to lie down and go to sleep. Even a simple act like drinking a cup of tea contains many reference points. You pour yourself a cup of tea; you pick up a spoonful of sugar and bring it toward your teacup; you dip the spoon into the cup and stir it around so that the sugar becomes thoroughly mixed with the tea; you put the spoon down; you pick up the cup by its handle and bring it toward your mouth; you drink a little bit of tea; and then you put the cup down. All of those processes are simple and ordinary reference points that show you how to conduct your journey through life.

Then you have reference points that are connected with how you express your emotions. You have love affairs, you have quarrels, and sometimes you get bored with life, so you read a newspaper or watch television. All of those emotional textures provide reference points in conducting your life.

The principles of warriorship are concerned, first of all, with learning to appreciate those processes, those mundane reference points. But then, by relating with the ordinary conditions of your life, you might make a shocking discovery. While drinking your cup of tea, you might discover that you are drinking tea in a vacuum. In fact, *you* are not even drinking the tea. The hollowness of space is drinking tea. So while doing any little ordinary thing, that reference point might bring an experience of non–reference point. When you put on your pants or your skirt, you might find that you are dressing up space. When you put on your makeup, you might discover that you are putting cosmetics on space. You are beautifying space, pure nothingness.

In the ordinary sense, we think of space as something vacant or dead. But in this case, space is a vast world that has capabilities of absorbing, acknowledging, and accommodating. You can put cosmetics on it, drink tea with it, eat cookies with it, polish your shoes in it. Something is there. But ironically, if you look into it, you can't find anything. If you try to put your finger on it, you find that you don't even have a finger to put! That is the primordial nature of basic goodness, and it is that nature which allows a human being to become a warrior, to become the warrior of all warriors.

The warrior, fundamentally, is someone who is not afraid of space. The coward lives in constant terror of space. When the coward is alone in the forest and doesn't hear a sound, he thinks there is a ghost lurking somewhere. In the silence, he begins to bring up all kinds of monsters and demons in his mind. The coward is afraid of darkness because he can't see anything. He is afraid of silence because he can't hear anything. Cowardice is turning the unconditional into a situation of fear by inventing reference points, or conditions, of all kinds. But for the warrior, unconditionality does not have to be conditioned or limited. It does not have to be qualified as either positive or negative, but it can just be neutral—as it is.

The setting-sun world is afraid of space, afraid of the truth of non–reference point. In that world, people are afraid to be vulnerable. They are afraid to expose their flesh, bone, and marrow to the world outside. They are afraid to transcend the conditions or reference points they have set up for themselves. In the setting-sun world, people believe, absolutely, in their reference points. They think that, if they open themselves, they will be exposing an open wound to germs and disease. A hungry vampire may be nearby and smell the blood and come to eat them up. The setting-sun world teaches that you should guard your flesh and blood, that you should wear a suit of armor to protect yourself. But what are you really protecting yourself from? *Space.*

If you succeed in encasing yourself completely, you may feel secure, but you will also feel terribly lonely. This is not the loneliness of the warrior but the loneliness of the coward—the loneliness of being trapped in the cocoon, cut off from basic human affection.

You don't know how to take off your suit of armor. You have no idea how to conduct yourself without the reference point of your own security. The challenge of warriorship is to step out of the cocoon, to step out into space, by being brave and at the same time gentle. You can expose your wounds and flesh, your sore points.

Usually, when you have a wound, you put a Band-Aid on until it heals. Then you take off the bandage and expose the healed flesh to the world outside. In this case, you expose an open wound, open flesh, unconditionally. You can be completely raw and exposed with your husband or your wife, your banker, your landlord, anyone you meet.

Out of that comes an extraordinary birth: the birth of the universal monarch. The Shambhala definition of a monarch is someone who is very raw and sensitive, willing to open his or her heart to others. That is how you become a king or queen, the ruler of your world. The way to rule the universe is to expose your heart, so that others can see your heart beating, see your red flesh, and see the blood pulsating through your veins and arteries.

Ordinarily, we think of a king in the negative sense, as someone who holds himself apart from others, hiding in his palace and creating a kingdom to shield himself from the world. Here we are speaking of opening yourself to other human beings in order to promote human welfare. The monarch's power, in the Shambhala world, comes from being very soft. It comes from opening your heart so that you share your heart with others. You have nothing to hide, no suit of armor. Your experience is naked and direct. It is even beyond naked—it is raw, uncooked.

This is the fruition of warriorship: the complete primordial realization of basic goodness. At that level, there is absolutely no doubt about basic goodness or, therefore, about yourself. When you expose your naked flesh to the universe, can you say: "Should I put a second skin on? Am I too naked?" You can't. At that point, there is no room for second thoughts. You have nothing to lose and nothing to gain. You simply expose your heart completely.

Shambhala: The Sacred Path of the Warrior, Pages 153–157

Part II
THE NOBLE WAY OF BUDDHA

By the examination of his own thoughts, emotions, concepts, and the other activities of mind, the Buddha discovered that there is no need to struggle to prove our existence. . . . There is no need to struggle to be free; the absence of struggle is in itself freedom. This egoless state is the attainment of Buddhahood. The process of transforming the material of mind from expressions of ego's ambitions into expressions of basic sanity and enlightenment through the practice of meditation—this might be said to be the true spiritual path.

INTRODUCTION

The True Spiritual Path

WALKING THE SPIRITUAL PATH properly is a very subtle process; it is not something to jump into naively. There are numerous sidetracks that lead to a distorted, ego-centered version of spirituality; we can deceive ourselves into thinking we are developing spiritually when instead we are strengthening our egocentricity through spiritual techniques. This fundamental distortion may be referred to as *spiritual materialism*.

The approach presented here is a classical Buddhist one—not in a formal sense, but in the sense of presenting the heart of the Buddhist approach to spirituality. Although the Buddhist way is not theistic, it does not contradict the theistic disciplines. Rather, the differences between the ways are a matter of emphasis and method. The basic problems of spiritual materialism are common to all spiritual disciplines. The Buddhist approach begins with our confusion and suffering and works toward the unraveling of their origin. The theistic approach begins with the richness of God and works toward raising consciousness so as to experience God's presence. But since the obstacles to relating with God are our confusions and negativities, the theistic approach must also deal with them. Spiritual pride, for example, is as much a problem in theistic disciplines as in Buddhism.

According to the Buddhist tradition, the spiritual path is the process of cutting through our confusion, of uncovering the awakened state of mind. When the awakened state of mind is crowded in by ego and its attendant paranoia, it takes on the character of an underlying instinct. So it is not a matter of building up the awakened state of mind but rather of burning out the confusions that obstruct it. In the process of burning out these confusions, we discover enlightenment. If the process were otherwise, the awakened state of mind would be a product, dependent upon cause and effect and therefore liable to dissolution. Anything that is created must, sooner or later, die. If enlightenment were created in such a way, there would always be the possibility of ego's reasserting itself, causing a return to the confused state. Enlightenment is permanent because we have not produced it; we have merely discovered it. In the Buddhist tradition, the analogy of the sun appearing from behind the clouds is often used to explain the discovery of enlightenment. In meditation practice, we clear away the confusion of ego in order to glimpse the awakened state. The absence of ignorance, of being crowded in, of paranoia, opens up a tremendous view of life. One discovers a different way of being.

The heart of the confusion is that human beings have a sense of self that seems to them to be continuous and solid. When a thought or an emotion or an event occurs, there is a sense of someone's being conscious of what is happening. You sense that *you* are reading these words. This sense of self is actually a transitory, discontinuous event, which in our confusion seems to be quite solid and continuous. Since we take our confused view as being real, we struggle to maintain and enhance this solid self. We try to feed it pleasures and shield it from pain. Experience continually threatens to reveal our transitoriness to us, so we continually struggle to cover up any possibility of discovering our real condition. "But," we might ask, "if our real condition is an awakened state, why are we so busy trying to avoid becoming aware of it?" It is because we have become so absorbed in our confused view of the world that we consider it real, the only possible world. This struggle to maintain the sense of a solid, continuous self is the action of ego.

Ego, however, is only partially successful in shielding us from pain. It is the dissatisfaction that accompanies ego's struggle that inspires us to examine what we are doing. Since there are always gaps in our self-consciousness, some insight is possible.

An interesting metaphor used in Tibetan Buddhism to describe the functioning of ego is that of the "Three Lords of Materialism": the "Lord of Form," the "Lord of Speech," and the "Lord of Mind." In the discussion of the Three Lords that follows, the words *materialism* and *neurotic* refer to the action of ego.

The Lord of Form refers to the neurotic pursuit of physical comfort, security, and pleasure. Our highly organized and technological society reflects our preoccupation with manipulating physical surroundings so as to shield ourselves from the irritations of the raw, rugged, unpredictable aspects of life. Push-button elevators, prepackaged meat, air-conditioning, flush toilets, private funerals, retirement programs, mass production, weather satellites, bulldozers, fluorescent lighting, nine-to-five jobs, television—all are attempts to create a manageable, safe, predictable, pleasurable world.

The Lord of Form does not signify the physically rich and secure life situations we create per se. Rather, it refers to the neurotic preoccupation that drives us to create them, to try to control nature. It is ego's ambition to secure and entertain itself, trying to avoid all irritation. So we cling to our pleasures and possessions, we fear change or force change, we try to create a nest or playground.

The Lord of Speech refers to the use of intellect in relating to our world. We adopt sets of categories that serve as handles, as ways of managing phenomena. The most fully developed products of this tendency are ideologies, the systems of ideas that rationalize, justify, and sanctify our lives. Nationalism, communism, existentialism, Christianity, Buddhism—all provide us with identities, rules of action, and interpretations of how and why things happen as they do.

Again, the use of intellect is not in itself the Lord of Speech. The Lord of Speech refers to the inclination on the part of ego to interpret anything that is threatening or irritating in such a way as to neutralize the threat or turn it into something "positive" from ego's point of view. The Lord of Speech refers to the use of concepts as filters to screen us from a direct perception of what is. The concepts are taken too seriously; they are used as tools to solidify our world and ourselves. If a world of nameable things exists, then "I" as one of the nameable things exists as well. We wish not to leave any room for threatening doubt, uncertainty, or confusion.

The Lord of Mind refers to the effort of consciousness to maintain awareness of itself. The Lord of Mind rules when we use spiritual and psychological disciplines as the means of maintaining our self-consciousness, of holding on to our sense of self. Drugs, yoga, prayer, meditation, trances, various psychotherapies—all can be used in this way.

Ego is able to convert everything to its own use, even spirituality. For example, if you have learned of a particularly beneficial meditation technique of spiritual practice, then ego's attitude is, first, to regard it as an object of fascination and, second, to examine it. Finally, since ego is seemingly solid and cannot really absorb anything, it can only mimic. Thus, ego tries to examine and imitate the practice of meditation and the meditative way of life. When we have learned all of the tricks and answers of the spiritual game, we automatically try to imitate spirituality, since real involvement would require the complete elimination of ego, and actually the last thing we want to do is to give up the ego completely. However, we cannot experience that which we are trying to imitate; we can only find some area within the bounds of ego that seems to be the same thing. Ego translates everything in terms of its own state of health, its own inherent qualities. It feels a sense of great accomplishment and excitement at having been able to create such a pattern. At last, it has created a tangible accomplishment, a confirmation of its own individuality.

If we become successful at maintaining our self-consciousness through spiritual techniques, then genuine spiritual development is highly unlikely. Our mental habits become so strong as to be hard to penetrate. We may even go so far as to achieve the totally demonic state of complete egohood.

Even though the Lord of Mind is the most powerful in subverting spirituality, still the other two Lords can also rule the spiritual practice. Retreat to nature; isolation; simple, quiet, high people—all can be ways of shielding oneself from irritation, all can be expressions of the Lord of Form. Or perhaps religion may provide us with a rationalization for creating a secure nest, a simple but comfortable home, for acquiring an amiable mate and a stable, easy job.

The Lord of Speech is involved in spiritual practice as well. In following a spiritual path, we may substitute a new religious ideology for our former beliefs but continue to use it in the old neurotic way. Regardless of how sublime our ideas may be, if we take them too seriously and use them to maintain our ego, we are still being ruled by the Lord of Speech.

Most of us, if we examine our actions, would probably agree that we are ruled by one or more of the Three Lords. "But," we might ask, "so what? This is simply a description of the human condition. Yes, we know that our technology cannot shield us from war, crime, illness, economic insecurity, laborious work, old age, and death; nor can our ideologies shield us from doubt, uncertainty, confusion, and disorientation; nor can our therapies protect us from the dissolution of the high states of consciousness that we may temporarily achieve and the disillusionment and anguish that follow. But what else are we to do? The Three Lords seem too powerful to overthrow, and we don't know what to replace them with."

The Buddha, troubled by these questions, examined the process by which the Three Lords rule. He questioned why our minds follow them and whether there is another way. He discovered that the Three Lords seduce us by creating a fundamental myth: that we are solid beings. But ultimately the myth is false, a huge hoax, a gigantic fraud, and it is the root of our suffering. In order to make this discovery, he had to break through very elaborate defenses erected by the Three Lords to prevent their subjects from discovering the fundamental deception that is the source of their power. We cannot in any way free ourselves from the domination of the Three Lords unless we, too, cut through, layer by layer, the elaborate defenses of these Lords.

The Lords' defenses are created out of the material of our

minds. This material of mind is used by the Lords in such a way as to maintain the basic myth of solidity. In order to see for ourselves how this process works, we must examine our own experience. "But how," we might ask, "are we to conduct the examination? What method or tool are we to use?" The method that the Buddha discovered is meditation. He discovered that struggling to find answers did not work. It was only when there were gaps in his struggle that insights came to him. He began to realize that there was a sane, awake quality within him that manifested itself only in the absence of struggle. So the practice of meditation involves "letting be."

There have been a number of misconceptions regarding meditation. Some people regard it as a trancelike state of mind. Others think of it in terms of training, in the sense of mental gymnastics. But meditation is neither of these, although it does involve dealing with neurotic states of mind. The neurotic state of mind is not difficult or impossible to deal with. It has energy, speed, and a certain pattern. The practice of meditation involves *letting be*— trying to go with the pattern, trying to go with the energy and the speed. In this way, we learn how to deal with these factors, how to relate with them, not in the sense of causing them to mature in the way we would like, but in the sense of knowing them for what they are and working with their pattern.

There is a story regarding the Buddha that recounts how he once gave teaching to a famous sitar player who wanted to study meditation. The musician asked, "Should I control my mind, or should I completely let go?" The Buddha answered, "Since you are a great musician, tell me how you would tune the strings of your instrument." The musician said, "I would make them not too tight and not too loose." "Likewise," said the Buddha, "in your meditation practice, you should not impose anything too forcefully on your mind, nor should you let it wander." That is the teaching of letting the mind *be* in a very open way, of feeling the flow of energy without trying to subdue it and without letting it get out of control, of going with the energy pattern of mind. This is meditation practice.

Such practice is necessary generally because our thinking pattern, our conceptualized way of conducting our life in the world, is either too manipulative, imposing itself upon the world, or else runs completely wild and uncontrolled. Therefore, our meditation practice must begin with ego's outermost layer, the discursive thoughts that continually run through our minds, our mental gossip. The Lords use discursive thought as their first line of defense, as the pawns in their effort to deceive us. The more we generate thoughts, the busier we are mentally and the more convinced we are of our existence. So the Lords are constantly trying to activate these thoughts, trying to create a constant overlapping of thoughts so that nothing can be seen beyond them. In true meditation, there is no ambition to stir up thoughts, nor is there an ambition to suppress them. They are just allowed to occur spontaneously and become an expression of basic sanity. They become the expression of the precision and the clarity of the awakened state of mind.

If the strategy of continually creating overlapping thoughts is penetrated, then the Lords stir up emotions to distract us. The exciting, colorful, dramatic quality of the emotions captures our attention as if we were watching an absorbing film show. In the practice of meditation, we neither encourage emotions nor repress them. By seeing them clearly, by allowing them to be as they are, we no longer permit them to serve as a means of entertaining and distracting us. Thus, they become the inexhaustible energy that fulfills egoless action.

In the absence of thoughts and emotions, the Lords bring up a still more powerful weapon, concepts. Labeling phenomena creates a feeling of a solid, definite world of "things." Such a solid world reassures us that we are a solid, continuous thing as well. The world exists, therefore I, the perceiver of the world, exist. Meditation involves seeing the transparency of concepts, so that labeling no longer serves as a way of solidifying our world and our image of self. Labeling becomes simply the act of discrimination. The Lords have still further defense mechanisms, but it would be too complicated to discuss them in this context.

By the examination of his own thoughts, emotions, concepts, and the other activities of mind, the Buddha discovered that there is no need to struggle to prove our existence, that we need not be subject to the rule of the Three Lords of Materialism. There is no need to struggle to be free; the absence of struggle is in itself freedom. This egoless state is the attainment of Buddhahood. The process of transforming the material of mind from expressions of ego's ambition into expressions of basic sanity and enlightenment through the practice of meditation—this might be said to be the true spiritual path.

Cutting Through Spiritual Materialism, Pages 3–11

Padmasambhava and
Spiritual Materialism

GURU RINPOCHE—OR Padmasambhava, as he is often called in the West—was an Indian teacher who brought the complete teachings of the Buddha, the *buddhadharma,* to Tibet. To begin with, we probably need some basic introduction to who Padmasambhava was, to how he fits into the context of the Buddhist teachings in general, and to how he came to be so admired by Tibetans in particular. He remains our source of inspiration, even now, here in the West. We have inherited his teachings, and from that point of view, I think we could say that Padmasambhava is alive and well.

I suppose the best way to characterize Padmasambhava for people with a Western or Christian cultural outlook is to say that he was a saint. We are going to discuss the depth of his wisdom and his lifestyle, his skillful way of relating with students. The students he had to deal with were Tibetans, who were extraordinarily savage and uncultured. He was invited to come to Tibet, but the Tibetans showed very little understanding of how to receive and welcome a great guru from another part of the world. They were very stubborn and very matter-of-fact—very earthy. They presented all kinds of obstacles to Padmasambhava's activity in Tibet. However, the obstacles did not come from the Tibetan people alone but also from differences in climate, landscape, and the social situation as a whole. In some ways, Padmasambhava's situation was very similar to our situation here. Americans are hospitable, but on the other hand, there is a very savage and rugged side to American culture. Spiritually, American culture is not conducive to just bringing out the brilliant light and expecting it to be accepted.

So there is an analogy here. In terms of that analogy, the Tibetans are the Americans and Padmasambhava is himself.

Before getting into details concerning Padmasambhava's life and teachings, I think it would be helpful to discuss the idea of a saint in the Buddhist tradition. The idea of a saint in the Christian tradition and the idea of a saint in the Buddhist tradition are somewhat conflicting. In the Christian tradition, a saint is generally considered to be someone who has direct communication with God, who perhaps is completely intoxicated with the Godhead and because of this is able to give out certain reassurances to people. People can look to the saint as an example of higher consciousness or higher development.

The Buddhist approach to spirituality is quite different. It is nontheistic. It does not have the principle of an external divinity. Thus, there is no possibility of getting promises from the divinity and bringing them from there down to here. The Buddhist approach to spirituality is connected with awakening within oneself rather than with relating to something external. So the idea of a saint as someone who is able to expand himself to relate to an external principle, get something out of it, and then share that with others is difficult or nonexistent from the Buddhist point of view.

A saint in the Buddhist context—for example, Padmasambhava or a great being like the Buddha himself—is someone who provides an example of the fact that completely ordinary, confused human beings can wake themselves up; they can put themselves together and wake themselves up through an accident of life of one kind or another. The pain, the suffering of all kinds, the misery, and the chaos that are part of life begin to wake them, shake them. Having been shaken, they begin to question: "Who am I? What am I? How is it that all these things are happening?" Then they go further and realize that there is something in them that is asking these questions, something that is, in fact, intelligent and not exactly confused.

This happens in our own lives. We feel a sense of confusion—it seems to be confusion—but that confusion brings out something that is worth exploring. The questions that we ask in the midst of our confusion are potent questions, questions that we really have. We ask: "Who am I? What am I? What is this? What is life?" and so forth. Then we explore further and ask: "In fact, who on earth asked that question? Who is that person who asked the question 'Who am I?' Who is the person who asked, 'What is?' or even 'What is what is?' " We go on and on with this questioning, further and further inward. In some way, this is nontheistic spirituality in its fullest sense. External inspirations do not stimulate us to model ourselves on further external situations. Rather, the external situations that exist speak to us of our confusion, and this makes us think more, think further. Once we have begun to do that, then, of course, there is the other problem: once we have found out who and what we are, how do we apply what we have learned to our living situation? How do we put it into practice?

There seem to be two possible approaches here. One is trying to live up to what we would *like* to be. The other is trying to live what we are. Trying to live up to what we would like to be is like pretending we are a divine being or a realized person, or whatever we might like to call the model. When we realize what is wrong with us, what our weakness is, what our problems and neuroses are, the automatic temptation is to try to act just the opposite, as though we have never heard of such a thing as our being wrong or confused. We tell ourselves: "Think positive! Act as though you're OK." Although we know that something is wrong with us on the level of the actual living situation, on the kitchen-sink level, we regard that as unimportant. "Let's forget those 'evil vibrations,' " we say. "Let's think the other way. Let's pretend to be good."

This approach is known in the Buddhist tradition as *spiritual materialism,* which means not being realistic, or to use hippie jargon, spacing out. "Let's forget the bad and pretend to be good." We could classify as spiritual materialism any approach—such as Buddhist, Hindu, Jewish, or Christian—that provides us with techniques to try to associate with the good, the better, the best—or the ultimately good, the divine.

When we begin associating ourselves with the good, it makes us happy. We feel full of delight. We think, "At last, I've found an answer!" That answer is that the only thing to do is regard ourselves as free already. Then, having established the position that we are free already, we just have to let all things flow.

Then we add a further touch to reinforce our spiritual materialism: everything that we do not know or did not understand in connection with our spiritual quest we connect with descriptions in various scriptures about that which is beyond mind, beyond words, ineffable—the ineffable Self, or whatever. We associate our own lack of understanding about what is going on with us with those unspoken, inexpressible things. This way, our ignorance is made into the greatest discovery of all. We can connect this "great discovery" with a doctrinal supposition; for example, "the savior" or some interpretation of the scriptures.

Whereas before we didn't know anything at all, now we "know" something that we actually don't know. There *is* something ahead of us now. We cannot describe it in terms of words, concepts, and ideas, but we have discovered that, to begin with, it is a matter of twisting ourselves into the good. So we have this one thing to start with: we can directly and deliberately translate our confusion as being something that is not confused. We do this just because we are seeking pleasure, spiritual pleasure. In doing it, we affirm that the pleasure we are seeking is of an unknowable nature, because we actually have no idea what kind of spiritual pleasure we are going to get out of this maneuver. And all the spiritual interpretations of the scriptures referring to the unknowable can be applied to the fact that we do not know what we are trying to do spiritually. Nevertheless, we are definitely involved in spiritual conviction now, because we have suppressed our original doubts about who we are and what we are—our feeling that perhaps we might not be anything. We have suppressed that; we may not even know about it anymore.

Having suppressed this embarrassment of ego that provided us with stepping-stones to the unknown, the nature of which we did not understand, we end up with two games of confusion going on: a game of the unknown and a game of the transcendental unknown. Both of these are part of spiritual materialism. We do not know who or what we are, but we do know that we would like to be someone or something. We decide to go ahead with what we would like to be even though we do not know what that is. That is the first game. Then on top of that, in connection with being something, we would also like to know that there is something about the world or the cosmos that corresponds to this "something" that we are. We have a sense of finding this something that we want to know, but we actually can't understand it, so that becomes the transcendental unknown. Since we can't understand it, we say, "Let's make that bigger and more gigantic confusion into the spirituality of the infiniteness of the Godhead," or something like that.

This should give us some understanding of spiritual materialism. The danger of spiritual materialism is that, under its influence, we make all kinds of assumptions. First, there are the domestic or personal-level assumptions, which we make because we want to be happy. Second, there are the spiritual assumptions that are made because that transcendental, gigantic, greater discovery is left mysterious. This brings further great assumptions: we do not know what we are actually going to achieve by achieving that unknown thing, but nevertheless, we give it some vague description, such as "being absorbed into the cosmos." And since nobody has yet gone that far, if anybody questions this discovery of "absorption into the cosmos," then we just make up further logic or look for reinforcement from the scriptures or other authorities.

The result of all this is that we end up confirming ourselves and confirming that the experience we are proclaiming is a true experience. Nobody can question it. At some stage, there's no room left for questioning at all. Our whole outlook becomes completely established with no room left at all for questioning. This is what we could call achieving egohood, as opposed to achieving enlightenment. At that point, if I would like to practice my aggression and passion on you and you don't accept that, then that's your fault. You do not understand the ineffable spirituality, so you are at fault. The only way left for me to help you is to reduce you to a shrunken head, to take out your brain and heart. You become a mere puppet under my command.

⌒

That is a rough portrait of spiritual materialism. It is the first of the two possible approaches: trying to live up to what you would *like* to be. Now let's talk about the second possible approach, that of trying to live what you are.

This possibility is connected with seeing our confusion, or misery and pain, but not making those discoveries into an answer. Instead, we explore further and further and further without looking for an answer. It is a process of working with ourselves, with our lives, with our psychology, without looking for an answer but seeing things as they are—seeing what goes on in our heads directly and simply, absolutely literally. If we can undertake a process like that, then there is a tremendous possibility that our confusion—the chaos and neurosis that goes on in our minds—might become a further basis for investigation. Then we look further and further and further. We don't make a big point or an answer out of any one thing. For example, we might think that because we have discovered one particular thing that is wrong with us, that must be *it*, that must be the problem, that must be the answer. No. We don't fixate on that, we go further. "Why is that the case?" We look further and further. We ask: "Why is this so? Why is there spirituality? Why is there awakening? Why is there this moment of relief? Why is there such a thing as discovering the pleasure of spirituality? Why, why, why?" We go on deeper and deeper and deeper and deeper, until we reach the point where there is no answer. There is not even a question. Both question and answer die simultaneously at some point. They begin to rub each other too closely, and they short-circuit each other in some way. At that point, we tend to give up hope of an answer, or of anything whatsoever, for that matter. We have no more hope, none whatsoever. We are purely hopeless. We could call this transcending hope, if you would like to put it in more genteel terms.

This hopelessness is the essence of crazy wisdom. It is hopeless, utterly hopeless. It is beyond hopelessness. (Of course, it would be possible, if we tried to turn that hopelessness itself into some kind of solution, to become confused again, to say the least.)

The process is one of going further in and in and in without any reference point of spirituality, without any reference point of a savior, without any reference point of goodness or badness—without any reference points whatsoever! Finally, we might reach the basic level of hopelessness, of transcending hope. This does not mean we end up as zombies. We still have all the energies; we have all the fascination of discovery, of seeing this process unfolding and unfolding and unfolding, going on and on. This process of discovery automatically recharges itself so that we keep going deeper and deeper and deeper. This process of going deeper and deeper is the process of crazy wisdom, and it is what characterizes a saint in the Buddhist tradition.

Padmasambhava appeared in eight different manifestations or aspects, which are connected with such a process of psychological penetration, of cutting through the surface of the psychological realm and then cutting through a further surface and infinitely further surfaces down through ever further depths of further surfaces, deeper and deeper. This is the process we involve ourselves in by discussing Padmasambhava's life, the eight aspects of Padmasambhava, and crazy wisdom.

In this context, we see that the Buddhist approach to spirituality is one of ruthlessly cutting through any chance we might have of confirming ourselves at any particular stage of development on the spiritual path. When we discover that we have made some progress on the spiritual path, that discovery of progress is regarded as a hindrance to further progress. So we don't get a chance to rest, to relax, or to congratulate ourselves at all. It is a one-shot, ongoingly ruthless spiritual journey. And that is the essence of Padmasambhava's spirituality.

Padmasambhava had to work with the Tibetan people of those days. You can imagine it. A great Indian magician and pandit, a great *vidyadhara*, or tantric master, comes to the Land of Snow, Tibet. The Tibetans think he is going to teach them some beautiful spiritual teaching about how to know the essence of the mind. The expectations built up by the Tibetans are enormous. Padmasambhava's work is to cut through the Tibetans' layers and layers of expectations, through all their assumptions as to what spirituality might be. Finally, at the end of Padmasambhava's mission in Tibet, when he manifested as Dorje Trolö, all those layers of expectation were completely cut through. The Tibetans began to realize that spirituality is cutting through hope and fear as well as being the sudden discovery of intelligence that goes along with this process.

Crazy Wisdom, Pages 3–13

STYLES OF IMPRISONMENT

Cosmic Joke

IN ORDER TO cut through the ambition of ego, we must understand how we set up me and my territory, how we use our projections as credentials to prove our existence. The source of the effort to confirm our solidity is an uncertainty as to whether or not we exist. Driven by this uncertainty, we seek to prove our own existence by finding a reference point outside ourselves, something with which to have a relationship, something solid to feel separate from. But the whole enterprise is questionable if we really look back and back and back. Perhaps we have perpetrated a gigantic hoax?

The hoax is the sense of the solidity of I and other. This dualistic fixation comes from nothingness. In the beginning, there is open space, zero, self-contained, without relationship. But in order to confirm zeroness, we must create one to prove that zero exists. But even that is not enough; we might get stuck with just one and zero. So we begin to advance, venture out and out. We create two to confirm one's existence, and then we go out again and confirm two by three, three by four, and so on. We set up a background, a foundation from which we can go on and on to infinity. This is what is called *samsara*, the continuous vicious cycle of confirmation of existence. One confirmation needs another confirmation needs another . . .

The attempt to confirm our solidity is very painful. Constantly, we find ourselves suddenly slipping off the edge of a floor that had appeared to extend endlessly. Then we must attempt to save ourselves from death by immediately building an extension to the floor in order to make it appear endless again. We think we are safe on our seemingly solid floor, but then we slip off again and have to build another extension. We do not realize that the whole process is unnecessary, that we do not need a floor to stand on, that we have been building all these floors on the ground level. There was never any danger of falling or need for support. In fact, our occupation of extending the floor to secure our ground is a big joke, the biggest joke of all, a cosmic joke. But we may not find it funny: it may sound like a serious double cross.

To understand more precisely the process of confirming the solidity of I and other—that is, the development of ego—it is helpful to be familiar with the five *skandhas*, a set of Buddhist concepts that describe ego as a five-step process.

The first step, or skandha, the birth of ego, is called "form" or basic ignorance. We ignore the open, fluid, intelligent quality of space. When a gap or space occurs in our experience of mind, when there is a sudden glimpse of awareness, openness, absence of self, then a suspicion arises: "Suppose I find that there is no solid me? That possibility scares me. I don't want to go into that." That abstract paranoia, the discomfort that something may be wrong, is the source of karmic chain reactions. It is the fear of ultimate confusion and despair. The fear of the absence of self, of the egoless state, is a constant threat to us. "Suppose it is true, what then? I am afraid to look." We want to maintain some solidity, but the only material available with which to work is space, the absence of ego, so we try to solidify or freeze that experience of space. Ignorance in this case is not stupidity, but it is a kind of stubbornness. Suddenly, we are bewildered by the discovery of selflessness and do not want to accept it; we want to hold on to something.

Then the next step is the attempt to find a way of occupying ourselves, diverting our attention from our aloneness. The karmic chain reaction begins. Karma is dependent upon the relativity of this and that—my existence and my projections—and karma is continually reborn as we continually try to busy ourselves. In other words, there is a fear of not being confirmed by our projections. One must constantly try to prove that one does exist by feeling one's projections as a solid thing. Feeling the solidity of something seemingly outside you reassures you that you are a solid entity as well. This is the second skandha, "feeling."

In the third stage, ego develops three strategies or impulses with which to relate to its projections: indifference, passion, and aggression. These impulses are guided by perception. Perception, in this case, is the self-conscious feeling that you must officially report back to central headquarters what is happening in any given moment. Then you can manipulate each situation by organizing another strategy.

In the strategy of indifference, we numb any sensitive areas that we want to avoid, that we think might hurt us. We put on a suit of armor. The second strategy is passion—trying to grasp things and eat them up. It is a magnetizing process. Usually, we do not grasp if we feel rich enough. But whenever there is a feeling of poverty, hunger, impotence, then we reach out, we extend our tentacles and attempt to hold on to something. Aggression, the third strategy, is also based upon the experience of poverty, the feeling that you cannot survive and therefore must ward off anything that threatens your property or food. Moreover, the more aware you are of the possibilities of being threatened, the more desperate your reaction becomes. You try to run faster and faster in order to find a way of feeding or defending yourself. This speeding about is a form a aggression. Aggression, passion, indifference are part of the third skandha, "perception/impulse."

Ignorance, feeling, impulse, and perception—all are instinctive processes. We operate a radar system that senses our territory. Yet we cannot establish ego properly without intellect, without the ability to conceptualize and name. By now, we have an enormously rich collection of things going on inside us. Since we have so many things happening, we begin to categorize them, putting them into certain pigeonholes, naming them. We make it official, so to speak. So "intellect" or "concept" is the next stage of ego, the fourth skandha, but even this is not quite enough. We need a very active and efficient mechanism to keep the instinctive and intellectual processes of ego coordinated. That is the last development of ego, the fifth skandha, "consciousness."

Consciousness consists of emotions and irregular thought patterns, all of which taken together form the different fantasy worlds with which we occupy ourselves. These fantasy worlds are referred to in the scriptures as the "six realms." The emotions are the highlights of ego, the generals of ego's army; subconscious thought, daydreams, and other thoughts connect one highlight to another. So thoughts form ego's army and are constantly in motion, constantly busy. Our thoughts are neurotic in the sense that they are irregular, changing direction all the time and overlapping one another. We continually jump from one thought to the next, from spiritual thoughts to sexual fantasies to money matters to domestic thoughts and so on. The whole development of the five skandhas—ignorance/form, feeling, impulse/perception, concept, and consciousness—is an attempt on our part to shield ourselves from the truth of our insubstantiality.

The practice of meditation is to see the transparency of this shield. But we cannot immediately start dealing with the basic ignorance itself; that would be like trying to push a wall down all at once. If we want to take this wall down, we must take it down brick by brick; we start with immediately available material, a stepping-stone. So the practice of meditation starts with the emotions and thoughts, particularly with the thought process.

The Myth of Freedom, Pages 19–23

Self-Absorption

THE SIX REALMS, the different styles of samsaric occupation, are referred to as "realms" in the sense that we dwell within a particular version of reality. We are fascinated with maintaining familiar surroundings, familiar desires and longings, so as not to give in to a spacious state of mind. We cling to our habitual patterns because confusion provides a tremendously familiar ground to sink into as well as a way of occupying ourselves. We are afraid to give up this security and entertainment, afraid to step into open space, into a meditative state of mind. The prospect of the awakened state is very irritating because we are uncertain how to handle it, so we prefer to run back to our prison rather than release ourselves from it. Confusion and suffering become an occupation, often quite secure and delightful.

The six realms are: the realm of the gods, the realm of the jealous gods, the human realm, the animal realm, the realm of the hungry ghosts, and the hell realm. The realms are predominantly emotional attitudes toward ourselves and our surroundings, emotional attitudes colored and reinforced by conceptual explanations and rationalizations. As human beings, we may, during the course of a day, experience the emotions of all of the realms, from the pride of the god realm to the hatred and paranoia of the hell realm. Nonetheless, a person's psychology is usually firmly rooted in one realm. This realm provides us with a style of confusion, a way of entertaining and occupying ourselves so as not to have to face our fundamental uncertainty, our ultimate fear that we may not exist.

The fundamental occupation of the god realm is mental fixation, a meditative absorption of sorts, which is based upon ego, upon the spiritually materialistic approach. In such meditation practice, the meditator maintains himself by dwelling upon something. The particular topic of meditation, no matter how seemingly profound, is experienced as a solid body rather than as transparent. This practice of meditation begins with a tremendous amount of preparation or "self-development." Actually, the aim of such practice is not so much to create the solidity of a place to dwell as it is to create the self-consciousness of the dweller. There is tremendous self-consciousness, which, of course, reaffirms the meditator's existence.

You do get very dramatic results from such practice if you are successful at it. One might experience inspiring visions or sounds, seemingly profound mental states, physical bliss, and mental bliss. All sorts of "altered states of consciousness" could be experienced or manufactured through the efforts of self-conscious mind. But these experiences are imitations, plastic flowers, manmade, manufactured, prefabricated.

We could dwell on a technique as well—repetition of a *mantra* or visualization. One is not completely absorbed into the visualization or mantra, but instead *you* are visualizing, *you* are repeating the mantra. Such practice, based upon "me," that "I am doing this," is once again the development of self-consciousness.

The realm of the gods is realized through tremendous struggle, is manufactured out of hope and fear. The fear of failure and the hope of gain build up and up and up to a crescendo. One moment you think you are going to make it, and the next moment you think you are going to fail. Alternation between these extremes produces enormous tension. Success and failure mean so much to us—"This is the end of me," or "This is my achievement of ultimate pleasure."

Finally, we become so excited that we begin to lose the reference points of our hope and fear. We lose track of where we are and what we were doing. And then there is a sudden flash in which pain and pleasure become completely one and the meditative state of dwelling on the ego dawns upon us. Such a breakthrough, such a tremendous achievement. And then pleasure begins to saturate our system, psychologically and physically. We no longer have to care about hope or fear. And quite possibly we might believe this to be the permanent achievement of enlightenment or union with God. At that moment, everything we see appears to be beautiful, loving, even the most grotesque situations of life seem heavenly. Anything that is unpleasant or aggressive seems beautiful because we have achieved oneness with ego. In other words, ego lost track of its intelligence. This is the absolute, ultimate achievement of bewilderment, the depths of ignorance—extremely powerful. It is a kind of spiritual atomic bomb, self-destructive in terms of compassion, in terms of communication, in terms of stepping out of the bondage of ego. The whole approach in the realm of the gods is stepping in and in and in, churning out more and more chains with which to bind oneself. The more we develop our practice, the more bondage we create. The scriptures cite the analogy of the silkworm, which binds itself with its own silk thread until it finally suffocates itself.

Actually, we have only been discussing one of two aspects of the realm of the gods, the self-destructive perversion of spirituality into materialism. However, the god realm's version of materialism can also be applied to so-called worldly concerns in the search for extreme mental and physical pleasure, the attempt to dwell on seductive goals of all kinds: health, wealth, beauty, fame, virtue, whatever. The approach is always pleasure-oriented, in the sense of maintenance of ego. What characterizes the realm of the gods is the losing track of hope and fear. And this might be achieved in terms of sensual concerns as well as in terms of spirituality. In both cases, in order to achieve such extraordinary happiness, we must lose track of who is searching and what is the goal. If our ambition expresses itself in terms of worldly pursuits, at first we search for happiness, but then we begin to enjoy the struggle toward happiness as well and we begin to relax into our struggle. Halfway to achieving absolute pleasure and comfort, we begin to give in and make the best of our situation. The struggle becomes an adventure and then a vacation or holiday. We are still on our adventurous journey to the actual ultimate goal, but at the same time, we consider every step along the way a vacation, a holiday.

So the realm of the gods is not particularly painful, in itself. The pain comes from the eventual disillusionment. You think you have achieved a continually blissful state, spiritual or worldly; you are dwelling on that. But suddenly, something shakes you, and you realize that what you have achieved is not going to last forever.

Your bliss becomes shaky and more irregular, and the thought of maintenance begins to reappear in your mind as you try to push yourself back into your blissful state. But the karmic situation brings you all kinds of irritations, and at some stage, you begin to lose faith in the continuity of the blissful state. A sudden violence arises, the feeling that you have been cheated, that you cannot stay in this realm of the gods forever. So when the karmic situation shakes you and provides extraordinary situations for you to relate with, the whole process becomes profoundly disappointing. You condemn yourself or the person who put you into the god realm or what brought you out of it. You develop anger and disappointment because you think you have been cheated. You switch into another style of relating to the world, another realm. This is what is called samsara, which literally means "continual circle," "whirlpool," the ocean of confusion that spins around again and again and again, without end.

The Myth of Freedom, Pages 23–28

Paranoia

THE DOMINANT characteristic of the next realm, the jealous god or asura realm, is paranoia. If you are trying to help those who have an asura mentality, they interpret your action as an attempt to oppress them or infiltrate their territory. But if you decide not to help them, they interpret that as a selfish act: you are seeking comfort for yourself. If you present both alternatives to them, then they think you are playing games with them. The asura mentality is quite intelligent: it sees all the hidden corners. You think that you are communicating with an asura face-to-face, but in actual fact, he is looking at you from behind your back. This intense paranoia is combined with an extreme efficiency and accuracy, which inspire a defensive form of pride. The asura mentality is associated with wind, speeding about, trying to achieve everything on the spot, avoiding all possibilities of being attacked. It is trying constantly to attain something higher and greater. To do so, one must watch out for every possible pitfall. There is no time to prepare, to get ready to put your action into practice. You just act without preparation. A false kind of spontaneity, a sense of freedom to act develops.

The asura mentality is preoccupied with comparison. In the constant struggle to maintain security and achieve greater things, you need points of reference, landmarks to plot your movement, to fix your opponent, to measure your progress. You regard life situations as games, in the sense of there being an opponent and yourself. You are constantly dealing with them and me, me and my friends, me and myself. All corners are regarded as being suspicious or threatening; therefore, one must look into them and be careful of them. But one is not careful in the sense of hiding or camouflaging oneself. You are very direct and willing to come out in the open and fight if there is a problem or if there is a plot or a seeming plot against you. You just come out and fight face-to-face, trying to expose the plot. At the same time that one is going out in the open and facing the situation, one is distrustful of the messages that you receive from the situation, so you ignore them. You refuse to accept anything, refuse to learn anything that is presented by outsiders, because everyone is regarded as the enemy.

The Myth of Freedom, Pages 28–29

Passion

PASSION IS THE major occupation in the human realm. Passion in this sense is an intelligent kind of grasping in which the logical reasoning mind is always geared toward the creation of happiness. There is an acute sense of the separateness of pleasurable objects from the experiencer, resulting in a sense of loss, poverty, often accompanied by nostalgia. You feel that only pleasurable objects can bring you comfort and happiness, but you feel inadequate, not strong or magnetic enough for the objects of pleasure to be drawn naturally into your territory. Nevertheless, you try actively to draw them in. This often leads to a critical attitude toward other people. You want to magnetize the best qualities, the most pleasurable, most sophisticated, most civilized situations.

This kind of magnetizing is different from that of the asura realm, which is not as selective and intelligent. The human realm, by comparison, involves a high degree of selectivity and fussiness. There is an acute sense of having your own ideology and your own style, of rejecting things not your style. You must have the right balance in everything. You criticize and condemn people who do not meet your standards. Or else you might be impressed by someone who embodies your style or is superior to you at achieving it, someone who is very intelligent and has very refined taste, who leads a pleasurable life and has the things you would like to have. It might be a historical figure or a mythological figure or one of your contemporaries who has greatly impressed you. He is very accomplished, and you would like to possess his qualities. It is not simply a matter of being jealous of another person; you want to draw that person into your territory. It is an ambitious kind of jealousy, in that you want to equal the other person.

The essence of the human realm is the endeavor to achieve

some high ideal. Often those who find themselves in this realm will have visions of Christ or Buddha or Krishna or Mohammed or other historical figures who have tremendous meaning for them because of their achievements. These great personages have magnetized everything that one could possibly think of—fame, power, wisdom. If they wanted to become rich, they could do so because of their enormous influence over other people. You would like to be like them—not necessarily better than but at least equal to them. Often people have visions in which they identify themselves with great politicians, statesmen, poets, painters, musicians, scientists, and so forth. There is a heroic attitude, the attempt to create monuments, the biggest, greatest historical monument. This heroic approach is based on fascination with what you lack. When you hear of someone who possesses remarkable qualities, you regard him or her as a significant being and yourself as insignificant. This continual comparing and selecting generates a never-ending procession of desires.

The human mentality places a strong emphasis on knowledge, learning, and education, on collecting all kinds of information and wisdom. The intellect is most active in the human realm. There is so much going on in your mind as a result of having collected so many things and having planned so many projects. The epitome of the human realm is to be stuck in a huge traffic jam of discursive thought. You are so busy thinking that you cannot learn anything at all. The constant churning out of ideas, plans, hallucinations, and dreams is a quite different mentality from that of the god realm. There you are completely absorbed in a blissful state, a kind of self-stuck sense of satisfaction. In the jealous god realm, you are completely drunk on competitiveness; there is less possibility of thought happening because your experiences are so strong that they overpower you, hypnotize you. In the case of the human realm, there are more thoughts happening. The intellectual or logical mind becomes much more powerful so that one is completely overwhelmed by the possibilities of magnetizing new situations. Thus, one tries to grasp new ideas, new strategies, relevant case histories, quotations from books, significant incidents that have occurred in one's life, and so on, and one's mind becomes completely full of thought. The things that have been recorded in the subconscious play back continually, much more so than in the other realms.

So it is a very intellectual realm, very busy and very disturbing. The human mentality has less pride than the mentalities of the other realms. In the other realms, you find some occupation to hang on to and derive satisfaction from, whereas in the human realm, there is no such satisfaction. There is a constant searching, constant looking for new situations or attempts to improve given situations. It is the least enjoyable state of mind because suffering is not regarded as an occupation nor as a way of challenging oneself; rather, it is a constant reminder of ambitions created out of suffering.

The Myth of Freedom, Pages 29–32

Stupidity

THE DESCRIPTIONS of the different realms are related to subtle but distinct differences in the ways individuals handle themselves in daily life—how they walk, talk, write letters, the way they read, eat, sleep, and so on. Everyone tends to develop a style that is peculiar to him or her. If we hear a tape recording of our voice or see a videotape or movie of ourselves, we are often shocked to see our style as someone else sees it. It feels extremely alien. Usually, we find other people's point of view irritating or embarrassing.

Blindness to our style, to how others see us, is most acute in the animal realm. I am not speaking of literally being reborn as an animal but of the animal quality of mind, a mentality that stubbornly pushes forward toward predetermined goals. The animal mentality is very serious. It even makes humor into a serious occupation. Self-consciously trying to create a friendly environment, a person will crack jokes or try to be funny, intimate, or clever. However, animals do not really smile or laugh; they just behave. They may play, but it is unusual for animals to actually laugh. They might make friendly noises or gestures, but the subtleties of a sense of humor are absent. The animal mentality looks directly ahead, as if wearing blinders. It never looks to the right or left but very sincerely goes straight ahead, trying to reach the next available situation, continually trying to adjust situations to make them conform to its expectations.

The animal realm is associated with stupidity: that is, preferring to play deaf and dumb, preferring to follow the rules of available games rather than redefine them. Of course, you might try to manipulate your perception of any given game, but you are really just following along, just following your instinct. You have some hidden or secret wish that you would like to put into effect, so when you come to obstacles, to irritations, you just push forward, regardless of whether or not you may hurt someone or destroy something of value. You just go out and pursue whatever is available, and if something else comes up, you take advantage of that as well and pursue it.

The ignorance or stupidity of the animal realm comes from a deadly honest and serious mentality, which is quite different from the bewilderment of the basic ignorance of the first skandha. In animal ignorance, you have a certain style of relating to your self and refuse to see that style from other points of view. You completely ignore such possibilities. If somebody attacks you or challenges your clumsiness, your unskilled way of handling a situation, you find a way of justifying yourself, find a rationale to keep your self-respect. You are not concerned with being truthful as long as your deception can be maintained in front of others. You are proud that you are clever enough to lie successfully. If you are attacked, challenged, criticized, you automatically find an answer. Such stupidity can be very clever. It is ignorance or stupidity in the sense that you do not see the environment around you, but you see only your goal and only the means to achieve that goal, and you invent all kinds of excuses to prove that you are doing the right thing.

The animal mentality is extremely stubborn, but this stubbornness can be sophisticated as well and quite skillful and ingenious, but without a sense of humor. The ultimate sense of humor is a free way of relating with life situations in their full absurdity. It is seeing things clearly, including self-deception, without blinders, without barriers, without excuses. It is being open and seeing with panoramic vision rather than trying to relieve tension. As long as humor is used as a way to relieve tension or self-consciousness or pressure, then it is the humor of the animal realm, which is actually extremely serious. It is a way of looking for a crutch. So the essence of the animal style is to try to fulfill your desires with extreme honesty, sincerity, and seriousness. Traditionally, this direct and mean way of relating with the world is symbolized by the pig. The pig does not look to the right or left but just sniffs along, consuming whatever comes in front of its nose; it goes on and on and on, without any sense of discrimination—a very sincere pig.

Whether we are dealing with simple domestic tasks or highly

sophisticated intellectual projects, we can have an animal style. It does not matter whether the pig eats expensive sweets or garbage. What is important is *how* he eats. The extreme animal mentality is trapped in a continual, self-contained, self-justifying round of activity. You are not able to relate with the messages given to you by your environment. You do not see yourself mirrored by others. You may be dealing with very intellectual matters, but the style is animal since there is no sense of humor, no way of surrendering or opening. There is a constant demand to move on from one thing to the next, regardless of failures or obstacles. It is like being a tank that rolls along, crushing everything in its path. It does not matter if you run over people or crash through buildings—you just roll along.

The Myth of Freedom, Pages 32–35

Poverty

IN THE *PRETA* or hungry ghost realm, one is preoccupied with the process of expanding, becoming rich, consuming. Fundamentally, you feel poor. You are unable to keep up the pretense of being what you would like to be. Whatever you have is used as proof of the validity of your pride, but it is never enough. There is always some sense of inadequacy.

The poverty mentality is traditionally symbolized by a hungry ghost who has a tiny mouth, the size of the eye of a needle, a thin neck and throat, skinny arms and legs, and a gigantic belly. His mouth and neck are too small to let enough food pass through them to fill his immense belly, so he is always hungry. And the struggle to satisfy his hunger is very painful since it is so hard to swallow what he eats. Food, of course, symbolizes anything you may want—friendship, wealth, clothes, sex, power, whatever.

Anything that appears in your life you regard as something to consume. If you see a beautiful autumn leaf falling, you regard it as your prey. You take it home or photograph it or paint a picture of it or write in your memoirs how beautiful it was. If you buy a bottle of Coke, it is exciting to hear the rattlings of the paper bag as you unpack it. The sound of the Coke spilling out of the bottle gives a delightful sense of thirst. Then you self-consciously taste it and swallow it. You have finally managed to consume it—such an achievement. It was fantastic; you brought the dream into reality. But after a while, you become restless again and look for something else to consume.

You are constantly hungering for new entertainment—spiritual, intellectual, sensual, and so on. Intellectually, you may feel inadequate and decide to pull up your socks by studying and listening to juicy, thoughtful answers, profound, mystical words.

You consume one idea after another, trying to record them, trying to make them solid and real. Whenever you feel hunger, you open your notebook or scrapbook or a book of satisfying ideas. When you experience boredom or insomnia or depression, you open your books, read your notes and clippings, and ponder over them, draw comfort from them. But this becomes repetitive at some point. You would like to remeet your teachers or find new ones. And another journey to the restaurant or the supermarket or the delicatessen is not a bad idea. But sometimes you are prevented from taking the trip. You may not have enough money, your child gets sick, your parents are dying, you have business to attend to, and so on. You realize that when more obstacles come up, then that much more hunger arises in you. And the more you want, the more you realize what you cannot get, which is painful.

It is painful to be suspended in unfulfilled desire, continually searching for satisfaction. But even if you achieve your goal, then there is the frustration of becoming stuffed, so full that one is insensitive to further stimuli. You try to hold on to your possession, to dwell on it, but after a while, you become heavy and dumb, unable to appreciate anything. You wish you could be hungry again so you could fill yourself up again. Whether you satisfy a desire or suspend yourself in desire and continue to struggle, in either case you are inviting frustration.

The Myth of Freedom, Pages 35–37

Anger

THE HELL REALM is pervaded by aggression. This aggression is based on such a perpetual condition of hatred that you begin to lose track of whom you are building your aggression toward as well as who is being aggressive toward you. There is a continual uncertainty and confusion. You have built up a whole environment of aggression to such a point that finally, even if you were to feel slightly cooler about your own anger and aggression, the environment around you would throw more aggression at you. It is like walking in hot weather: you might feel physically cooler for a while, but hot air is coming at you constantly so you cannot keep yourself cool for long.

The aggression of the hell realm does not seem to be your aggression, but it seems to permeate the whole space around you. There is a feeling of extreme stuffiness and claustrophobia. There is no space in which to breathe, no space in which to act, and life becomes overwhelming. The aggression is so intense that if you were to kill someone to satisfy your aggression, you would achieve only a small degree of satisfaction. The aggression still lingers around you. Even if you were to try to kill yourself, you would find that the killer remains; so you would not have managed to murder yourself completely. There is a constant environment of aggression in which one never knows who is killing whom. It is like trying to eat yourself from the inside out. Having eaten yourself, the eater remains, and he must be eaten as well, and so on and so on. Each time the crocodile bites his own tail, he is nourished by it; the more he eats, the more he grows. There is no end to it.

You cannot really eliminate pain through aggression. The more you kill, the more you strengthen the killer, who will create new things to be killed. The aggression grows until finally there is no space: the whole environment has been solidified. There are not even gaps in which to look back or do a double take. The whole space has become completely filled with aggression. It is outrageous. There is no opportunity to create a watcher to testify to your destruction, no one to give you a report. But at the same time, the aggression grows. The more you destroy, the more you create.

Traditionally, aggression is symbolized by the sky and earth radiating red fire. The earth turns into a red-hot iron, and space becomes an environment of flame and fire. There is no space to breathe any cool air or feel coldness. Whatever you see around you is hot, intense, extremely claustrophobic. The more you try to destroy your enemies or win over your opponents, the more you generate resistance, counteraggression bouncing back at you.

In the hell realm, we throw out flames and radiations that are continually coming back to us. There is no room at all in which to experience any spaciousness or openness. Rather, there is a constant effort, which can be very cunning, to close up all the space. The hell realm can only be created through your relationships with the outside world, whereas in the jealous god realm, your own psychological hang-ups could be the material for creating the asura mentality. In the hell realm, there is a constant situation of relationship; you are trying to play games with something, and the attempt bounces back on you, constantly recreating extremely claustrophobic situations; so that finally there is no room in which to communicate at all.

At that point, the only way to communicate is by trying to re-create your anger. You thought you had managed to win a war of one-upmanship, but finally you did not get a response from the other person; you one-upped him right out of existence. So you are faced only with your own aggression coming back at you, and it manages to fill up all the space. You are left lonely once more, without excitement, so you seek another way of playing the game, again and again and again. You do not play for enjoyment but because you do not feel protected or secure enough. If you have no way to secure yourself, you feel bleak and cold, so you must rekindle the fire. In order to rekindle the fire, you have to fight constantly to maintain yourself. You cannot help playing the game; you just find yourself playing it, all the time.

The Myth of Freedom, Pages 37–40

MEDITATION

Afterthought

Such a precious human body,
Difficult to rediscover;
Such precious pain,
Not difficult to discover;
Such an old story
Is by now a familiar joke.
You and I know the facts and the case history;
We have a mutual understanding of each other
Which has never been sold or bought by anyone.
Our mutual understanding keeps the thread of sanity.
Sometimes the thread is electrified,
Sometimes it is smeared with honey and butter;
Nevertheless, we have no regrets.
Since I am here,
Seemingly you are here too.
Let us practice!
Sitting is a jewel that ornaments our precious life.

Timely Rain, Page 36

Meditation and Mind

For the follower of the buddhadharma, the teachings of Buddhism, there is a need for a great emphasis on the practice of meditation. One must see the straightforward logic that mind is the cause of confusion and that by transcending confusion, one attains the enlightened state. This can only take place through the practice of meditation. The Buddha himself experienced this, by working on his own mind; and what he learned has been handed down to us.

Mindfulness is a basic approach to the spiritual journey that is common to all traditions of Buddhism. But before we begin to look closely at that approach, we should have some idea of what is meant by spirituality itself. Some say that spirituality is a way of attaining a better kind of happiness, transcendental happiness. Others see it as a benevolent way to develop power over others. Still others say the point of spirituality is to acquire magical powers so we can change our bad world into a good world or purify the world through miracles. It seems that all of these points of view are irrelevant to the Buddhist approach. According to the buddhadharma, spirituality means relating with the working basis of one's existence, which is one's state of mind.

There is a problem with one's basic life, one's basic being. This problem is that we are involved in a continual struggle to survive, to maintain our position. We are continually trying to grasp on to some solid image of ourselves. And then we have to defend that particular fixed conception. So there is warfare, there is confusion, and there is passion and aggression; there are all kinds of conflicts. From the Buddhist point of view, the development of true spirituality is cutting through our basic fixation, that clinging, that stronghold of something-or-other, which is known as ego.

In order to do that, we have to find out what ego is. What is this all about? Who are we? We have to look into our already existing state of mind. And we have to understand what practical step we can take to do that. We are not involved here in a metaphysical discussion about the purpose of life and the meaning of spirituality on an abstract level. We are looking at this question from the point of view of a working situation. We need to find some simple thing we can do in order to embark on the spiritual path.

People have difficulty beginning a spiritual practice because they put a lot of energy into looking for the best and easiest way to get into it. We might have to change our attitude and give up looking for the best or the easiest way. Actually, there is no choice. Whatever approach we take, we will have to deal with what we are already. We have to look at who we are. According to the Buddhist tradition, the working basis of the path and the energy involved in the path is the mind—one's own mind, which is working in us all the time.

Spirituality is based on mind. In Buddhism, mind is what distinguishes sentient beings from rocks or trees or bodies of water. That which possesses discriminating awareness, that which possesses a sense of duality—which grasps or rejects something external—that is mind. Fundamentally, it is that which can associate with an "other"—with any "something" that is perceived as different from the perceiver. That is the definition of mind. The traditional Tibetan phrase defining mind means precisely that: "That which can think of the other, the projection, is mind."

So by *mind* we mean something very specific. It is not just something very vague and creepy inside our heads or hearts, something that just happens as part of the way the wind blows and the grass grows. Rather, it is something very concrete. It contains perception—perception that is very uncomplicated, very basic, very precise. Mind develops its particular nature as that perception begins to linger on something other than oneself. Mind makes the fact of perceiving something else stand for the existence of oneself. That is the mental trick that constitutes mind. In fact, it should be the opposite. Since the perception starts from oneself, the logic should be: "I exist, therefore the other exists." But somehow the hypocrisy of mind is developed to such an extent that mind lingers on the other as a way of getting the feedback that it itself exists, which is a fundamentally erroneous belief. It is the fact that the existence of self is questionable that motivates the trick of duality.

This mind is our working basis for the practice of meditation and the development of awareness. But mind is something more than the process of confirming self by the dualistic lingering on the other. Mind also includes what are known as *emotions,* which are the highlights of mental states. Mind cannot exist without emotions. Daydreaming and discursive thoughts are not enough. Those alone would be too boring. The dualistic trick would wear too thin. So we tend to create waves of emotion that go up and down: passion, aggression, ignorance, pride—all kinds of emotions. In the beginning, we create them deliberately, as a game of trying to prove to ourselves that we exist. But eventually, the game becomes a hassle; it becomes more than a game and forces us to challenge ourselves more than we intended. It is like a hunter who, for the sport of practicing his shooting, decides to shoot one leg of a deer at a time. But the deer runs very fast, and it appears it might get away altogether. This becomes a total challenge to the hunter, who rushes after the deer, now trying to kill it completely, to shoot it in the heart. So the hunter has been challenged and feels defeated by his own game.

Emotions are like that. They are not a requirement for survival; they are a game we developed that went wrong at some point—it went sour. In the face of this predicament, we feel terribly frustrated and absolutely helpless. Such frustration causes some people to fortify their relationship to the "other" by creating a god or other projections, such as saviors, gurus, and mahatmas. We create all kinds of projections as henchmen, hitmen, to enable us to redominate our territory. The implicit sense is that if we pay homage to such great beings, they will function as our helpers, as the guarantors of our ground.

So we have created a world that is bittersweet. Things are amusing but, at the same time, not so amusing. Sometimes things seem terribly funny but, on the other hand, terribly sad. Life has the quality of a game of ours that has trapped us. The setup of mind has created the whole thing. We might complain about the government or the economy of the country or the prime rate of interest, but those factors are secondary. The original process at the root of the problems is the competitiveness of seeing oneself only as a reflection of the other. Problematic situations arise automatically as expressions of that. They are our own production, our own neat work. And that is what is called mind.

A gigantic world of mind exists to which we are almost totally unexposed. This whole world—this tent and this microphone, this light, this grass, the very pair of spectacles that we are wearing—is made by mind. Minds made this up, put these things together. Every bolt and nut was put in by somebody-or-other's mind. This whole world is mind's world, the product of mind. This is needless to say; I am sure everybody knows this. But we might remind ourselves of it so that we realize that meditation is not an exclusive activity that involves forgetting this world and getting into something else. By meditating, we are dealing with the very mind that devised our eyeglasses and put the lenses in the rims, and the very mind that put up this tent. Our coming here is the product of our minds. Each of us has different mental manifestations, which permit others to identify us and say, "This guy is named so-and-so, this girl is named so-and-so." We can be identified as individuals because we have different mental approaches, which also shape the expressions of our physical features. Our physical characteristics are part of our mental activity as well. So this is a living world, mind's world. Realizing this, working with mind is no longer a remote or mysterious thing to do. It is no longer dealing with something that is hidden or somewhere else. Mind is right here. Mind is hanging out in the world. It is an open secret.

The Heart of the Buddha, Pages 21–28

Mindfulness and Awareness

HAVING LAID THE basic groundwork regarding the practice of meditation, we can now go further and discuss the point that the practice of meditation involves a basic sense of continuity. Meditation does not involve discontinuing one's relationship with oneself and looking for a better person or searching for possibilities of reforming oneself and becoming a better person. The practice of meditation is a way of continuing one's confusion, chaos, aggression, and passion—but working with it, seeing it from the enlightened point of view. That is the basic purpose of meditation practice as far as this approach is concerned.

There is a Sanskrit term for basic meditation practice, *shamatha,* which means "development of peace." In this case, peace refers to the harmony connected with accuracy rather than to peace from the point of view of pleasure rather than pain. We have experienced pain, discomfort, because we have failed to relate with the harmony of things as they are. We haven't seen things as they are precisely, directly, properly, and because of that, we have experienced pain, chaotic pain. But in this case, when we talk about peace, we mean that, for the first time, we are able to see ourselves completely, perfectly, beautifully *as what we are,* absolutely as what we are.

This is more than raising the level of our potentiality. If we talk in those terms, it means we are thinking of an embryonic situation that will develop: this child may be highly disturbed, but he has enormous potentiality of becoming a reasonable, less disturbed personality. We have a problem with language here, an enormous problem. Our language is highly involved with the realm of possessions and achievements. Therefore, we have a problem in expressing with this language the notion of unconditional potentiality, which is the notion that is applicable here.

Shamatha meditation practice is the vanguard practice for developing our mindfulness. I would like to call your attention to this term, *mindfulness*. Generally, when we talk about mindfulness, it has to do with a warning sign, like the label on your cigarette package where the surgeon general tells you this is dangerous to your health—beware of this, be mindful of this. But here mindfulness is not connected with a warning. In fact, it is regarded as more of a welcoming gesture: you could be fully minded, mindful. Mindfulness means that you could be a wholesome person, a completely wholesome person, rather than that you should not be doing this or that. Mindfulness here does not mean that you should look this way or that way so you can be cured of your infamous problems, whatever they are, your problems of being mindless. Maybe you think like this: you are a highly distracted person, you have problems with your attention span. You can't sit still for five minutes or even one minute, and you should control yourself. Everybody who practices meditation begins as a naughty boy or naughty girl who has to learn to control himself or herself. They should learn to pay attention to their desk, their notebook, their teacher's blackboard.

That is the attitude that is usually connected with the idea of mindfulness. But the approach here has nothing to do with going back to school, and mindfulness has nothing to do with your attention span as you experienced it in school at all. This is an entirely new angle, a new approach, a development of peace, harmony, openness.

The practice of meditation, in the form of shamatha at the beginner's level, is simply being. It is bare attention that has nothing to do with a warning. It is just simply being and keeping a watchful eye, completely and properly. There are traditional disciplines, techniques, for that, mindfulness techniques. But it is very difficult actually to explain the nature of mindfulness. When you begin trying to develop mindfulness in the ordinary sense, a novice sense, your first flash of thought is that you are unable to do such a thing. You feel that you may not be able to accomplish what you want to do. You feel threatened. At the same time, you feel very romantic: "I am getting into this new discipline, which is a unique and very powerful thing for me to do. I feel joyous, contemplative, monkish (or 'nunkish'). I feel a sense of renunciation, which is very romantic."

Then the actual practice begins. The instructors tell you how to handle your mind and your body and your awareness and so on. In practicing shamatha under those circumstances, you feel like a heavily loaded pack donkey trying to struggle across a highly polished stream of ice. You can't grip it with your hooves, and you have a heavy load on your back. At the same time, people are hitting you from behind, and you feel so inadequate and so embarrassed. Every beginning meditator feels like an adolescent donkey, heavily loaded and not knowing how to deal with the slippery ice. Even when you are introduced to various mindfulness techniques that are supposed to help you, you still feel the same thing—that you are dealing with a foreign element, which you are unable to deal with properly. But you feel that you should at least show your faith and bravery, show that you are willing to go through the ordeal of the training, the challenge of the discipline.

The problem here is not so much that you are uncertain how to practice meditation but that you haven't identified the teachings as personal experience. The teachings are still regarded as a foreign element coming into your system. You feel you have to do your best with that sense of foreignness, which makes you a clumsy young donkey. The young donkey is being hassled by his master a great deal, and he is already used to carrying a heavy load and to being hit every time there is a hesitation. In that picture, the master becomes an external entity rather than the donkey's own conviction. A lot of the problems that come up in the practice of meditation have to do with a fear of foreignness, a sense that you are unable to relate with the teachings as part of your basic being. That becomes an enormous problem.

The practice of shamatha meditation is one of the most basic practices for becoming a good Buddhist, a well-trained person. Without that, you cannot take even a step toward a personal understanding of the true buddhadharma. And the buddhadharma, at this point, is no myth. We know that this practice and technique were devised by the Buddha himself. We know that he went through the same experiential process. Therefore, we can follow his example.

The basic technique here is identification with one's breath or, when doing walking meditation, identification with one's walking. There is a traditional story that Buddha told an accomplished musician that he should relate to controlling his mind by keeping it not too tight and not too loose. He should keep his mind at the right level of attention. So as we practice these techniques, we should put 25 percent of our attention on the breathing or the walking. The rest of our mental activities should be let loose, left open. This has nothing to do with the vajrayana or crazy wisdom or anything like that at all. It is just practical advice. When you tell somebody to keep a high level of concentration, to concentrate 100 percent and not make any mistakes, that person becomes stupid and is liable to make more mistakes because he's so concentrated on what he's doing. There's no gap. There's no room to open himself, no room to relate with the back-and-forth play between the reference point of the object and the reference point of the subject. So the Buddha quite wisely advised that you put only tentative attention on your technique, not to make a big deal out of concentrating on the technique (this method is mentioned in the *Samadhiraja Sutra*). Concentrating too heavily on the technique brings all kinds of mental activities, frustrations, and sexual and aggressive fantasies of all kinds. So you keep just on the verge of your technique, with just 25 percent of your attention. Another 25 percent is relaxing, a further 25 percent relates to making friends with oneself, and the last 25 percent connects with expectation—your mind is open to the possibility of something happening during this practice session. The whole thing is synchronized completely.

These four aspects of mindfulness have been referred to in the *Samadhiraja Sutra* as the four wheels of a chariot. If you have only three wheels, there's going to be a strain on the chariot as well as the horse. If you have two, the chariot will be heavy to the point of not being functional—the horse will have to hold up the whole thing and pull as well. If, on the other hand, you had five or six wheels on your chariot, that would create a bumpy ride and the passengers would not feel all that comfortable. So the ideal number of wheels we should have on our chariot is four, the four techniques of meditation: concentration, openness, awareness, expectation. That leaves a lot of room for play. That is the approach of the buddhadharma, and we know that a lot of people in the lineage have practiced that way and have actually achieved a perfect state of enlightenment in one lifetime.

The reason why the technique is very simple is that, that way, we cannot elaborate on our spiritual-materialism trip. We all breathe, unless we are dead. We all walk, unless we are in a wheelchair. And those techniques are the simplest and the most powerful, the most immediate, practical, and relevant to our life. In the case of breathing, there is a particular tradition that has developed from a commentary on the *Samadhiraja Sutra* written by Gampopa. There we find the notion, related to breathing, of mixing mind and space, which is also used in tantric meditative practices. But even at the hinayana level, there is a mixing of mind and space. This has become one of the very important techniques of meditation. Sometimes this particular approach is also referred to as *shilhak sung juk*, which is a Tibetan expression meaning "combining shamatha and vipashyana meditation practices." *Vipashyana* is a Sanskrit term for awareness. It is often translated as "insight." The term for awareness in Tibetan is *lhakthong*, which literally means "clear seeing."

Combining shamatha and vipashyana plays an important part in the meditator's development. Mindfulness becomes awareness. Mindfulness is taking an interest in precision of all kinds, in the simplicity of the breath, of walking, of the sensations of the body, of the experiences of the mind—of the thought process and memories of all kinds. Awareness is acknowledging the totality of the whole thing. In the Buddhist tradition, awareness, or vipashyana, has been described as the first experience of egolessness. There is an expression in Tibetan: *lhakthong dagme tokpe sherap*, which means "the knowledge that realizes egolessness through awareness." Vipashyana is the first introduction to the understanding of egolessness. Awareness in this case is totality rather than one-sidedness. A person who has achieved awareness or who is working on the discipline of awareness has no direction, no bias in one direction or another. He is just simply aware, totally and completely. This awareness also includes precision, which is the main quality of awareness in the early stage of the practice of meditation.

Awareness brings egolessness because there is no object of awareness. You are aware of the whole thing completely, of you and other and of the activities of you and other at the same time. So everything is open. There is no particular object of the awareness.

If you're smart enough, you might ask the question, "Who is being aware of this whole thing?" That's a very interesting question, the sixty-four-dollar question. And the answer is, nobody is being aware of anything but *itself*. The razor blade cuts itself. The sun shines by itself. Fire burns by itself. Water flows by itself. Nobody watches—and that is the very primitive logic of egolessness.

I'm sure the mahayanists would sneer and think that this is terrible logic, very crude. They probably would not hold high opinions of it. But from the point of view of hinayana, that's extraordinarily fantastic logic. Razor blade cuts itself; fire burns itself; water quenches thirst by itself. This is the egolessness of vipashyana practice.

Traditionally, we have the term *smriti-upasthana* in Sanskrit, or *satipatthana* in Pali, which means resting in one's intelligence. This is the same as awareness. Awareness here does not mean that the person practicing vipashyana meditation gives up his or her shamatha techniques of, say, *anapanasati*—mindfulness of the coming and going of the breath—or of walking in walking meditation practice. The meditator simply relates with that discipline in a more expansive way. He or she begins to relate with the whole thing. This is done in connection with what is known as the four foundations of mindfulness: mindfulness of body, of mind, of livelihood, and of effort.

If you relate with every move you make in your sitting practice of meditation, if you take note of every detail, every aspect of the movement of your mind, of the relationships in everything that you do, there's no room for anything else at all. Every area is taken over by meditation, by vipashyana practice. So there is no one to practice and nothing to practice. No "you" actually exists. Even if you think, "I am practicing this particular technique," you really have no one there to relate to, no one to talk to. Even at the moment when you say, "I am practicing," that, too, is an expression of awareness at the same time, so you have nothing left, nothing whatsoever, even no "I am practicing." You can still say the empty words, but they are like a lion's corpse, as it has been traditionally described. When the lion is dead, the lion's corpse remains lying in the jungle, and the other animals continue to be frightened of the lion. The only ones who can destroy the lion's corpse are the worms who crawl up from underneath and do not see it from the outside. They eat through it, so finally the lion's corpse disintegrates on the ground. So the worms are like the awareness, the knowledge that realizes egolessness through awareness—vipashyana.

The Path Is the Goal, Pages 14–24

Cool Boredom

WE MUST USE the human body as an analogy to describe the development of ego. In this analogy, feeling, impulse, and concepts—the fundamental dualism—are like the bones of the body. Emotions are like the muscles of the body, and subconscious gossip and all the little mental activities are the circulatory system that feeds and sustains the muscles. So in order to have a completely functioning body, we need to have a muscle system and a circulatory system and bones to support them.

We begin meditation practice by dealing with thoughts, the fringe of ego. The practice of meditation is an undoing process. If you want to dissect and examine the body of ego, you start by cutting a slit in the skin, and then you cut through the arteries. So the practitioner who is not involved with credentials begins with an operation. Credentials are an illness, and you need an operation to remove them. With your sickness, you are trying to prove that you exist. "I am sick; therefore, I am real, I feel pain." So the operation is to eliminate the notion of being an important person simply because you are sick. Of course, you can attract all kinds of attention if you declare that you are sick. Then you can phone your relatives and friends and tell them that you are sick, and they will come and help you.

That is a very wretched way of proving your existence. That is precisely what the credentials do. They prove that you are sick so that you can have attention from your friends. We have to operate on this person to eliminate the credential sickness. But if we give this person an anesthetic, he will not realize how much he has to give up. So we should not use anesthetics at all. It should be like natural childbirth. The mother sees her child being born, how it comes out of her body, how it enters into the outside world.

Giving birth to buddhadharma without credentials should be the same; you should see the whole process. You are taken straight to the operating room. Now, in the operating theater, the first step of the operation is to make a little slit in the area of complaint with an extraordinarily sharp surgical knife, the sword of Manjushri, the sword of compassion and wisdom. Just a little slit is made, which is not as painful as we expected.

Sitting and meditating is the little slit in your artery. You may have been told that sitting meditation is extremely boring and difficult to accomplish. But you do not find it all that difficult. In fact, it seems quite easy. You just sit. The artery, which is the subconscious gossip in your mind, is cut through by using certain techniques—either working on breathing or walking or whatever. It is a very humble gesture on your part—just sit and cut through your thoughts, just welcome your breathing going out and in, just natural breathing, no special breathing, just sit and develop the watchfulness of your breathing. It is not concentrating on breathing. Concentration involves something to grasp, something to hold on to. You are "here" trying to concentrate on something "there." Rather than concentration, we practice mindfulness. We see what is happening there rather than developing concentration, which is goal-oriented. Anything connected with goals involves a journey toward somewhere from somewhere. In mindfulness practice, there is no goal, no journey; you are just mindful of what is happening there.

There is no promise of love and light or visions of any kind—no angels, no devils. Nothing happens: it is absolutely boring. Sometimes you feel silly. One often asks the question, "Who is kidding whom? Am I on to something or not?" You are not on to something. Traveling the path means you get off everything; there is no place to perch. Sit and feel your breath, be with it. Then you begin to realize that actually the slitting of the artery did not take place when you were introduced to the practice. The actual slitting takes place when you begin to feel the boredom of the practice—real boredom. "I'm supposed to get something out of Buddhism and meditation. I'm supposed to attain different levels of realization. I haven't. I'm bored stiff." Even your watcher is unsympathetic to you, begins to mock you. Boredom is important because boredom is anticredential. Credentials are entertaining, always bringing you something new, something lively, something fantastic, all kinds of solutions. When you take away the idea of credentials, then there is boredom.

We had a film workshop in Colorado in which we discussed whether it was important to entertain people or make a good film. And what I said was that perhaps the audience might be bored with what we have to present, but we must raise the intelligence, the standards of the audience, up to the level of what we are presenting, rather than trying to constantly match their expectations, their desire for entertainment. Once you begin to try to satisfy the audience's desire for entertainment, you constantly bend down and bend down and bend down, until the whole thing becomes absurd. If a filmmaker presents his own ideas with dignity, his work might be ill received in the beginning but possibly well received once people begin to catch up to it. The film might raise the audience's level of sophistication.

Similarly, boredom is important in meditation practice; it increases the psychological sophistication of the practitioners. They begin to appreciate boredom, and they develop their sophistication until the boredom begins to become cool boredom, like a mountain river. It flows and flows and flows, methodically and repetitiously, but it is very cooling, very refreshing. Mountains never get tired of being mountains, and waterfalls never get tired of being waterfalls. Because of their patience, we begin to appreciate them. There is something in that. I don't want to sound especially romantic about the whole thing, I am trying to paint a black picture, but I slipped a bit. It is a good feeling to be bored, constantly sitting and sitting. First gong, second gong, third gong, more gongs yet to come. Sit, sit, sit, sit. Cut through the artery until the boredom becomes extraordinarily powerful. We have to work hard at it.

At this point, we cannot really study the vajrayana or, for that matter, even the mahayana. We are not up to it because we have not actually made a relationship with boredom yet. To begin with, we have to relate with the hinayana. If we are to save ourselves from spiritual materialism and from buddhadharma with credentials, if we are to become the dharma without credentials, the introduction of boredom and repetitiousness is extremely important. Without it, we have no hope. It is true—no hope.

There are definite styles of boredom. The Zen tradition in Japan creates a definite style of boredom in its monasteries. Sit, cook, eat. Sit zazen and do your walking meditation and so on. But to an American novice who goes to Japan or takes part in traditional Japanese practice in this country, the message of boredom is not communicated properly. Instead, if I may say so, it turns into a militant appreciation of rigidity, or an aesthetic appreciation of simplicity, rather than actually being bored, which is strange. Actually, it was not designed to be that way. To the Japanese, Zen practice is an ordinary Japanese life-situation in which you just do your daily work and sit a lot of zazen. But Americans appreciate the little details—how you use your bowl and how you eat consciously in zazen posture. This is only supposed to create a feeling of boredom, but to American students, it is a work of art. Cleaning your bowl, washing it out, folding your white napkin, and so forth becomes living theater. The black cushion is supposed to suggest no color, complete boredom. But for Americans, it inspires a mentality of militant blackness, straightforwardness.

The tradition is trying to bring out boredom, which is a necessary aspect of the narrow path of discipline, but instead, the practice turns out to be an archeological, sociological survey of interesting things to do, something you could tell your friends about: "Last year, I spent the whole fall sitting in a Zen monastery for six months. I watched autumn turn into winter, and I did my zazen practice, and everything was so precise and beautiful. I learned how to sit, and I even learned how to walk and eat. It was a wonderful experience, and I did not get bored at all."

You tell your friends, "Go, it's great fun," and you collect another credential. The attempt to destroy credentials creates another credential. The first point in destroying ego's game is the strict discipline of sitting meditation practice. No intellectual speculation, no philosophizing. Just sit and do it. That is the first strategy in developing buddhadharma without credentials.

The Myth of Freedom, Pages 51–56

The Way of
the Buddha

BOREDOM HAS MANY aspects: there is the sense that nothing is happening, that something might happen, or even that what we would like to happen might replace that which is not happening. Or one might appreciate boredom as a delight. The practice of meditation could be described as relating with cool boredom, refreshing boredom, boredom like a mountain stream. It refreshes because we do not have to do anything or expect anything. But there must be some sense of discipline if we are to get beyond the frivolity of trying to replace boredom. That is why we work with the breath as our practice of meditation. Simply relating with the breath is very monotonous and unadventurous—we do not discover that the third eye is opening or that cakras are unfolding. It is like a stone-carved Buddha sitting in the desert. Nothing, absolutely nothing, happens.

As we realize that nothing is happening, strangely we begin to realize that something dignified is happening. There is no room for frivolity, no room for speed. We just breathe and are there. There is something very satisfying and wholesome about it. It is as though we had eaten a good meal and were satisfied with it, in contrast to eating and trying to satisfy oneself. It is a very simple-minded approach to sanity.

It is recorded that the Buddha was given many Hindu meditation practices. He scorched himself in fires. He related with the energy of tantra by visualizing all kinds of things. He saw a neurological light by pressing his eyeballs, and he heard a neurological buzz of supposedly yogic sound by pressing his ears. He went through all of this himself and realized that these phenomena were gimmicks rather than real samadhi or meditation. Maybe the Buddha was a dumb yoga student without any imagination. However, we follow his dumbness, his example as the enlightened one, the *samyaksambuddha,* the completely enlightened one.

As the Buddha's approach to the practice of meditation evolved, he realized that gimmicks are merely neurotic affectations. He decided to look for what is simple, what is actually there, to discover the relationship between mind and body, his relationship with the kusha grass mat on which he sat and the bodhi tree above his head. He looked into his relationships with everything very simply and directly. It was not especially exciting—there were no flashes of anything—but it was reassuring. At the dawn of his enlightenment, someone asked the Buddha, "What are your credentials? How do we know that you are enlightened?" He touched his hand to the ground. "This solid earth is my witness. This solid earth, this sane earth, is my witness." Sane and solid and definite, no imaginings, no concepts, no emotions, no frivolity, but being basically what is: this is the awakened state. And this is the example we follow in our meditation practice.

As far as Buddha was concerned, at that point it was not the message but the implications that were more important. And as followers of Buddha, we have this approach, which is the idea of *vipashyana,* literally meaning "insight." Insight is relating not only with what you see but also with the implications of it, the totality of the space and objects around it. Breath is the object of meditation, but the environment around the breath is also part of the meditative situation.

The Buddha then turned the wheel of the dharma, expounding the four noble truths: pain, the origin of pain, the goal, and the path. All this was inspired by his discovery that there is tremendous space in which the universality of inspiration is happening. There is pain, but there is also the environment around the origin of pain. The whole thing becomes more expansive, more open. He wasn't such a bad yoga student after all. Quite possibly he was not good at hatha yoga, but he saw the environment around hatha yoga and *pranayama.*

The Buddha's demonstrations of basic sanity were spontaneous. He did not preach or teach in the ordinary sense, but as he unfolded, the energy of compassion and the endless resources of generosity developed within him, and people began to find this out. That kind of activity of the Buddha is the vipashyana practice that we are attempting. It is realizing that space contains matter, that matter makes no demands on space, and that space makes no demands on matter. It is a reciprocal and open situation. Everything is based on compassion and openness. Compassion is not particularly emotional in the sense that you feel bad that someone is suffering, that you are better than others and that you have to help them. Compassion is that total openness in which the Buddha had no ground, no sense of territory. So much so, that he was hardly an individual. He was just a grain of sand living in the vast desert. Through his insignificance, he became the "world enlightened one," because there was no battle involved. The dharma he taught was passionless, without aggression. Passion is grasping, holding on to your territory.

So our practice of meditation, if we follow the Buddha's way, is the practice of passionlessness or nonaggression. It is dealing with the possessiveness of aggression: "This is my spiritual trip, and I don't want you to interfere with it. Get out of my territory." Spirituality, or the vipashyana perspective, is a panoramic situation in which you can come and go freely and your relationship with the world is open. It is the ultimate nonviolence.

The Myth of Freedom, Pages 56–59

Art in
Everyday Life

IN AWARENESS PRACTICE, called vipashyana in Sanskrit, there seems to be a need for a general sense of appreciation or artfulness. Awareness practice is highly psychological: it brings a lot of new material into our lives as well as utilizing the material we already have. We could say that an appreciation of mind brings an appreciation of everyday life. So we find that we are surrounded by all kinds of ways of experiencing and expressing our artistic talent, so to speak.

There is a difference between a mindfulness [Sanskrit: *shamatha*] approach to art and an awareness [Sanskrit: *vipashyana*] approach to art. In the case of mindfulness, there is a sense of duty and restriction; a demand is made on us to develop acute, precise mindfulness. Although the tension of being mindful may be very light—we are just touching the verge of the breathing process, and there is a sense of freedom—nevertheless, it is still a demand we place on ourselves. In the case of awareness experience, there is simply appreciation. Nothing is hassling us or demanding anything from us. Instead, by means of awareness practice, we could simply tune in to the phenomenal world both inwardly and outwardly.

The idea of the artist is very important and seems to be necessary at this point. When we talk about art, we could be referring to somebody deliberately expressing the beauty and delightfulness or the mockery and crudeness of the world that we live in, in the form of poetry, pictures, or music. That kind of art could be said to be somewhat deliberate art. It is not so much for yourself, but it is more an exhibition, however honest and genuine the artist may be. Such an artist may say that he simply composed his poem because he felt that way. But if that's the case, why should he write it down on a piece of paper and date it? If it's just purely for himself, it does not need to be recorded. Whenever a need for recording your work of art is involved, then there is a tendency toward awareness of oneself: "If I record that brilliant idea I've developed, in turn, quite possibly accidentally, somebody might happen to see it and think well of it." There's that little touch involved, however honest and genuine it may be.

A work of art from that point of view is exhibition. I'm not saying that is wrong—by no means. In fact, if we develop a moralistic approach toward art, the whole thing becomes heavy-handed. We try to save ourselves from ego-tripping and just show an inch or a corner of our work of art, afraid that if we do the whole thing completely, we might be indulging our ego and our pride, and so forth. In that approach, there's a lot of hesitation, a pulling back and forth involved. In exhibitionistic art, until you begin to realize that the discipline and training you have received are your possession and you can do what you like with them, until you have that sense of ownership, you will be regarded as halfhearted. That goes with any kind of artwork. The training and discipline you have received are completely inherent; you possess them completely and thoroughly, and it's now up to you how you present them. It's the same as the wisdom of the lineage, which is handed down to a particular lineage holder, and that lineage holder exercises his own authority as to how to present it to his particular generation.

In the practical art of brushstroke paintings, you might assume the painters are free and they can do what they want. The paintings are just blobs of ink put together, and it seems to be coincidental that they make some sense. But those brush painters had long, painful training at the beginning, all of them, in a very orthodox style. In that conservative approach, once the training is completed, then you can do what you want. So even the work of a seemingly freestyle person has its root in that conservative interpretation. I think that the tradition of the East has always been of that nature. But in the West, particularly in the twentieth century, people don't always go through a thorough training process first. They purely use their talent, imitating the free style of trained people. And that's very chancy—sometimes they hit and make a tremendous success, and sometimes they miss, and the whole thing becomes a tremendous mess. So in order to develop a really freestyle work of art, you have to have the awkwardness of seeing yourself being awkward. That kind of watcher seems to be necessary, actually. We have no other choice. The only thing that makes things less serious is to have some kind of humor about the whole thing—not rebellious humor, but appreciating the games that are going on. And that creates further improvisation in brushing one's teeth, or whatever.

Generally, the Tibetan approach is very conservative. Also, the cultural attitude is that there is no secular art in Tibet. If you're going to paint even a freestyle thangka, the subject has to be a religious one: different gurus, different deities, or different protectors. So in Tibet, you can't have too much of a free hand, whereas in the Zen tradition of China and Japan, often people depict secular art in the language of Zen. As far as social psychology is concerned, their pattern of thinking was much superior to the Tibetans'. They didn't stick very faithfully to the doctrine, but they found a way of expressing the teachings in secular art, which seems to have different cultural implications.

The art of meditative experience might be called genuine art. Such art is not designed for exhibition or broadcast. Instead, it is a perpetually growing process in which we begin to appreciate our surroundings in life, whatever they may be—it doesn't necessarily have to be good, beautiful, and pleasurable at all. The definition of art, from this point of view, is to be able to see the uniqueness of everyday experience. Every moment we might be doing the same things—brushing our teeth every day, combing out hair every day, cooking our dinner every day. But that seeming repetitiveness becomes unique every day. A kind of intimacy takes place with the daily habits that you go through and the art involved in it. That's why it is called art in everyday life.

In this country, there are many traditions and schools of thought in regard to awareness practice. Attempts are made to develop awareness through awareness of body, awareness of surroundings, and also through encounter groups of various kinds. Those could also be included as works of art. But there's a problem if we are unable to relate with and appreciate the insignificant details of our everyday life. Doing special body awareness practices devoid of everyday life—going to class and doing your thing and coming back—might seem extraordinarily fruitful and liberating; nevertheless, there's still a dichotomy in your life. You feel the importance and the seriousness of the artwork or awareness practice in which you're involved, but in fact, the more you feel that the whole thing is important and serious, the more your development of awareness is going to be destroyed. Real awareness cannot develop if you are trying to chop your experience into categories and put it into pigeonholes.

One of the things we should overcome in order to become a genuine artist is aggression. The attitude of aggression is one in which everything's the same, so what's the difference? It brings with it an outlook on life that the whole world is involved in a plot against you and there's no point even attempting to make it workable. There's no point being involved in details. Everything is the same, so what? It's the attitude of a street fighter. That attitude of aggression is the seed of crudeness, as opposed to artistry. Such crudeness is extremely dumb and blind and misses most of the subtleties of life and its interesting points. If we begin to see even a part of that, the attitude of aggression deliberately shuts us down. That attitude of aggression brings with it the idea of the needlessness of being meticulous or of repetitive effort in trying to relate with things. If you are not able to see a particular situation clearly the first time, you might go back a second time and third time and fourth time—but aggression kills that potential of going back and developing the patience actually to experience it. So we could quite safely categorize aggression and impatience as antiart, the source of crudeness.

In the awareness experience, you are able to see the shadow of your watcher by being patient. You do not want to get hold of just one chunk of mindfulness and stick with it, but you experience the mindfulness *and* its shadow, the environment around it. There is a tremendous appreciation of life and of how to conduct one's life. So awareness practice is not just formal sitting meditation or meditation in action alone. It is a unique training practice in how to behave as an inspired human being, or inspired sentient being. That is what is meant by being an artist.

While other artists take a deliberately artistic or exhibitionistic approach, with awareness practice your entire ability and all your potentials are completely opened. (I'm not using the term *exhibitionistic* pejoratively, but in a neutral way.) You don't need very much inspiration at all. Actually, you don't need that much vocabulary or tricks of any kind to create good works of art— poetry, painting, music, or whatever. You just simply say the experience you've experienced—just say it, just play it, just paint it. Once you've begun to break through that kind of backwater, there are gushes of all kinds of energies. And since the first attempt was free and clear and resourceful, then the second and third and fourth creations of art are no problem at all. It comes naturally, quite simply. However, if you are concerned, thinking, "Oh, I can't write poetry; I've never done it. I used to do it in school, but I was a rather bad one. I can't even draw a circle. I can't even sing"—that is simply hesitation. This has nothing to do with artistic talent. Professional, mechanical talent is not the obstacle—it is the psychological aggression that has to be worked on. When that psychological aggression is transmuted into the energy of artistic talent, you begin to realize that you can do all kinds of things—to your amazement.

There are a lot of implications of art in vipashyana experience, not only for painting and other artistic media but also for relationships generally—how to communicate, how to speak, how to cook, how to choose one's clothes in a shop, how to select food at the supermarket—all those little details. Some people get extremely paranoid because they weren't brought up in cultured society, so to speak, and did not have any opportunities for learning how to go about such things. People become paranoid, aggressive, and "hufty-pufty" and come down on gentility as just being another trip: "I don't have to do that; I'm quite happy with my crudeness." But again, the aggression is the problem. It is not that you have to tune in to special information or a certain tradition, a particular style of eating, a particular style of dressing. This has nothing to do with a particular culture; rather, it has something to do with your instinct—that your instinct is open and has the room to exercise its potentialities into action. Then, for the very fact of being a genteel animal, human beings bring out their own man-animal–like, apelike, or genteel-ape tastes, whatever comes through.

Particularly in this country, the present conventional art is concentrated on the mere representation of sarcasm and crudeness, and it is ultimately unbearable, ugly, dirty—and thought-provoking, no doubt. It seems that artists find it comfortable to produce that kind of art, because they are afraid to put a positive message out to the masses. Any positive messages they might have are a problem. The safest way of putting out some kind of artistic message is to do so from the angle of criticizing the existing flow of society, which is very safe. That might be said to be the same trick as Nagarjuna's logic, which is that one should not dwell on anything, one should not have any philosophy at all. If we don't have any philosophy, we are safe, and we could criticize the nihilist and the eternalist and even those who dwell in the middle—and that's our philosophy. But somehow there's something not quite straightforward about that. After all, as Buddhists, we are followers of the Buddha, the Maharishi, the Great Rishi who followed the straightforward path. Likewise, in art, it seems to be necessary and important that we create a target of ourselves. We may become a target of criticism by presenting positive art, but that might be the best approach. It is the same thing in our daily life: not negating everything that happens in our lives, negation being a lifestyle, but getting into and presenting certain positive steps, like an appreciation of beauty. So art in the transcendental sense becomes the real practice of awareness, or vipashyana.

In the past, we have talked about becoming good students of a tea maker, learning how to make a perfect cup of tea and how to entertain friends. From the ordinary way of looking, that seems to be just like parents' wishes that their children grow up and become society boys and society girls—that you entertain your friends ideally and occupy them and say the right things at the right moment, and everything runs smoothly. But in this case, it's much more than that. If you link that with the idea of awareness practice, then it is becoming a bodhisattva, which is the highest, most supreme society person that we could ever imagine. The bodhisattva is known as the great host, the ship, the bridge, the highway, the mountain, the earth—all of which deal with interactions with people. So there is a lot of potential in us. And that element could be applied at the beginning level of vipashyana practice as well; we don't have to start on such a big scale. Our energy and money and space and experience may be limited, but at least we can start on the practical level of developing an awareness of that potential.

We can start with the possibility of vipashyana experience, which is that everyday life is a work of art if you see it from a point of view of nonaggression. That point is extremely important, particularly in order to overcome clumsiness and crudeness, which, in this case, is not ordinary clumsiness and crudeness but fundamental, phenomenological clumsiness and crudeness. Aggression is antiart. If you are not in an aggressive state of mind, you feel you are rich and resourceful and infinitely inspired. When somebody is angry and uptight—even such ordinary, literal aggression as anger—then it cuts all possibilities of improvising what exists in your life as part of your artistic talent. It is not there anymore, because if things potentially improvisable come up, you become angry at them and they become a nuisance. You would like to kick them out, destroy them. It is like an angry person who comes home and, not finding a way to express his anger, starts throwing chairs and hitting the table. That is a very unartistic thing to do and, to say the least, rather pathetic.

At the same time, anger and aggression are different. If you relate with your anger in such a way that it also inspires a work of poetry, there must be some generosity involved or at least some kind of awareness. So art is not just creating beauty; it is anything workable and rich. And as far as art in everyday life and the awareness experience is concerned, transcending aggression is the root of all the artistic talent one can ever imagine.

Dharma Art, Pages 25–31

How Typical Student Poetry Should Be

When the enlightened one was with us,
When he talked to us,
When he walked with us,
When he fixed his robes,
When he washed his hands after a meal,
The enlightened one was always precise, accurate.
He possessed ideal total *shinjang*,[1] without reference point.
He was playful and he was accurate.
He was clean, neat, tidy.
Watching his fingers, it was beautiful
The way Buddha handled his begging bowl.
He had no discrimination against or, for that matter, rejection of the way
    phenomena work:
Buddha worked with a blade of grass,
Pebbles, dirt, in his begging bowl.
He washed his robes with such precision.

We like the way the Buddha is in action.
Watching working Buddha is magnificent.
There is no discrepancy.
Buddha is the best friend,
He is the best at working with the unworkables.
Therefore he is the king.
The best monarch we could ever find is the Buddha.
The Buddha's gaze and the Buddha's hands—
The way he washes his hands—
He washes his hands as a monarch would.
He is not arrogant,
He is humble and genuine and imperial.
We like Buddha's way:
Imperial humbleness.
There is no one like him.
That is why we call him *samyaksambuddha*.[2]

---

1. The quality of being tamed or processed, which results from the practice of meditation.
2. A Sanskrit epithet for the Buddha that means "the completely perfect awakened one."

O how much I love you Buddha!
The way you do things properly,
The way you feel the world around you,
You have no aggression—
O Buddha! O Tathagata![3]
You are so tamed,
You are so beautiful,
You are so royal,
You are so humble.
O to be like you, the genuine Buddha
Who need not clarify or validate
You are buddha as Buddha.
O how gorgeous to be Buddha!

We love your simplicity.
We are glad that you took human birth and that you conducted yourself
    in the human realm.
O Buddha, samyaksambuddha,
We love you.
Astonished that you are Buddha,
Fascinated that you are Buddha,
Totally captivated that you are Buddha,
We are inspired to follow your example.
Shakyamuni,[4] O Buddha, we love you.
We are your best friend, O best friend.

Homage to the Sambuddha,[5] the perfect being.
I, Chögyam, emulate you.
O Buddha,
Namo buddhaya
Buddham sharanam gacchami.[6]

By Dharma Sagara, Ananda, Buddha Das, Hotei[7]

---

3. Another epithet that means "he who has gone beyond."
4. The name of the historical Buddha, which means "sage of the shakya [clan]."
5. The perfect buddha, or the perfectly awake one.
6. The last two lines of the poem are Sanskrit and mean: "Homage to the Buddha, I take refuge in the Buddha."
7. Chögyam Trungpa signed this poem with four names, or titles. *Dharma Sagara* is Sanskrit for Chögyam and means "Dharma Ocean." *Ananda* was the servant and a close disciple of Shakyamuni Buddha. *Buddha Das* is a mixture of Sanskrit and Hindi, which means "servant of the Buddha." *Hotei* is the name of a legendary Chinese Zen master, known for his crazy wisdom teachings. He is the model for the fat, round-bellied figures that traditionally bring good luck and wealth.

MAHAYANA: WORKING WITH OTHERS

The Manure of Experience and the Field of Bodhi

How to give birth to bodhi, the awakened state of mind? There is always great uncertainty when you don't know how to begin and you seem to be perpetually caught up in the stream of life. A constant pressure of thoughts, of wandering thoughts and confusion and all kinds of desires, continually arises. If you speak in terms of the person in the street, he or she doesn't seem to have a chance. People are never really able to look inward, unless perhaps they read some book on the subject and have the desire to enter into a disciplined way of life, and even then there seems to be no chance, no way to begin. People tend to make a very sharp distinction between spiritual life and everyday life. They will label a person as "worldly" or "spiritual," and they generally make a hard-and-fast division between the two. So if one speaks about meditation, awareness, and understanding, then the ordinary person, who has never heard of such things, obviously would not have a clue and probably would not even be sufficiently interested to listen properly. And because of this division, a person finds it almost impossible to take the next step and can never really communicate with self or with others in this particular way. The teachings, the instructions, the mystical writings, may all be very profound, but somehow one is never able to penetrate through to them, so one comes to a kind of dead end. Either a person is "spiritually inclined" or else he or she is a "worldly person," and there seems to be no way to bridge this gap. I think this is one of the great hindrances to the birth of bodhi. It also happens that people who have started on the path have doubts and want to give it up. They may perhaps think that they would be happier if they gave it up and just remained agnostics.

So there is something not quite flowing, there is a failure to relate one thing to another, and this is what prevents us from giving birth to bodhi. Therefore, we have to study this problem. We have to provide some clue for the man and woman in the street, some way of finding out, some concept that they can understand and that will still be related to their lives and will still be part of their lives. Of course, there is no magic word or miraculous thing that could suddenly change someone's mind. One wishes it were possible, by saying only a few words, to enlighten someone, but even great teachers like Christ or Buddha were unable to perform such a miracle. They had always to find the right opportunity and create the right situation. If one examines the character of the person and one studies the blockage, the difficulties, then one simply goes further and further, because one is trying to untie a knot that is already there and it would take ages and ages to unravel this entanglement and confusion. So one has to approach from another angle and start off by just accepting the character of that person, who may be completely worldly minded, and then choose one particular aspect of his or her activity or mentality and use it as a ladder, as an anchor, as a vehicle, so that even the person in the street could give birth to bodhi. It is all very well to say that Buddha was an awakened person and that he is continuously living as far as the essence of the Buddha and his teachings are concerned—the universal law permeates everything—and to talk of the sangha, the highest and most open community that can influence things. But still the majority of people could never even think of taking refuge along those lines. So somehow one has to find the right approach. And one always finds that a person has within himself or herself a specific character. A person may be regarded as having no intelligence and no personality at all, but each person in fact has his or her own particular quality. It may be a great kind of violence or great laziness, but one has just to take that particular quality and not regard it necessarily as a fault or blockage, for that *is* the bodhi which is in oneself; it is the seed, or rather the full potentiality for giving birth—one is already impregnated by bodhi. As one particular scripture says, "Since Buddha-nature pervades all beings, there is no such thing as an unsuitable candidate."

This scripture was composed after the death of Buddha, after the parinirvana. In the world of gods and men, everyone began to doubt whether the teachings of Buddha would remain because it seemed that now the wonderful teacher was gone and all that remained was a group of mendicant monks, and they did not seem to do very much, or they were not able to do so. So one of the disciples was lamenting and saying that now the world of samsara will go on and on, with its waves of passion, desire, hatred, and delusion; we will never have the chance to hear the Buddha's teaching and instructions, we are again plunged into darkness. So what shall we do? And as he lamented, the answers came to his mind, that Buddha had never died, that his teaching is always present, and that the birth and death of Buddha is merely a concept, an idea. In fact, no one is excluded, and all beings—anyone who possesses consciousness, anyone who possesses mind, or the unconscious mind—all are candidates for bodhisattvahood; anyone can become an awakened person.

In this sense, there is no such thing as a "secret doctrine" or a teaching that is only for the few. As far as the teaching is concerned, it is always open; so open, in fact, so ordinary and so simple, that it is contained within the character of that particular person. He may be habitually drunk or habitually violent, but that character is his potentiality. And in order to help give birth to bodhi, one must first of all respect that person's character and open one's heart to that violence in the other. Then one must go into him fully and respect him so that the energetic, the dynamic aspect of violence can be made to serve as the energy aspect of the spiritual life. In this way, the first step is taken and the first link is made. Probably the person feels very bad, that she is doing something wrong or that something is not quite right. She may feel that she has big difficulties, that she has a problem that she wants to solve. But she cannot solve it, and probably, in the search for a solution, she merely substitutes other activities for the ones she has renounced. Therefore, it is through simple, direct, and ordinary things in the person's mind and behavior that she arrives at the realization of the awakened state of mind.

Of course, one cannot apply this in a general way. It is no use generalizing or trying to explain philosophical concepts to a person in this state. One has to study that particular moment of the person, that very moment of nowness. And there is always a kind of spark, a kind of gap. One's character is not just one thing. There is active behavior, then passive, then active, continuously changing, and the first moment producing and giving birth to the next moment. So there is always a gap between these two periods, and one has to take that as the starting point. Probably one has to begin with some form of theory, because without respecting samsara, the world of confusion, one cannot possibly discover the awakened state of mind, or nirvana. For samsara is the entrance, samsara is the vehicle for nirvana. Therefore, one should say that the violent character is good. It is a wonderful thing; it is something positive. And then you begin to realize this, though at first you may be perplexed and wonder what is good in it, but somehow, if you get beyond the fascination part of it, you at least begin to feel good; and you begin to realize that you are not just a "sinner" but that there is something very positive in you. It is exactly the same thing when one practices meditation. A person may begin to detect his or her own weaknesses. It may be in a mild form, as a wandering mind or planning for one's future, but certain things begin to come, and it is as though one were sitting specially to think these things over rather than to practice meditation. Through this, one discovers certain things, and this is very valuable; it provides a wonderful opportunity.

It is often mentioned in the scriptures that without theories, without concepts, one cannot even start. So start with concepts and then build up theory. And then you use up the theory, and it gradually gives way to wisdom, to intuitive knowledge, and that knowledge finally links with reality. So to start with, one should allow and not react against things. And if one wants to help a person, for example, there are two ways of doing it: one is that you want to help because you want the person to be different, you would like to mold her according to your idea, you would like her to follow your way. That is still compassion with ego, compassion with an object, compassion finally with results that will benefit you as well—and that is not quite true compassion. This plan to help other people may be a very good one, but nevertheless, the emotional approach of wanting to save the world and bring peace is not quite enough. There has to be more than that; there has to be more depth. So first, one has to start by respecting concepts and then build from there. Though actually, in Buddhist teachings, concepts are generally regarded as a hindrance. But being a hindrance does not mean that it prevents anything. It is a hindrance, and it is also the vehicle—it is everything. Therefore, one must pay special attention to concepts.

It is said, I think in the *Lankavatara Sutra,* that unskilled farmers throw away their rubbish and buy manure from other farmers, but those who are skilled go on collecting their own rubbish, in spite of the bad smell and the unclean work, and when it is ready to be used, they spread it on their land, and out of this, they grow their crops. That is the skilled way. In exactly the same way, the Buddha says, those who are unskilled will divide clean from unclean and will try to throw away samsara and search for nirvana, but those who are skilled bodhisattvas will not throw away desire and the passions and so on but will first gather them together. That is to say, one should first recognize and acknowledge them, and study them and bring them to realization. So the skilled bodhisattva will acknowledge and accept all these negative things. And this time, one really knows that one has all these terrible things in oneself, and although it is very difficult and unhygienic, as it were, to work on, that is the only way to start. And then one will scatter them on the field of bodhi. Having studied all these concepts and negative things, when the time is right, one does not keep them anymore but scatters them and uses them as manure. So out of these unclean things comes the birth of the seed that is realization. This is how one has to give birth. And the very idea that concepts are bad, or such and such a thing is bad, divides the whole thing, with the result that you are not left with anything at all to deal with. And in that case, you have to either be completely perfect or else battle through all these things and try to knock them all out. But when you have this hostile attitude and try to suppress things, then each time you knock one thing out, another springs up in its place, and when you attack that one, another one comes up from somewhere else. There is this continual trick of the ego, so that when you try to disentangle one part of the knot, you pull on the string and only make it tighter somewhere else, so you are continually trapped in it. Therefore, the thing is not to battle anymore, not to try to sort out the bad things and only achieve good, but respect them and acknowledge them. So theory and concepts are very good, like wonderful manure. Through thousands and thousands of lives, we have been collecting so much rubbish that now we have a wonderful wealth of this manure. It has everything in it, so it would be just the right thing to use, and it would be such a shame to throw it away. Because if you do throw it away, then all your previous life until today—maybe twenty, thirty, or forty years—will have been wasted. Not only that, but lives and lives and lives will have been wasted, so one would have a feeling of failure. All that struggle and all that collecting would have been wasted, and you would have to start all over again from the beginning. Therefore, there would be a great feeling of disappointment, and it would be more a defeat than anything having been gained. So one has to respect the continual pattern. One may have broken away from the origin, and all sorts of things may have happened. These may not be particularly good things. They are rather undesirable and negative. At this stage, there are good things and bad things, but this collection contains good things disguised as bad and bad things disguised as good.

One must respect the flowing pattern of all one's past lives and the early part of one's present life right up to today. And there is a wonderful pattern in it. There is already a very strong current where many streams meet in a valley. And this river is very good and contains this powerful current running through it, so instead of trying to block it, one should join this current and use it. This does not mean that one should go on collecting these things over and over again. Whoever does that would be lacking in awareness and wisdom and would not have understood the idea of collecting manure. One should collect it together and acknowledge it, and by acknowledging it, one would have reached a certain point and would understand that this manure is ready to be used.

There is a story in the teachings of tantra about two close friends who both wanted to search for the truth. They went to a master, and the master said, "Do not abandon anything; accept everything. And once having accepted, use it in the right way." And the first one thought, "Well, this is wonderful. I can go on being just the way I am." So he set up hundreds of brothels and hundreds of butcher's shops and hundreds of drinking places, which in India was regarded as something that only a lower-caste person would do. He began to run all these big businesses, and he thought this was what he was supposed to do. But the other friend thought this was not quite right, and he began to examine himself; and by examining himself, he came to the conclusion that he had enough material already and did not have to collect any more. He did not have to do any particular practice of meditation, but by acknowledging the already existing heap, he achieved enlightenment, or at least a certain stage of realization, a kind of satori. Then one day, they met each other and talked together and compared their experiences. The first one was not at all awakened; he was still struggling and collecting and doing all these things. In fact, he had fallen into an even worse trap and had not even started to examine himself. But each of them was quite sure that he was right, so they both decided to go and consult the teacher. And the teacher said, "I am afraid your way is wrong" to the one who was running the businesses. And he was so disappointed that he drew his sword and murdered the teacher on the spot.

There are these two possible approaches, and there may perhaps be some confusion between the two. Nevertheless, if a person is skilled enough—not necessarily intelligent, but skilled enough—and patient enough to sift through his or her rubbish and study it thoroughly, then the person will be able to use it. So coming back to the subject of concepts, which is a very important example, the idea behind this is to develop a positive outlook and to recognize your great wealth. And having recognized one's concepts and ideas, one must also, in a sense, cultivate them. One has a tendency to try to abandon them or throw them away. But one should cultivate them, not in the sense of reading more books and having more discussions and philosophical disputes—that would be the other way, the way of the friend who ran the businesses—but simply, since you already have enough wealth, just go through it. Just as a person who wants to buy something has to first check through and see how much money he has. Or else it is like going back to your old diaries and studying them, and seeing your different stages of development; or going up to the attic and opening up all the old boxes to find the old dolls and toys that were given to you when you were three years old, and looking at them and examining them together with their associations. In this way, you gain a complete understanding of what you are, and that is more important than continuously creating. The point of realization is not to try to understand only the awakened state and pretend not to understand the other side, because that becomes a way of cheating oneself. You see, you are your own best friend, your own closest friend, you are the best company for yourself. One knows one's own weaknesses and inconsistency, one knows how much wrong one has done, one knows it all in detail, so it doesn't help to try to pretend you don't know it or to try not to think of that side and only think of the good side; that would mean that one was still storing one's rubbish. And if you stored it like that, you would not have enough manure to raise a crop from this wonderful field of bodhi. So you should go through and study even right back to your childhood, and of course, if you have the great ability to go back to your previous lives, you should do so and try to understand them.

There is also a story about Brahma, who came one day to hear the Buddha preach, and the Buddha asked "Who are you?" And Brahma for the first time began to look and check into himself (Brahma personifying the ego), and when he first looked into himself, he couldn't bear it. He said, "I'm Brahma, the Great Brahma, the Supreme Brahma." So Buddha asked, "Why do you come and listen to me?" And Brahma said, "I don't know." Buddha then said to him, "Now, look back into your past." So Brahma, with his wonderful ability to see his many past lives, looked; and he couldn't bear it. He simply broke down and wept in front of Buddha. Then Buddha said, "Well done, well done, Brahma! That is good." You see, this was the first time that Brahma had used his wonderful ability to see into his distant past, and so he finally saw things clearly. This does not mean that a person has to break down and feel bad about it, but it is very important to check and go through everything so that nothing is unexplored. Having started from there, one gains a complete view of the whole thing—like an aerial view that takes in the whole landscape, all the trees and the road and everything—without there being anything that one pretends not to see.

One must also examine fear and expectation. If there is fear of death, one examines that; if one fears old age, one examines that. If one feels uneasy about a certain ugliness in oneself, or a certain disability or physical weakness of any kind, one examines that as well. And one should also examine one's mental image of oneself and anything one may feel bad about. It is very painful in the beginning—as Brahma showed by breaking down—when you first go through it and see it. But this is the only way to do it. Sometimes one touches on a very painful spot where one is almost too shy to look into it, but somehow one still has to go through it. And by going into it, one finally achieves a real command of oneself; one gains a thorough knowledge of oneself for the first time. Now, we have explored the negative aspects and have also probably gained some idea of the positive side. We still have not attained anything; we have just started the basic collection of manure, and now we have to study it and see how to put it to use.

By now, one has developed this positive outlook and one has achieved a certain amount of understanding, and that is what is known as real theory. It is still theory, but you do not throw it overboard. In fact, you cultivate this kind of theory, and you continuously work on and on intellectually—intellectualizing only up to a certain point, of course, but still working on and on—without having reference to books or talks or discussions. It has to be a kind of contemplation and firsthand study. One's theory then begins to develop and takes on a shape of its own. And then you begin to discover not only the positive things you have done but also the element of bodhi that is in you. You begin to realize that you have this great ability to create such a wonderful theory. At this stage, of course, a person often feels that she has reached a state of enlightenment, a state of satori, but this is a mistake. Naturally, at this first discovery, there is great excitement, great joy, bliss, but she still has to go on. So having gone through these things, and having studied and explored them, one finds that one's theory does not stop, as ordinary theory does after reading books on philosophy—or scriptures, for that matter. But this theory continues. There is a continual investigation, a continual finding out. Sometimes, of course, this theory does stop. One reaches a certain point where one becomes too much fascinated by the whole thing; one searches with too much eagerness, and then one comes to a stop and can't go any further. That doesn't mean there is a breakdown or a blockage; it means one is trying too much with an idea, one is trying too much with the inquisitive mind. Then one has to channel it differently, without the eagerness and without the fascination, but going step-by-step—as it says in the scriptures: at an elephant's pace. You have to walk very slowly, unemotionally. But walk with dignity, step-by-step, like an elephant walking in the jungle.

So your continual struggle may be a very slow one, but Milarepa, a great teacher in the Kagyü lineage of Tibetan Buddhism, says, "Hasten slowly and you will soon arrive." By this time, theory is no longer theory. Well, it is also a kind of imagination. So many imaginary things come in. And this imagination may even be a kind of hallucination, but again, one does not abandon that. One does not regard it as a wrong track, as though one had to go back to the right one. In fact, one uses imagination. So theory brings imagination, which is the beginning of intuitive knowledge. One then discovers that one has a great imaginative energy, and so one goes on, gradually, step-by-step. In the next stage, one goes beyond just imagination—and this is not hallucination at all. There is something in us that is more real than merely imagination, though it is still colored by imagination. It is somehow ornamented by this sort of imaginary outline, but at the same time, there is something in it. It is like reading a children's book, for example; it is written for children and it is entirely imaginary, but there is something in it as well. Perhaps the writer simplifies his experience or tries to be childlike, so one finds something in it. And the same is true of any story, for that matter. And that imagination is not just hallucination but real imagination. If one looks back to theory, or if one traces back to the first steps one took, it may seem a bit tiring or even unnecessary, but it isn't so. One hasn't wasted time at all.

You have scattered the manure very evenly over the field, and now is the time to sow the seed and wait for the crop to grow. That is the first preparation, and now one is ready to discover. And that discovery has already begun to develop. There are many questions one would like to ask, and many things are still not certain. But in fact, at that stage, one doesn't really need to ask questions at all; perhaps one simply needs an external person to say that it is so, although the answer is already in one. The question is like the first layer, like the skin of an onion, and when you remove it, the answer is there. This is what the great logician and philosopher of Buddhism, Asanga, described as "the intuitive Mind." In the intuitive mind, if one studies true logic, one finds that the answers—and the opponent's attitude—are in us. So we don't have to search for the answer, because the question contains the answer in it. It is a matter of going into it in depth; that is the true meaning of logic. At this stage, one has reached a kind of feeling; the imagination becomes a kind of feeling. And with that feeling, it is as though one has reached the entrance hall.

Meditation in Action, Pages 19–29

The Bodhisattva Vow

BEFORE WE COMMIT ourselves to walking the open path of mahayana, we must first walk the hinayana, or narrow path. This path begins formally with the student's taking refuge in the buddha, the dharma, and the sangha—that is, in the lineage of teachers, the teachings, and the community of fellow pilgrims. We expose our neurosis to our teacher, accept the teachings as the path, and humbly share our confusion with our fellow sentient beings. Symbolically, we leave our homeland, our property, and our friends. We give up the familiar ground that supports our ego, admit the helplessness of ego to control its world and secure itself. We give up our clingings to superiority and self-preservation. But taking refuge does not mean becoming dependent upon our teacher or the community or the scriptures. It means giving up searching for a home, becoming a refugee, a lonely person who must depend upon himself. A teacher or fellow traveler or the scriptures might show us where we are on a map and where we might go from there, but we have to make the journey ourselves. Fundamentally, no one can help us. If we seek to relieve our loneliness, we will be distracted from the path. Instead, we must make a relationship with loneliness until it becomes aloneness.

In the hinayana, the emphasis is on acknowledging our confusion. In the mahayana, we acknowledge that we are a buddha, an awakened one, and act accordingly, even though all kinds of doubts and problems might arise. The stepping-stone, the starting point in becoming awake, in joining the family of buddhas, is the taking of the bodhisattva vow. (A bodhisattva is literally "one who is awake.") In the scriptures, taking the bodhisattva vow and walking on the bodhisattva path are described as being the act of awakening bodhi or "basic intelligence." Becoming "awake" involves seeing our confusion more clearly. We can hardly face the embarrassment of seeing our hidden hopes and fears, our frivolousness and neurosis. It is such an overcrowded world. And yet it is a very rich display. The basic idea is that if we are going to relate with the sun, we must also relate with the clouds that obscure the sun. So the bodhisattva relates positively to both the naked sun and the clouds hiding it. But at first, the clouds, the confusion, which hide the sun are more prominent. When we try to disentangle ourselves, the first thing we experience is entanglement.

Traditionally, the bodhisattva vow is taken in the presence of a spiritual teacher and images of the buddhas and the scriptures in order to symbolize the presence of the lineage, the family of Buddha. One vows: From today until the attainment of enlightenment, I devote my life to work with sentient beings and renounce my own attainment of enlightenment. Actually, we cannot attain enlightenment until we give up the notion of "me" personally attaining it. As long as the enlightenment drama has a central character, "me," who has certain attributes, there is no hope of attaining enlightenment, because it is nobody's project; it is an extraordinarily strenuous project, but nobody is pushing it. Nobody is supervising it or appreciating its unfolding. We cannot pour our being from our dirty old vessel into a new clean one. If we examine our old vessel, we discover that it is not a solid thing at all. And such a realization of egolessness can only come through the practice of meditation, relating with discursive thoughts and gradually working back through the five skandhas. When meditation becomes a habitual way of relating with daily life, a person can take the bodhisattva vow. At that point, discipline has become ingrown rather than enforced. It is like becoming involved in an interesting project upon which we automatically spend a great deal of time and effort. No one needs to encourage or threaten us; we just find ourselves intuitively doing it. Identifying with buddha nature is working with our intuition, with our ingrown discipline.

The bodhisattva vow acknowledges confusion and chaos— aggression, passion, frustration, frivolousness—as part of the path. The path is like a busy, broad highway, complete with roadblocks, accidents, construction work, and police. It is quite terrifying. Nevertheless, it is majestic; it is the great path. "From today onward until the attainment of enlightenment, I am willing to live with my chaos and confusion as well as with that of all other sentient beings. I am willing to share our mutual confusion." So no one is playing a one-upmanship game. The bodhisattva is a very humble pilgrim who works in the soil of samsara to dig out the jewel embedded in it.

The Myth of Freedom, Pages 103–105

Compassion

BODHICHITTA IS THE principle of inherent wakefulness. It literally means the seed or spark of enlightenment. It is the awakened heart of all sentient beings. The ultimate or absolute principle of bodhichitta is based on developing the *paramita,* or practice, of generosity, which is symbolized by a wish-fulfilling jewel. The Tibetan word for generosity, *jinpa,* means "giving," "opening," or "parting" [as when you part or draw open a curtain]. So the notion of generosity means not holding back but giving constantly. Generosity is self-existing openness, complete openness. You are no longer subject to cultivating your own scheme or project. And the best way to open yourself up is to make friends with yourself and with others.

Traditionally, there are three types of generosity. The first one is ordinary generosity, giving material goods or providing comfortable situations for others. The second one is the gift of fearlessness. You reassure others and teach them that they don't have to feel completely tormented and freaked out about their existence. You help them to see that there is basic goodness and spiritual practice, that there is a way for them to sustain their lives. That is the gift of fearlessness. The third type of generosity is the gift of dharma. You show others that there is a path that consists of discipline, meditation, and intellect or knowledge. Through all three types of generosity, you can open up other people's minds. In that way, their closedness, wretchedness, and small thinking can be turned into a larger vision.

That is the basic vision of mahayana altogether: to let people think bigger, think greater. We can afford to open ourselves and join the rest of the world with a sense of tremendous generosity, tremendous goodness, and tremendous richness. The more we give, the more we gain—although what we might gain should not particularly be our reason for giving. Rather, the more we give, the more we are inspired to give constantly. And the gaining process happens naturally, automatically, always.

The opposite of generosity is stinginess, holding back—having a poverty mentality, basically speaking. The basic principle of ultimate bodhichitta is to rest in the eighth consciousness, or *alaya,* and not follow our discursive thoughts. *Alaya* is a Sanskrit word meaning "basis," or sometimes "abode" or "home," as in *Himalaya,* "abode of snow." So it has that idea of a vast range. It is the fundamental state of consciousness, before it is divided into "I" and "other," or into the various emotions. It is the basic ground where things are processed, where things exist. In order to rest in the nature of alaya, you need to go beyond your poverty attitude and realize that your alaya is as good as anybody else's alaya. You have a sense of richness and self-sufficiency. You can do it, and you can afford to give out as well.

Ultimate bodhichitta is similar to the absolute *shunyata* principle. And whenever there is the absolute shunyata principle, we have to have a basic understanding of absolute compassion at the same time. *Shunyata* literally means "openness" or "emptiness." Shunyata is basically understanding nonexistence. When you begin realizing nonexistence, then you can afford to be more compassionate, more giving. A problem is that usually we would like to hold on to our territory and fixate on that particular ground. Once we begin to fixate on that ground, we have no way to give. Understanding shunyata means that we begin to realize that there is no ground to get, that we are ultimately free, nonaggressive, open. We realize that we are actually nonexistent ourselves. We are not—*no,* rather. Then we can give. We have lots to gain and nothing to lose at that point. It is very basic.

Compassion is based on some sense of "soft spot" in us. It is as if we had a pimple on our body that was very sore—so sore that we do not want to rub it or scratch it. During our shower, we do not want to rub too much soap over it because it hurts. There is a sore point or soft spot that happens to be painful to rub, painful to put hot or cold water over.

That sore spot on our body is an analogy for compassion.

Why? Because even in the midst of immense aggression, insensitivity in our life, or laziness, we always have a soft spot, some point we can cultivate—or at least not bruise. Every human being has that kind of basic sore spot, including animals. Whether we are crazy, dull, aggressive, ego-tripping, whatever we might be, there is still that sore spot taking place in us. An open wound, which might be a more vivid analogy, is always there. That open wound is usually very inconvenient and problematic. We don't like it. We would like to be tough. We would like to fight, to come out strong, so we do not have to defend any aspect of ourselves. We would like to attack our enemy on the spot, single-handedly. We would like to lay our trips on everybody completely and properly, so that we have nothing to hide. That way, if somebody decides to hit us back, we are not wounded. And hopefully, nobody will hit us on that sore spot, that wound that exists in us. Our basic makeup, the basic constituents of our mind, are based on passion and compassion at the same time. But however confused we might be, however much of a cosmic monster we might be, still there is an open wound or sore spot in us always. There always will be a sore spot.

Sometimes people translate that sore spot or open wound as "religious conviction" or "mystical experience." But let us give that up. It has nothing to do with Buddhism, nothing to do with Christianity, and moreover, nothing to do with anything else at all. It is just an open wound, a very simple open wound. That is very nice—at least we are accessible somewhere. We are not completely covered with a suit of armor all the time. We have a sore spot somewhere, some open wound somewhere. Such a relief! Thank earth!

Because of that particular sore spot, even if we are a cosmic monster—Mussolini, Mao Tse-tung, or Hitler—we can still fall in love. We can still appreciate beauty, art, poetry, or music. The rest of us could be covered with cast-iron shields, but some sore spot always exists in us, which is fantastic. That sore spot is known as embryonic compassion, potential compassion. At least we have some kind of gap, some discrepancy in our state of being that allows basic sanity to shine through.

Our level of sanity could be very primitive. Our sore spot could be just purely the love of tortillas or the love of curries. But that's good enough. We have some kind of opening. It doesn't matter what it is love *of* as long as there is a sore spot, an open wound. That's good. That is where all the germs could get in and begin to impregnate and take possession of us and influence our system. And that is precisely how the compassionate attitude supposedly takes place.

Not only that, but there is also an inner wound, which is called *tathagatagarbha,* or buddha nature. Tathagatagarbha is like a heart that is sliced and bruised by wisdom and compassion. When the external wound and the internal wound begin to meet and to communicate, then we begin to realize that our whole being is made out of one complete sore spot altogether, which is called "bodhisattva fever." That vulnerability is compassion. We really have no way to defend ourselves anymore at all. A gigantic cosmic wound is all over the place—an inward wound and an external wound at the same time. Both are sensitive to cold air, hot air, and little disturbances of atmosphere that begin to affect us both inwardly and outwardly. It is the living flame of love, if you would like to call it that. But we should be very careful what we say about love. What is love? Do we know love? It is a vague word. In this case, we are not even calling it love. Nobody before puberty would have any sense of sexuality or of love affairs. Likewise, since we haven't broken through to understand what our soft spot is all about, we cannot talk about love; we can only talk about passion. It might sound too grandiose to talk about compassion. It sounds fantastic, but it actually doesn't say as much as love, which is very heavy. Compassion is a kind of passion, com-passion, which is easy to work with.

There is a slit in our skin, a wound. It's very harsh treatment, in some sense; but on the other hand, it's very gentle. The intention is gentle, but the practice is very harsh. By combining the intention and the practice, you are being "harshed," and also you are being "gentled," so to speak—both together. That makes you into a bodhisattva. You have to go through that kind of process. You have to jump into the blender. It is necessary for you to do that. Just jump into the blender and work with it. Then you will begin to feel that you are swimming in the blender. You might even enjoy it a little bit, after you have been processed. So an actual understanding of ultimate bodhichitta only comes from compassion. In other words, a purely logical, professional, or scientific conclusion doesn't bring you to that.

A lot of you seemingly, very shockingly, are not particularly compassionate. You are not saving your grandma from drowning, and you are not saving your pet dog from getting killed. Therefore, we have to go through this subject of compassion. Compassion is a very, very large subject, an extraordinarily large subject, which includes how to *be* compassionate. And actually, ultimate bodhichitta is preparation for relative bodhichitta. Before we cultivate compassion, we first need to understand how to *be* properly. How to love your grandma and how to love your flea or your mosquito—that comes later. The relative aspect of compassion comes much later. If we do not have an understanding of ultimate bodhichitta, then we do not have any understanding of the actual working basis of being compassionate and kind to somebody. We might just join the Red Cross and make nuisances of ourselves and create further garbage.

According to the mahayana tradition, we are told that we can actually arouse twofold bodhichitta: relative bodhichitta and ultimate bodhichitta. We could arouse both of them. Then, having aroused bodhichitta, we can continue further and practice according to the bodhisattva's example. We can be active bodhisattvas.

In order to arouse absolute or ultimate bodhichitta, we have to join shamatha and vipashyana together. Having developed the basic precision of shamatha and the total awareness of vipashyana, we put them together so that they cover the whole of our existence—our behavior patterns and our daily life—everything. In that way, in both meditation and postmeditation practice, mindfulness and awareness are happening simultaneously, all the time. Whether we are sleeping or awake, eating or wandering, precision and awareness are taking place all the time. That is quite a delightful experience.

Beyond that delight, we also tend to develop a sense of friendliness to everything. The early level of irritation and aggression has been processed through, so to speak, by mindfulness and awareness. There is instead a notion of basic goodness, which is described in the Kadam texts as the natural virtue of alaya. This is an important point for us to understand. Alaya is the fundamental state of existence, or consciousness, before it is divided into "I" and "other," or into the various emotions. It is the basic ground where things are processed, where things exist. And its basic state, and natural style, is goodness. It is very benevolent. There is a basic state of existence that is fundamentally good and that we can rely on. There is room to relax, room to open ourselves up. We can make friends with ourselves and with others. That is fundamental virtue or basic goodness, and it is the basis of the possibility of absolute bodhichitta.

Once we have been inspired by the precision of shamatha and the wakefulness of vipashyana, we find that there is room, which gives us the possibility of total naïveté, in the positive sense. The Tibetan word for naïveté is *pak-yang*, which means "carefree" or "let loose." We can be carefree with our basic goodness. We do not have to scrutinize or investigate wholeheartedly to make sure that there are no mosquitoes or eggs inside our alaya. Basic goodness can be cultivated and connected with quite naturally and freely, in a pak-yang way. We can develop a sense of relaxation and release from torment—from this-and-that altogether.

Training the Mind, Pages 11–21

The Lion's Roar

THE BODHISATTVA, the committed mahayana practitioner, takes a vow to work with all sentient beings and with every life-situation. Working with the emotions is a powerful part of this path. The lion's roar is the fearless proclamation that any state of mind, including the emotions, is a workable situation, a reminder in the practice of meditation. We realize that chaotic situations must not be rejected. Nor must we regard them as regressive, as a return to confusion. We must respect whatever happens to our state of mind. Chaos should be regarded as extremely good news.

There are several stages in relating with the emotions—the stages of seeing, hearing, smelling, touching, and transmuting. In the case of seeing the emotions, we have a general awareness that the emotions have their own space, their own development. We accept them as part of the pattern of mind, without question, without reference back to the scriptures, without help from credentials, but we directly acknowledge that they are so, that these things are happening. And then hearing involves experiencing the pulsation of such energy, the energy upsurge as it comes toward you. Smelling is appreciating that the energy is somewhat workable, as when you smell food and the smell becomes an appetizer, whetting your appetite before you eat. It smells like a good meal, it smells delicious, although you have not eaten it yet. It is somewhat workable. Touching is feeling the nitty-gritty of the whole thing, that you can touch and relate with it, that your emotions are not particularly destructive or crazy but just an upsurge of energy, whatever form they take—aggressive, passive, or grasping. Transmutation is not a matter of rejecting the basic qualities of the emotions. Rather, as in the alchemical practice of changing lead into gold, you do not reject the basic qualities of the material, but you change its appearance and substance somewhat. So you experience emotional upheaval as it is but still work with it, become one with it. The usual problem is that when emotions arise, we feel that we are being challenged by them, that they will overwhelm our self-existence or the credentials of our existence. However, if we become the embodiment of hatred or passion, then we do not have any personal credentials anymore. Usually, that is why we react against the emotions, because we feel we might be taken over by them, that we might freak out, lose our heads. We are afraid that aggression or depression will become so overwhelming that we will lose our ability to function normally, that we will forget how to brush our teeth, how to dial a telephone.

There is a fear that emotion might become too much, that we might fall into it and lose our dignity, our role as human beings. Transmutation involves going through such fear. Let yourself be in the emotion, go through it, give in to it, experience it. You begin to go toward the emotion rather than just experiencing the emotion coming toward you. A relationship, a dance, begins to develop. Then the most powerful energies become absolutely workable rather than taking you over, because there is nothing to take over if you are not putting up any resistance. Whenever there is no resistance, a sense of rhythm occurs. The music and the dance take place at the same time. That is the lion's roar. Whatever occurs in the samsaric mind is regarded as the path; everything is workable. It is a fearless proclamation—the lion's roar. As long as we create "patches" to cover what we regard as unworkable situations—metaphysical, philosophical, religious patches—then our action is not the lion's roar. It is a coward's scream—very pathetic.

Usually, whenever we feel that we cannot work with something, automatically we look back and try to find some external resource, some patch to conceal our insufficiency. Our concern is to save face, avoid being embarrassed, avoid being challenged by our emotions. How might we put another patch on top of another patch in order to get out of this situation? We could burden ourselves with millions upon millions of patches, one on top of the other. If the first one is too delicate, then the second may be stronger, so we end up creating a suit of patches, a suit of armor.

But here we have some problems. The joints in our armor begin to squeak, and there are holes in the armor where the joints are. It is difficult to put patches on the joints, because we still want to move, still want to dance, but we do not want to squeak. We want to have joints in order to move. So unless one is completely mummified, which is death, being a corpse, there is no way to completely protect oneself. For a living human being, patchwork is an absolutely impractical idea.

So the buddhadharma without credentials is, from this point of view, the same thing as the lion's roar. We do not need patches anymore. We could transmute the substance of the emotions, which is an extremely powerful act. Indian Ashokan art depicts the lion's roar with four lions looking in the four directions, which symbolizes the idea of having no back. Every direction is a front, symbolizing all-pervading awareness. The fearlessness covers all directions. Once you begin to radiate your fearlessness, it is all-pervading, radiated in all directions. In the traditional iconography, certain Buddhas are represented as having a thousand faces or a million faces, looking in all directions in panoramic awareness. Since they look everywhere, there is nothing to defend.

The lion's roar is fearlessness in the sense that every situation in life is workable. Nothing is rejected as bad or grasped as good. But everything we experience in our life-situations, any type of emotion, is workable. We can see quite clearly that trying to apply the reference point of credentials is useless. We have to really work into the situation completely and thoroughly. If we are extremely interested in eating food, really hungry, there is no time to read the menu because we want to eat. We really want to relate with food. So forget about the menu. It is an immediate interest, a direct relationship.

The basic point of the lion's roar is that if we are able to deal with emotions directly, able to relate with them as workable, then there is no need for external aid or explanations. It is a self-maintained situation. Any help from outsiders becomes credentials. So self-existing help develops. At that point, one does not need to avoid the credential problem anymore, because there is no room for speculation or rationalization. Everything becomes obvious and immediate, workable. And there is no chance or time or space to speculate on how to become a charlatan, how to con other people, because the situation is so immediate. So the idea of charlatanism does not appear at all, because there is no room for the idea of a game.

The Myth of Freedom, Pages 69–72

Acknowledging Death

WORKING WITH OTHERS as a healer, or a health practitioner, is an opportunity to practice the openness and compassion of the mahayana path. One's attitude toward death is central to any healing process. Although it is frequently ignored, it is always in the background. No one actually wants to face the possibility of death or even the idea of death. Even a mild sickness points to the possibility of nothingness: we might lose control of our physical and mental situation; we might become lost in midair. Since, as healers, we are dealing constantly with the fear of loss, we should actually bring that possibility into the picture. Facing it will not exactly solve the problem, but to begin with, the problem should at least be faced.

Many people are confused in their attitude toward death and toward dying persons: should we try to conceal the situation, or should we talk about it? Sometimes we do not want to talk about what is happening because it seems that to do so would be to suggest that something is basically wrong. Because of such attitudes, there is often a loss of spirit on the part of both the patient and the physician. But when we are willing to acknowledge what is really happening, we pick up spirit, or buoyancy. One could even go so far as to say that by such acknowledgment, some kind of sanity develops. So I think it is very important to present the possibility to people that they might have to face some kind of loss, some sense of bewilderment. In fact, the vanguard of death is uncertainty and complete bewilderment. It would be much healthier and more helpful to relate directly to this possibility rather than just ignoring it. The healer should encourage people who are sick to confront their uncertainty. Such open communication will allow a real meeting to take place, an honest relationship.

We do not have to try to conceal the unspeakable; on the other hand, we do not have to push it to the extreme. At the least, we should help a person to have some understanding of the idea of loss—of the possibility of nonexistence and of dissolving into the unknown. The whole point of any relationship is to share some degree of honesty and to explore how far we can go with it. In that way, relationships can become extremely powerful and intense, and beautiful. Sometimes we might only be able to get a hint of this intensity; we might only open up to just the bare minimum. Still, even then it is worthwhile. It is a step in the right direction.

In the healer-patient relationship, we are not concerned with trying to change people, particularly. Sickness and health are not black-and-white situations but are part of an organic process. We are simply working with sickness and the potential of death rather than relying on any particular doctrine. We are not talking about converting people. Nevertheless, the materials we have to work with are very rich; as we go along, we can see the seed changing into a flower. We do not really change people; they simply grow. Encouraging patients to accept death or uncertainty does not mean that they have to face the devil. Instead, such acceptance is something positive in people's lives; conquering the final fear of the unknown is very powerful.

Some people talk about healing in a magical sense, as when so-called healers put their hands on a sick person and miraculously heal him or her; others talk about the physical approach to healing, using drugs, surgery, and so forth. But I think the important point is that any real healing has to come out of some kind of psychological openness. There are constant opportunities for such openness—constant gaps in our conceptual and physical structures. If we begin to breathe out, then we create room for fresh air to rush in. If we do not breathe, there is no way for the fresh air to enter. It is a question of psychological attitude rather than of being taken over by external powers that heal us. Openness seems to be the only key to healing. And openness means we are willing to acknowledge that we are worthy; we have some kind of ground to relate with whatever is happening to us.

The role of the healer is not just to cure the disease; it is to cut through the tendency to see disease as an external threat. By providing companionship and some kind of sympathy, the healer creates a suggestion of health or underlying sanity, which then undermines naive conceptions of disease. The healer deals with the mishandling of the gaps that occur in one's life, with one's losses of spirit.

People tend to feel that their particular sickness is something special, that they are the only person with such an illness. But in fact, their illness is not so special—nor so terrible. It is a question of acknowledging that we are born alone and that we die alone, but that it is still OK. There is nothing particularly terrible or special about it.

Often the whole notion of sickness is taken as a purely mechanical problem: something is wrong with one's machine, one's body. But somehow that is missing the point. It is not the sickness that is the big problem but the psychological state behind it. We could not have gotten sick in the first place without some kind of loss of interest and attention. Whether we were run down by a car or we caught a cold, there was some gap in which we did not take care of ourselves—an empty moment in which we ceased to relate to things properly. There was no ongoing awareness of our psychological state. So to the extent that we invite it to begin with, all sickness—and not just those diseases traditionally considered to be psychosomatic—is psychological. All diseases are instigated by one's state of mind. And even after we have dealt with the disease and the symptoms have disappeared, by pretending that the problem is over we only plant seeds for further neurosis.

It seems that we generally avoid our psychological responsibility, as though diseases were external events imposing themselves upon us. There is a quality of sleepiness and of missing the gaps in the seemingly solid structure of our lives. Out of that sense of carelessness comes an immense message. Our bodies demand our attention; our bodies demand that we actually pay attention to what is going on with our lives. Illness brings us down to earth, making things seem much more direct and immediate.

Disease is a direct message to develop a proper attitude of mindfulness: we should be more intelligent about ourselves. Our minds and bodies are both very immediate. You alone know how your body feels. No one else cares; no one else can know but you.

So there is a natural wakefulness about what is good for you and what is not. You can respond intelligently to your body by paying attention to your state of mind.

Because of this, the practice of meditation may be the only way to really cure ourselves. Although the attempt to use meditation as some sort of cure may seem materialistic, the practice itself soon cuts through any materialistic attitude. Basically, mindfulness is a sense of composure. In meditation, we are not accomplishing anything; we are just there, seeing our lives. There is a general sense of watchfulness and an awareness of the body as an extremely sensitive mechanism that gives us messages constantly. If we have missed all the rest of the opportunities to relate with these messages, we find ourselves sick. Our bodies force us to be mindful on the spot. So it is important not to try to get rid of the sickness but to use it as a message.

We view our desire to get rid of disease as a desire to live. But instead, it is often just the opposite: it is an attempt to avoid life. Although we seemingly want to be alive, in fact we simply want to avoid intensity. It is an ironic twist: we actually want to be healed in order to avoid life. So the hope for cure is a big lie; it is the biggest conspiracy of all. In fact, all entertainment—whether it is the movies or various programs for so-called self-growth—lures us into feeling that we are in touch with life while in fact we are putting ourselves into a further stupor.

The healing relationship is a meeting of two minds: that of the healer and patient or, for that matter, of the spiritual teacher and student. If you and the other person are both open, some kind of dialogue can take place that is not forced. Communication occurs naturally because both are in the same situation. If the patient feels terrible, the healer picks up that sense of the patient's wretchedness: for a moment, he feels more or less the same, as if he himself were sick. For a moment, the two are not separate, and a sense of authenticity takes place. From the patient's point of view, that is precisely what is needed: someone acknowledges his existence and the fact that he needs help very badly. Someone actually sees through his sickness. The healing process can then begin to take place in the patient's state of being, because he realizes that someone has communicated with him completely. There has been a mutual glimpse of common ground. The psychological under-pinning of the sickness then begins to come apart, to dissolve. The same thing applies to meetings between a meditation teacher and his or her student. There is a flash of understanding—nothing particularly mystical or "far-out," as they say—just very simple, direct communication. The student understands and the teacher understands at the same moment. In this common flash of under-standing, knowledge is imparted.

At this point, I am not making any distinction between phy-sicians and psychiatrists: whether we are dealing at the psychologi-cal or the medical level, the relationship with one's patient has to be exactly the same. The atmosphere of acceptance is extremely simple but very effective. The main point is that the healer and the patient are able to share their sense of pain and suffering—their claustrophobia or fear or physical pain. The healer has to feel her-self to be part of that whole setup. It seems that many healers avoid that kind of identification; they do not want to get involved in such an intense experience. Instead, they try to play extremely cool and unconcerned, taking a more businesslike approach.

We all speak the same language; we experience a similar type of birth and a similar exposure to death. So there is bound to always be some link, some continuity between you and the other. It is something more than just mechanically saying "Yes, I know; it hurts very badly." Rather than just sympathizing with the pa-tient, it is important to actually feel her pain and share her anxiety. You can then say, "Yes, I feel that pain," in a different way. To relate with total openness means that you are completely captured by someone's problem. There may be a sense of not knowing quite how to handle it and just having to do your best, but even such clumsiness is an enormously generous statement. So complete openness and bewilderment meet at a very fine point.

There is much more involved in the healer-patient relation-ship than just going by the books and looking up the appropriate medicine. According to Buddhism, the human essence is compas-sion and wisdom. So you do not have to acquire skillful communi-cation from outside yourself; you have it already. It has nothing to do with mystical experience or any kind of higher spiritual ecstasy; it is just the basic working situation. If you have an interest in something, that is openness. If you have an interest in people's suffering and conflicts, you have that openness constantly. And then you can develop some sense of trust and understanding, so that your openness becomes compassion.

It is possible to work with sixty people a day and have something click with each of them. It requires a sense of complete dedication and a willingness to stay alert, without trying to achieve a specific goal. If you have a goal, then you are trying to manipulate the interaction and healing cannot take place. You need to understand your patients and encourage them to communicate, but you cannot force them. Only then can the patient, who is feeling a sense of separation, which is also a sense of death, begin to feel that there is hope. At last someone really cares for him, someone really does listen, even if it is only for a few seconds. That allows intense, very genuine communication to take place. Such communication is simple: there is no trick behind it and no complicated tradition to learn. It is not a question of learning *how* to do it but of just going ahead with it.

Psychiatrists and physicians, as well as their patients, have to come to terms with their sense of anxiety about the possibility of nonexistence. When there is that kind of openness, the healer does not have to solve a person's problem completely. The approach of trying to repair everything has always been a problem in the past; such an approach creates a successive string of cures and deceptions, which seem to go hand in hand. Once the basic fear is acknowledged, continuing with the treatment becomes very easy. The path comes to you: there is no need to try to create the path for yourself. Healing professionals have the advantage of being able to develop themselves by working with the great variety of situations that come to them. There are endless possibilities for developing one's awareness and openness. Of course, it is always easier to look down on your patients and their predicament, thinking how lucky you are that you do not have their diseases. You can feel somewhat superior. But the acknowledgment of your common ground—your common experience of birth, old age, sickness, and death, and the fear that underlies all of those—brings a sense of humility. That is the beginning of the healing process. The rest seems to follow quite easily and naturally, based on one's inherent wisdom and compassion. This is not a particularly mystical or spiritual process; it is simple, ordinary human experience. The first time you try to approach a person in this way, it may seem to be difficult. But you just do it on the spot.

And finally, what do we mean when we say that a patient has been healed? To be healed, ironically, means that a person is no longer embarrassed by life; she is able to face death without resentment or expectation.

The Heart of the Buddha, Pages 177–184

The Spiritual Friend

COMING TO THE STUDY of spirituality, we are faced with the problem of our relationship with a teacher, lama, guru, whatever we call the person we suppose will give us spiritual understanding. These words, especially the term *guru*, have acquired meanings and associations in the West that are misleading and that generally add to the confusion around the issue of what it means to study with a spiritual teacher. This is not to say that people in the East understand how to relate to a guru while Westerners do not; the problem is universal. People always come to the study of spirituality with some ideas already fixed in their minds of what it is they are going to get and how to deal with the person from whom they think they will get it. The very notion that we will *get* something from a guru—happiness, peace of mind, wisdom, whatever it is we seek—is one of the most difficult preconceptions of all. So I think it would be helpful to examine the way in which some famous students dealt with the problems of how to relate to spirituality and a spiritual teacher. Perhaps these examples will have some relevance for our own individual search.

One of the most renowned Tibetan masters and also one of the main gurus of the Kagyü lineage, of which I am a member, was Marpa, student of the Indian teacher Naropa and guru to Milarepa, his most famous spiritual son. Marpa is an example of someone who was on his way to becoming a successful self-made man. He was born into a farming family, but as a youth, he became ambitious and chose scholarship and the priesthood as his route to prominence. We can imagine what tremendous effort and determination it must have taken for the son of a farmer to raise himself to the position of priest in his local religious tradition. There were only a few ways for such a man to achieve any kind of position in tenth-century Tibet—as a merchant, as a bandit, or especially as a priest. Joining the local clergy at that time was roughly equivalent to becoming a doctor, lawyer, and college professor, all rolled into one.

Marpa began by studying Tibetan, Sanskrit, several other languages, and the spoken language of India. After about three years of such study, he was proficient enough to begin earning money as a scholar, and with this money, he financed his religious study, eventually becoming a Buddhist priest of sorts. Such a position brought with it a certain degree of local prominence, but Marpa was more ambitious, and so, although he was married by now and had a family, he continued to save his earnings until he had amassed a large amount of gold.

At this point, Marpa announced to his relatives his intentions to travel to India to collect more teachings. India at this time was the world center for Buddhist studies, home of Nalanda University and the greatest Buddhist sages and scholars. It was Marpa's intention to study and collect texts unknown in Tibet, bring them home, and translate them, thus establishing himself as a great scholar-translator. The journey to India was at that time, and until fairly recently, a long and dangerous one, and Marpa's family and elders tried to dissuade him from it. But he was determined and so set out accompanied by a friend and fellow scholar.

After a difficult journey of some months, they crossed the Himalayas into India and proceeded to Bengal, where they went their separate ways. Both men were well qualified in the study of language and religion, and so they decided to search for their own teachers, to suit their own tastes. Before parting, they agreed to meet again for the journey home.

While he was traveling through Nepal, Marpa had happened to hear of the teacher Naropa, a man of enormous fame. Naropa had been abbot of Nalanda University, perhaps the greatest center for Buddhist studies the world has ever known. At the height of his career, feeling that he understood the sense but not the real meaning of the teachings, he had abandoned his post and set out in search of a guru. For twelve years, he endured terrific hardship at the hands of his teacher Tilopa, until finally he achieved realization. By the time Marpa heard of him, he was reputed to be one of the greatest Buddhist saints ever to have lived. Naturally, Marpa set out to find him.

Eventually, Marpa found Naropa living in poverty in a simple house in the forests of Bengal. He had expected to find so great a teacher living in the midst of a highly evolved religious setting of some sort, and so he was somewhat disappointed. However, he was a bit confused by the strangeness of a foreign country and willing to make some allowances, thinking that perhaps this was the way Indian teachers lived. Also, his appreciation of Naropa's fame outweighed his disappointment, and so he gave Naropa most of his gold and asked for teachings. He explained that he was a married man, a priest, scholar, and farmer from Tibet, and that he was not willing to give up this life he had made for himself but that he wanted to collect teachings to take back to Tibet to translate in order to earn more money. Naropa agreed to Marpa's requests quite easily, gave Marpa instruction, and everything went smoothly.

After some time, Marpa decided that he had collected enough teachings to suit his purposes and prepared to return home. He proceeded to an inn in a large town where he rejoined his traveling companion, and the two sat down to compare the results of their efforts. When his friend saw what Marpa had collected, he laughed and said, "What you have here is worthless! We already have those teachings in Tibet. You must have found something more exciting and rare. I found fantastic teachings that I received from very great masters."

Marpa, of course, was extremely frustrated and upset, having come such a long way and with so much difficulty and expense, so he decided to return to Naropa and try once more. When he arrived at Naropa's hut and asked for more rare and exotic and advanced teachings, to his surprise Naropa told him, "I'm sorry, but you can't receive these teachings from me. You will have to go and receive these from someone else, a man named Kukuripa. The journey is difficult, especially so because Kukuripa lives on an island in the middle of a lake of poison. But he is the one you will have to see if you want these teachings."

By this time, Marpa was becoming desperate, so he decided to try the journey. Besides, if Kukuripa had teachings that even the great Naropa could not give him and, in addition, lived in the middle of a poisonous lake, then he must be quite an extraordinary teacher, a great mystic.

So Marpa made the journey and managed to cross the lake to the island, where he began to look for Kukuripa. There he found an old Indian man living in filth in the midst of hundreds of female dogs. The situation was outlandish, to say the least, but Marpa nevertheless tried to speak to Kukuripa. All he got was gibberish. Kukuripa seemed to be speaking complete nonsense.

Now the situation was almost unbearable. Not only was Kukuripa's speech completely unintelligible, but Marpa had to constantly be on guard against the hundreds of bitches. As soon as he was able to make a relationship with one dog, another would bark and threaten to bite him. Finally, almost beside himself, Marpa gave up altogether, gave up trying to take notes, gave up trying to receive any kind of secret doctrine. And at that point, Kukuripa began to speak to him in a totally intelligible, coherent voice, and the dogs stopped harrassing him, and Marpa received the teachings.

After Marpa had finished studying with Kukuripa, he returned once more to his original guru, Naropa. Naropa told him, "Now you must return to Tibet and teach. It isn't enough to receive the teachings in a theoretical way. You must go through certain life experiences. Then you can come back again and study further."

Once more, Marpa met his fellow searcher, and together they began the long journey back to Tibet. Marpa's companion had also studied a great deal, and both men had stacks of manuscripts, and as they proceeded, they discussed what they had learned. Soon Marpa began to feel uneasy about his friend, who seemed more and more inquisitive to discover what teachings Marpa had collected. Their conversations together seemed to turn increasingly around this subject, until finally his traveling companion decided that Marpa had obtained more valuable teachings than himself, and so he became quite jealous. As they were crossing a river in a ferry, Marpa's colleague began to complain of being uncomfortable and crowded by all the baggage they were carrying. He shifted his position in the boat, as if to make himself more comfortable and, in so doing, managed to throw all of Marpa's manuscripts into the river. Marpa tried desperately to rescue them, but they were gone. All the texts he had gone to such lengths to collect had disappeared in an instant.

So it was with a feeling of great loss that Marpa returned to Tibet. He had many stories to tell of his travels and studies, but he had nothing solid to prove his knowledge and experience. Nevertheless, he spent several years working and teaching until, to his surprise, he began to realize that his writings would have been useless to him, even had he been able to save them. While he was in India, he had only taken written notes on those parts of the teachings he had not understood. He had not written down those teachings that were part of his own experience. It was only years later that he discovered that they had actually become a part of him.

With this discovery, Marpa lost all desire to profit from the teachings. He was no longer concerned with making money or achieving prestige but instead was inspired to realize enlightenment. So he collected gold dust as an offering to Naropa and once again made the journey to India. This time he went full of longing to see his guru and desire for the teachings.

However, Marpa's next encounter with Naropa was quite different from before. Naropa seemed very cold and impersonal, almost hostile, and his first words to Marpa were, "Good to see you again. How much gold have you for my teachings?" Marpa had brought a large amount of gold but wanted to save some for his expenses and the trip home, so he opened his pack and gave Naropa only a portion of what he had. Naropa looked at the offering and said, "No, this is not enough. I need more gold than this for my teaching. Give me all your gold." Marpa gave him a bit more, and still Naropa demanded all, and this went on until finally Naropa laughed and said, "Do you think you can buy my teaching with your deception?" At this point, Marpa yielded and gave Naropa all the gold he had. To his shock, Naropa picked up the bags and began flinging the gold dust in the air.

Suddenly Marpa felt extremely confused and paranoid. He could not understand what was happening. He had worked hard for the gold to buy the teaching he so wanted. Naropa had seemed to indicate that he needed the gold and would teach Marpa in return for it. Yet he was throwing it away! Then Naropa said to him, "What need have I of gold? The whole world is gold for me!"

This was a great moment of opening for Marpa. He opened and was able to receive teaching. He stayed with Naropa for a long time after that, and his training was quite austere, but he did not simply listen to the teachings as before; he had to work his way through them. He had to give up everything he had; not just his material possessions but whatever he was holding back in his mind had to go. It was a continual process of opening and surrender.

In Milarepa's case, the situation developed quite differently. He was a peasant, much less learned and sophisticated than Marpa had been when he met Naropa, and he had committed many crimes, including murder. He was miserably unhappy, yearned for enlightenment, and was willing to pay any fee that Marpa might ask. So Marpa had Milarepa pay on a very literal physical level. He had him build a series of houses for him, one after the other, and after each was completed, Marpa would tell Milarepa to tear the house down and put all the stones back where he had found them, so as not to mar the landscape. Each time Marpa ordered Milarepa to dismantle a house, he would give some absurd excuse, such as having been drunk when he ordered the house built or never having ordered such a house at all. And each time Milarepa, full of longing for the teachings, would tear the house down and start again.

Finally, Marpa designed a tower with nine stories. Milarepa suffered terrific physical hardship in carrying the stones and building the house, and when he had finished, he went to Marpa and once more asked for the teachings. But Marpa said to him, "You want to receive teachings from me, just like that, merely because you built this tower for me? Well, I'm afraid you will still have to give me a gift as an initiation fee."

By this time, Milarepa had no possessions left whatsoever, having spent all his time and labor building towers. But Damema, Marpa's wife, felt sorry for him and said, "These towers you have built are such a wonderful gesture of devotion and faith. Surely my husband won't mind if I give you some sacks of barley and a roll of cloth for your initiation fee." So Milarepa took the barley and cloth to the initiation circle where Marpa was teaching and offered them as his fee, along with the gifts of the other students. But Marpa, when he recognized the gift, was furious and shouted at Milarepa, "These things belong to me, you hypocrite! You try to deceive me!" And he literally kicked Milarepa out of the initiation circle.

At this point, Milarepa gave up all hope of ever getting Marpa to give him the teachings. In despair, he decided to commit suicide and was just about to kill himself when Marpa came to him and told him that he was ready to receive the teaching.

The process of receiving teaching depends upon the student's giving something in return; some kind of psychological surrender is necessary, a gift of some sort. This is why we must discuss surrendering, opening, giving up expectations, before we can speak of the relationship between teacher and student. It is essential to surrender, to open yourself, to present whatever you are to the guru rather than trying to present yourself as a worthwhile student. It does not matter how much you are willing to pay, how correctly you behave, how clever you are at saying the right thing to your teacher. It is not like having an interview for a job or buying a new car. Whether or not you will get the job depends upon your credentials, how well you are dressed, how beautifully your shoes are polished, how well you speak, how good your manners are. If you are buying a car, it is a matter of how much money you have and how good your credit is.

But when it comes to spirituality, something more is required. It is not a matter of applying for a job, of dressing up to impress our potential employer. Such deception does not apply to an interview with a guru, because she sees right through us. She is amused if we dress up especially for the interview. Making ingratiating gestures is not applicable in this situation; in fact, it is futile. We must make a real commitment to being open with our teacher; we must be willing to give up all our preconceptions. Milarepa expected Marpa to be a great scholar and a saintly person, dressed in yogic costume with beads, reciting mantras, meditating. Instead, he found Marpa working on his farm, directing the laborers and plowing his land.

I am afraid the word *guru* is overused in the West. It would be better to speak of one's "spiritual friend," because the teachings emphasize a mutual meeting of two minds. It is a matter of mutual communication rather than a master-servant relationship between a highly evolved being and a miserable, confused one. In the master-servant relationship, the highly evolved being may appear not even to be sitting on his or her seat but may seem to be floating, levitating, looking down at us. The guru's voice is penetrating, pervading space. Every word, every cough, every movement is a gesture of wisdom. But this is a dream. A guru should be a spiritual friend who communicates and presents his or her qualities to us, as Marpa did with Milarepa and Naropa with Marpa. Marpa presented his quality of being a farmer-yogi. He happened to have seven children and a wife, and he looked after his farm, cultivating the land and supporting himself and his family. But these activities were just an ordinary part of his life. He cared for his students as he cared for his crops and family. He was so thorough, paying attention to every detail of his life, that he was able to be a competent teacher as well as a competent father and farmer. There was no physical or spiritual materialism in Marpa's lifestyle at all. He did not emphasize spirituality and ignore his family or his physical relationship to the earth. If you are not involved with materialism, either spiritually or physically, then there is no emphasis made on any extreme.

Nor is it helpful to choose someone for your guru simply because that person is famous, someone who is renowned for having published stacks of books and converted thousands or millions of people. Instead, the guideline is whether or not you are able actually to communicate with the person, directly and thoroughly. How much self-deception are you involved in? If you really open yourself to your spiritual friend, then you are bound to work together. Are you able to talk to him or her thoroughly and properly? Does he or she know anything about you? Does she know anything about herself, for that matter? Is the guru really able to see through your masks, communicate with you properly, directly? In searching for a teacher, this seems to be the guideline rather than fame or wisdom.

There is an interesting story of a group of people who decided to go and study under a great Tibetan teacher. They had already studied somewhat with other teachers but had decided to concentrate on trying to learn from this particular person. They were all very anxious to become his students and so sought an audience with him, but this great teacher would not accept any of them. "Under one condition only will I accept you," he said. "If you are willing to renounce your previous teachers." They all pleaded with him, telling him how much they were devoted to him, how great his reputation was, and how much they would like to study with him. But he would not accept any of them unless they would meet his condition. Finally, all except one person in the party decided to renounce their previous teachers, from whom they had in fact learned a great deal. The guru seemed to be quite happy when they did so and told them all to come back the next day. But when they returned, he said to them, "I understand your hypocrisy. The next time you go to another teacher, you will renounce me. So get out." And he chased them all out except for the one person who valued what he had learned previously. The person he accepted was not willing to play any more lying games, was not willing to try to please a guru by pretending to be different from what he was. If you are going to make friends with a spiritual master, you must make friends simply, openly, so that the communication takes place between equals rather than your trying to win the master over to you.

In order to be accepted by your guru as a friend, you have to open yourself completely. And in order that you might open, you will probably have to undergo tests by your spiritual friend and by life-situations in general, all of these tests taking the form of disappointment. At some stage, you will doubt that your spiritual friend has any feeling, any emotion toward you at all. This is dealing with your own hypocrisy. The hypocrisy, the pretense and basic twist of ego, is extremely hard; it has a very thick skin. We tend to wear suits of armor, one over the other. This hypocrisy is so dense and multileveled that as soon as we remove one layer of our suit of armor, we find another beneath it. We hope we will not have to completely undress. We hope that stripping off only a few layers will make us presentable. Then we appear in our new suit of armor with such an ingratiating face, but our spiritual friend does not wear any armor at all; he is a naked person. Compared with his nakedness, we are wearing cement. Our armor is so thick that our friend cannot feel the texture of our skin, our bodies. He cannot even see our faces properly. There are many stories of teacher-student relationships in the past in which the student had to make long journeys and endure many hardships until the fascination and impulses began to wear out. This seems to be the point: the impulse of searching for something is, in itself, a hang-up. When this impulse begins to wear out, then our fundamental basic nakedness begins to appear and the meeting of the two minds begins to take place.

It has been said that the first stage of meeting one's spiritual friend is like going to a supermarket. You are excited, and you dream of all the different things that you are going to buy: the richness of your spiritual friend and the colorful qualities of his personality. The second stage of your relationship is like going to court, as though you were a criminal. You are not able to meet your friend's demands, and you begin to feel self-conscious, because you know that she knows as much as you know about yourself, which is extremely embarrassing. In the third stage, when you go to see your spiritual friend, it is like seeing a cow happily grazing in a meadow. You just admire its peacefulness and the landscape, and then you pass on. Finally, the fourth stage with one's spiritual friend is like passing a rock in the road. You do not even pay attention to it; you just pass by and walk away.

At the beginning, a kind of courtship with the guru is taking place, a love affair. How much are you able to win this person over to you? There is a tendency to want to be closer to your spiritual friend, because you really want to learn. You feel such admiration for him. But at the same time, he is very frightening; he puts you off. Either the situation does not coincide with your expectations or there is a self-conscious feeling that "I may not be able to open completely and thoroughly." A love-hate relationship, a kind of surrendering and running away process develops. In other words, we begin to play a game, a game of wanting to open, wanting to be involved in a love affair with our guru, and then wanting to run away from him. If we get too close to our spiritual friend, then we begin to feel overpowered by him. As it says in the old Tibetan proverb: "A guru is like a fire. If you get too close, you get burned;

if you stay too far away, you don't get enough heat." This kind of courtship takes place on the part of the student. You tend to get too close to the teacher, but once you do, you get burned. Then you want to run away altogether.

Eventually, the relationship begins to become very substantial and solid. You begin to realize that wanting to be near and wanting to be far away from the guru are simply your own game. It has nothing to do with the real situation but is just your own hallucination. The guru or spiritual friend is always there burning, always a life-fire. You can play games with him or not, as you choose.

Then the relationship with one's spiritual friend begins to become very creative. You accept the situations of being overwhelmed by her and distant from her. If she decides to play the role of cold icy water, you accept it. If she decides to play the role of hot fire, you accept it. Nothing can shake you at all, and you come to a reconciliation with her.

The next stage is that, having accepted everything your spiritual friend might do, you begin to lose your own inspiration because you have completely surrendered, completely given up. You feel yourself reduced to a speck of dust. You are insignificant. You begin to feel that the only world that exists is that of this spiritual friend, the guru. It is as though you were watching a fascinating movie; the movie is so exciting that you become part of it. There is no you and no cinema hall, no chairs, no people watching, no friends sitting next to you. The movie is all that exists. This is called the "honeymoon period," in which everything is seen as a part of this central being, the guru. You are just a useless, insignificant person who is continuously being fed by this great, fascinating central being. Whenever you feel weak or tired or bored, you go and just sit in the cinema hall and are entertained, uplifted, rejuvenated. At this point, the phenomenon of the personality cult becomes prominent. The guru is the only person in the world who exists, alive and vibrant. The very meaning of your life depends upon him. If you die, you die for him. If you live, you survive for him and are insignificant.

However, this love affair with your spiritual friend cannot last forever. Sooner or later, its intensity must wane, and you must face your own life-situation and your own psychology. It is like having married and finished the honeymoon. You not only feel conscious of your lover as the central focus of your attention, but you begin to notice his or her lifestyle as well. You begin to notice what it is that makes this person a teacher, beyond the limits of her individuality and personality. Thus, the principle of the "universality of the guru" comes into the picture as well. Every problem you face in life is a part of your marriage. Whenever you experience difficulties, you hear the words of the guru. This is the point at which one begins to gain one's independence from the guru as lover, because every situation becomes an expression of the teachings. First, you surrendered to your spiritual friend. Then you communicated and played games with her. And now you have come to the state of complete openness. As a result of this openness, you begin to see the guru-quality in every life-situation, that all situations in life offer you the opportunity to be as open as you are with the guru, and so all things can become the guru.

Milarepa had a vivid vision of his guru Marpa while he was meditating in very strict retreat in Red Rock Jewel Valley. Weak with hunger and battered by the elements, he had fainted while trying to collect firewood outside his cave. When he regained consciousness, he looked to the east and saw white clouds in the direction where Marpa lived. With great longing, he sang a song of supplication, telling Marpa how much he longed to be with him. Then Marpa appeared in a vision, riding a white snow lion, and said to him something like, "What is the matter with you? Have you had a neurotic upheaval of some sort? You understand the dharma, so continue to practice meditation." Milarepa took comfort and returned to his cave to meditate. His reliance and dependence upon Marpa at this point indicate that he had not yet freed himself from the notion of guru as personal, individual friend.

However, when Milarepa returned to his cave, he found it full of demons with eyes as big as saucepans and bodies the size of thumbs. He tried all kinds of ploys to get them to stop mocking and tormenting him, but they would not leave until Milarepa finally stopped trying to play games, until he recognized his own hypocrisy and gave in to openness. From this point on, you see a tremendous change of style in Milarepa's songs, because he had learned to identify with the universal quality of guru rather than solely relating to Marpa as an individual person.

The spiritual friend becomes part of you as well as being an individual, external person. As such, the guru, both internal and external, plays a very important part in penetrating and exposing our hypocrisies. The guru can be a person who acts as a mirror, reflecting you, or else your own basic intelligence takes the form of the spiritual friend. When the internal guru begins to function, then you can never escape the demand to open. The basic intelligence follows you everywhere; you cannot escape your own shadow. "Big Brother is watching you." Though it is not external entities who are watching us and haunting us; we haunt ourselves. Our own shadow is watching us.

We could look at it in two different ways. We could see the guru as a ghost, haunting and mocking us for our hypocrisy. There could be a demonic quality in realizing what we are. And yet there is always the creative quality of the spiritual friend that also becomes a part of us. The basic intelligence is continuously present in the situations of life. It is so sharp and penetrating that, at some stage, even if you want to get rid of it, you cannot. Sometimes it has a stern expression, sometimes an inspiring smile. It has been said in the tantric tradition that you do not see the face of the guru, but you see the expression of his or her face all the time. Either smiling, grinning, or frowning angrily, it is part of every life-situation. The basic intelligence, tathagatagarbha, buddha nature, is always in every experience life brings us. There is no escaping it. Again, it is said in the teachings: "Better not to begin. Once you begin, better to finish it." So you had better not step onto the spiritual path unless you must. Once you have stepped foot on the path, you have really done it; you cannot step back. There is no way of escaping.

Cutting Through Spiritual Materialism, Pages 31–47

The Lonely Journey

WE ARE WORKING on the karmic pattern of America. We are trying to infiltrate it. That is quite dangerous. The magical powers of materialism and spirituality are waging war, so to speak, all the time. From the beginning, it has worked that way. Spirituality is against worldliness, and worldliness is against spirituality. So we are facing tremendous danger.

We are working on the infiltration of the materialistic world. According to history, a lot of people who attempted to become teachers or outstanding students were struck down by the power and energy of materialism—whether through a direct physical attack or through a psychological attack. So it is very dangerous—to the extent that we should not be involved. If you insist on being involved in it, then you should be brave enough to work with it and go along with the infiltration.

The next subject is the practice of meditation, which is the technique of infiltration, or how to transmute negative hostile forces into positive creative situations. That is what we are doing. Your involvement is not going to be easy by any means. It is going to be extremely difficult. It is a lonely journey. It is a lonely journey with bridges, ladders, cliffs, and waves. It includes turbulent rivers that we have to cross, shaky bridges that we have to walk on, slippery steps that we have to tread on among hailstorms, rains, snowstorms, and powerful winds. Constant patience is needed as well: we are going to cross an inexhaustible stretch of desert without water. All of this is very frightening. And you cannot blame the situation on anyone: you can't blame it on the teacher who led you to it, and you can't blame it on yourself, that you started on it. Blaming doesn't help. Going along on the path is the only way.

At the same time, some energy and encouragement continue

on the path as well—it's not as black as that, by any means. Your first inspiration to step in or involve yourself in such a path is based on the communication and the connection between you and me. Some of you are involved with the work of Suzuki Roshi in California, and you also decided to become involved with my work. This situation contains tremendous power, reinforcement, and energy behind it. It is not only that the teachers themselves are particularly forceful teachers or powerful as individuals. They are just human beings. But the energy behind that inspiration comes from a lineage of twenty-five hundred years of effort, energy, and spiritual power. Nobody in that lineage took advantage of that power, but they received inspiration from it, and everybody worked, practiced, and achieved. And their inspiration has been handed down generation by generation. As the scriptures would say, it is like good gold, which is put on the fire and beaten, hammered, twisted, refined, until it comes out as pure gold—living pure gold. Or it is like hot baked bread. The knowledge of baking bread has been handed down generation by generation, so present-day bakers who belong to that particular lineage can still provide hot, living, tasty bread straight from the oven and feed you. Such a living quality of inspiration continues. It is that which keeps us continuing on the path, going through the deserts, going through the storms, bridges, ladders, and so on.

The whole thing is really based on our relationship to ourselves. Nobody particularly has to belong to a syndicate, or to a spiritual scene, just for the sake of belonging. It is the relationship of ourself to ourself that seems to be important. That inspiration of belonging to ourself, working with ourself, relating with ourself, has different facets, which are the six realms or the six types of world—the world of the gods, the world of hell, the worlds of the hungry ghosts, human beings, animals, and jealous gods. Making friends with ourselves is not easy. It is a very profound thing. At the same time, we can do it. Nevertheless, making a long story too short, involvement with ourselves means making an honest relationship with ourselves, looking into ourselves as what we are and realizing that external comfort will be temporary, that our comforters may not be there all the time. There is the possibility of our being alone. Therefore, there is more reason to work and go along with the practices that are involved. What happened to me is that I established a relationship with my guru, Jamgön Kongtrül Rinpoche. I learned from him and spent time with him. There were also certain times when I couldn't see him and I couldn't talk to him. Later I would be able to talk to him again and relate my experiences to him. When I saw him for the last time, I felt I really had communication, with real commitment and understanding of his teachings. I was very pleased about it. I regarded that as the beginning of our relationship. But then I had to go on without him. I had achieved tremendous insight, understanding, as to what he was and what he had to say, and I was dying to relate that to him, just to tell him. That would be so beautiful. It would be such a beautiful moment to relate to him that at last I had heard him, I had understood him. I was waiting for the occasion to do that—and it never took place; nothing happened. Jamgön Kongtrül was captured by the Communist Chinese, and he died in jail. I never met him or saw him again.

A similar situation happened with Gampopa and Milarepa. Milarepa told Gampopa, his chief disciple, that he should practice certain meditations and relate with his experience—and Gampopa did that; he achieved it. But it happened that he forgot the particular date he was supposed to come and see Milarepa, which was the fifteenth day of the first month of the year, according to the Tibetan calendar. He was about ten days late. He suddenly remembered on the twenty-fifth day that he must go and see Milarepa on the fifteenth, so he decided to set out. He rushed, but halfway there, some travelers came to him with the message that Milarepa was dead. He had sent a piece of his robe and a message for Gampopa. So Gampopa was never able to relate that last experience to Milarepa.

Situations like that take place all the time. They are a kind of encouragement, showing us that we are able to work with ourselves and that we will achieve the goal—but we will not receive the congratulations of the guru anymore. Again, you are alone: you are a lonely student, or you are a lonely teacher. You are continuously becoming alone again. With such independence, relating with spiritual scenes or other such situations is not so important.

But relating with *ourselves* is very important and more necessary. There is a real living quality in that.

I'm not saying these things because I want to raise your paranoia. But as in the historical cases, nobody is going to congratulate you, that finally you are buddha. And in fact, your enthronement ceremony will never take place. If it did take place, it would be dangerous, the wrong time—it would not be real anymore. So the lonely journey is important. And many of you are going to try to practice by yourselves and work hard on all this, trying to relate with the different realms of the world. But at the same time, no teacher or situation should be providing comfort to anybody. I suppose that is the point we are getting at. In other words, nobody is going to be initiated as a fully enlightened person decorated by the guru. It is just about to happen, you think you are just about to get a decoration—but it doesn't take place; it never happens. So any external reliance does not work. It is working on oneself with individual, personal intuition that is important.

Transcending Madness, Pages 166–170

Looking into the World

Looking into the world
I see alone a chrysanthemum,
Lonely loneliness,
And death approaches.
Abandoned by guru and friend,
I stand like the lonely juniper
Which grows among rocks,
Hardened and tough.
Loneliness is my habit—
I grew up in loneliness.
Like a rhinoceros
Loneliness is my companion—
I converse with myself.
Yet sometimes also,
Lonely moon,
Sad and Happy
Come together.

Do not trust.
If you trust, you are in
Others' hands.
It is like the single yak
That defeats the wolves.
Herds panic and in trying to flee
Are attacked.
Remaining in solitude
You can never be defeated.
So do not trust,
For trust is surrendering oneself.
Never, never trust.

But be friendly.
By being friendly toward others
You increase your non-trusting.
The idea is to be independent,
Not involved,

Not glued, one might say, to others.
Thus one becomes ever more
Compassionate and friendly.
Whatever happens, stand on your own feet
And memorize this incantation:
Do not trust.

Timely Rain, Pages 13–14

TANTRA: THE DIAMOND PATH

Listen, Abushri*

You who enjoy the union of bliss and emptiness
Seated motionless on the lunar disc
Above a beautiful hundred-petaled flower
Radiant with white light,
I pay homage to you the Divine Guru, Vajrasattva.

Listen, Abushri,
You miserable, daydreaming fool,
You remember how delusions
Confused you in the past?
Watch out for delusions in the present,
And don't lead a hypocritical life.

Stop unnecessary speculations.
You've made hundreds of plans
That never came off
And only led to disappointment.
Unfinished acts are like
The overlapping action of the waves.
Stay alone and stop
Making your own head spin.

You've studied hundreds of philosophies
Without grasping any of them.

---

*Chögyam Trungpa produced this translation for his first book of poems, *Mudra.* It is the work of a famed and much-loved Tibetan teacher, Petrül Rinpoche, who lived at the end of the nineteenth century. Chögyam Trungpa described him as "a renowned Nyingmapa teacher, particularly interested in bringing the philosophy and practice of meditation together. He refused to live in an institutionalized monastery and became a great traveler."

What's the point of further study?
You've studied without remembering
Anything when you needed it.
What's the point of contemplation?
Forget about your "meditation"!
It doesn't seem to be
The cure for conflicting emotions.

You may have recited the set number of mantras,
But you still haven't mastered the concrete visualizations.
You may have mastered the concrete visualizations,
But you still haven't loosened the grip of duality.
You may have subdued apparent evils,
But you still haven't tamed your ego.

Forget your set periods of meditation
And following an obsessive schedule.
High and clear but not letting go,
Low and steady but lacking clarity,
Penetrating insight but only stabbing—
That's your meditation!
Forget the stare of concentration
And the tethered mind.

Lectures sound interesting,
But they don't help your mind.
The logical mind seems sharp,
But it's really the seed of confusion.
Oral instruction sounds very profound,
But it doesn't help if it isn't practiced.
Forget about browsing through books,
Which causes distraction and eyestrain.

You bang your antique prayer-drum,
But just for the novelty of playing (with) it.
You offer up your body,
But in fact you're still attached to it.
You play clear-sounding cymbals,
But your mind is heavy and dull.
Forget about these tricks,
Attractive though they are.

Your disciples seem to be studying,
But they never follow through;

One day there's a glimmer of understanding,
But the next day it has gone.
They learn one thing out of a hundred,
But they don't retain even that.
Forget these apparently fervent disciples!

One's closest friend is full of love
Today and indifferent tomorrow.
He is humble one minute and proud the next.
The more one loves him, the more distant he becomes.
Forget the dear friend who smiles
Because the friendship is still a novelty!

Your girlfriend puts on a smiling face,
But who knows what she really feels?
For one night of pleasure, it's nine months of heartache.
You can spend a month trying to bed her and still not succeed.
It's really not worth all the scandal and gossip,
So forget about her.

Never-ending chatter stirs up likes and dislikes.
It may be amusing and enjoyable,
But it's merely imitating the faults of others.
The listeners seem receptive,
But they may be critical at heart.
It only gives you a dry throat,
So forget about idle talk!

Preaching without firsthand experience
Of the subject is like dancing on books.
The audience may seem willing to listen,
But they're not really interested at all.
If you do not practice what you preach,
You'll be ashamed of it sooner or later,
So forget about hollow rhetoric!

When you haven't any books,
You feel the need for them;
When you have them, you don't.
It's only a few pages,
But to copy them is endless.
All the books in the world
Would give you no satisfaction,

So forget about copying—
Unless you get a fee for it!

One day you're relaxed,
The next you are tense.
You will never be happy
If you're swayed by people's moods.
Sometimes they are pleasant,
But maybe not when you need them,
And you might be disappointed.
So forget about politeness and flattery!

Political and religious activities
Are only for gentlemen.
That's not for you, my dear boy.
Remember the example of an old cow:
She's content to sleep in a barn.
You have to eat, sleep, and shit—
That's unavoidable—anything
Beyond that is none of your business.
Do what you have to do,
And keep yourself to yourself.

You're as low as the lowest,
So you ought to be humble.
There's a whole hierarchy above you,
So stop being proud.
You shouldn't have too many close associates
Because differences would surely arise.
Since you're not involved
In religious and political activities,
Don't make demands on yourself.
Give up everything, that's the point!

This teaching is given by Yogi Trimê Lodrö from his own experience to
his dear friend Abushri. Do practice it, although there is nothing to
practice. Give up everything—that's the whole point. Don't get angry
with yourself even if you can't practice the dharma.

Mudra, Pages 15–19

Vajra Nature

THE VAJRAYANA SEEMS to have been widely misunderstood in the West. People have projected a lot of ideas onto it, believing it to be an expression of wildness and freedom. However, the cultivation of vajrayana has to be based on a very subtle, definite, ordinary, and real foundation. Otherwise, we are lost. Not only are we lost, but we are destroying ourselves.

In talking about the tantric tradition, we are not talking about playing with sex or aggression or colors or the phenomenal world. At this point, we are simply developing a basic understanding of how tantra works. We have to be very conservative. We have to be very, very concerned with the fundamentals. I could say: "Don't worry. If you worry, that's your problem. If you don't worry, everything is going to be OK. Let's dance together. Let's play music together. Let's drink milk and honey." But that does not work, not at all. Talking about tantra is not such an easy matter.

Working with the energy of vajrayana is like dealing with a live electric wire. We can use switches, gloves, and all sorts of buffers in handling this live wire, but we also have the choice of using our bare hands and touching the live wire directly—in which case, we are in trouble. The institution of tantra, not only Buddhist tantra but Hindu tantra as well, has been presented very generously to American students by many competent and great teachers. Still, many students get into trouble. They can't take it. They simply can't take it. They end up destroying themselves. They end up playing with the energy until it becomes a spiritual atomic bomb.

We might feel that working with tantra is like planting a little seed: we nourish it, make it germinate and send out shoots of greenery, and finally it will blossom as a beautiful flower. That is wishful thinking. We cannot approach tantra in that way. Instead, we have to realize that taking care of such a plant is not ordinary gardening. An extraordinary process is needed. Dealing with our state of being, our state of mind, is extraordinary in many ways. Moreover, dealing with our state of mind from the subtle tantric point of view is extremely dangerous—highly dangerous and equally highly productive. Therefore, we should be very careful and open when we talk about vajrayana. Nonexistence is the only preparation for tantra, and we should realize that there is no substitute.

The experience of nonexistence brings a sense of delightful humor and, at the same time, complete openness and freedom. In addition, it brings an experience of complete indestructibility that is unchallengeable, immovable, and completely solid. The experience of indestructibility can only occur when we realize that nonexistence is possible, in the sense of being without reference points, without philosophical definitions, without even the notion of nonexistence.

The development of indestructibility or immovability is extremely important to understand. Such indestructibility can only come out of the state of nothingness, egolessness, or nonexistence. According to the Buddha, tantra is greater liberation, greater discipline, and greater vision. But this greater liberation is based on working with the potentialities and energies that exist within us. Therefore, without having some understanding of nonexistence, there is no point in discussing indestructibility.

When we consider someone to be indestructible, we generally mean that he is well established in his discipline, such as a person who has mastered the art of warfare or studied philosophy in great depth. Because such a person has mastered all sorts of techniques and training, we therefore consider him to be immovable or indestructible. In fact, from the tantric point of view, the attempt to secure oneself with gadgetry is a source of vulnerability rather than indestructibility. In this case, we are not talking about indestructibility based on collecting information, tricks, or ideas. Instead, we are referring to a basic attitude of trust in the nonexistence of our being.

In the tantric notion of indestructibility, there is no ground, no basic premise, and no particular philosophy except one's own experience, which is extremely powerful and dynamic. It is a question of being rather than figuring out what to be, how to be. Usually, we rely upon reference points, conceptual ideas, and feedback to give us guidelines as to how to be good or bad boys and girls, but such dependence is questionable. If you say to your doctor, "I have insomnia; how can I fall asleep?" the doctor responds by saying, "Take these pills. Then you will have no problem." In America in particular, that approach has become a problem. In tantra, the point is not *how* to handle ourselves but that we simply have to do it. We cannot trick ourselves into realizing the state of immovability, or indestructibility. Indestructibility is based on our experience, which is solid, dynamic, and unyielding.

In that way, tantric discipline does not cooperate with any deception at all; therefore, it is regarded as indestructible, immovable. The tantric approach of nonparticipation in the games that go on in the samsaric world, however, is something more than boycotting. When we boycott something, we do so in the name of a protest. We disagree with certain systems or certain ideas, and therefore, we make a nuisance of ourselves. In this case, instead of boycotting the samsaric setup, we are fully and personally involved with it. We realize all the so-called benefits that the samsaric world might present to us—spiritual, psychological, and material goods of all kinds. We are fully aware of all the alternatives, but we do not yield to any of them at all. We are straightforward and hardheaded. That is the quality of immovability.

The word *hardheaded* is very interesting. When we say somebody is hardheaded, we mean that he is not taken in by anything. That is precisely what is meant by the term *vajra nature*: hardheadedness, vajra-headedness. Vajra is a quality of toughness and not being taken in by any kind of seduction. We also talk about "hard truth." Such truth is hard, unyielding, and uncomplimentary. When we receive news of someone's death, it is the hard truth. We cannot go back and say that it is not true. We cannot hire an attorney to argue the case or spend our money trying to bring the person back to life, because it is the hard truth. In the same way, vajra nature is hard truth. We cannot challenge or manipulate it in any way at all. It is both direct and precise.

The term *vajra* in Sanskrit or *dorje (rdo–rje)* in Tibetan means "having the qualities of a diamond." Like a diamond, vajra is tough and at the same time extremely precious. Unless we understand this basic vajra quality of tantra, or of the tantrika—this almost bullheaded quality of not yielding to any kind of seductions, to any little tricks or plays on words—we cannot understand vajrayana Buddhism at all.

Fundamentally speaking, indestructibility, or vajra nature, is basic sanity. It is the total experience of tantra, the experience of the enlightened state of being. This sanity is based on the experience of clarity, which comes from the practice of meditation. Through the meditation practice of the three yanas, we discover a sense of clarity, unconditional clarity. Such clarity is ostentatious and has immense brilliance. It is very joyful, and it has potentialities of everything. It is a real experience. Once we have experienced this brilliance—this farseeing, ostentatious, colorful, opulent quality of clarity—then there is no problem. That *is* vajra nature. It is indestructible. Because of its opulence and its richness, it radiates constantly, and immense, unconditional appreciation takes place. That combination of indestructibility and clarity is the basic premise of tantric Buddhist teachings.

We should understand how the vajrayana notion of brilliance differs from the notion of clear light as described in the *Tibetan Book of the Dead* and how it differs from the mahayana notion of luminosity. Clear light, according to the *Tibetan Book of the Dead*, is purely a phenomenological experience. You see whiteness as you die or as your consciousness begins to sink. Because the physical data of your body's habitual patterns are beginning to dissolve, you begin to enter another realm. You feel whitewashed, as if you were swimming in milk or drowning in milk. You feel suffocated with whiteness, which is known as clear light. That is purely a phenomenological experience, not the true experience of clarity. On the other hand, the mahayana Buddhists talk about luminosity, called *prabhasvara* in Sanskrit, or *ösel* ('od-gsal) in Tibetan. *Ösel* means seeing things very precisely, clearly, logically, and skillfully. Everything is seen very directly; things are seen as they are. Nevertheless, neither prabhasvara nor the notion of clear light matches the tantric notion of vajra clarity.

Vajrayana clarity has more humor. It also has more subtlety

and dignity. Moreover, it is utterly, totally outrageous. Things are seen as they are, precisely; but at the same time, things are also seeing us precisely. Because we are totally exposed and open and not afraid to be seen, a meeting point occurs. Something makes us realize that we cannot chicken out and say that our life is just a rehearsal. Something makes us realize that it is real. That state of being is not merely a phenomenological experience. It is a real state of being, a true state of being that is full and complete. That indestructibility and clarity are vajra nature, which is superior to any other approach to spirituality, even within the Buddhist tradition.

Journey without Goal, Pages 25–29

The Five Buddha Families

TANTRA IS extraordinarily special and extremely real and personal. The question in this chapter is how to relate our own ordinary existence or daily situation to tantric consciousness. The tantric approach is not just to make sweeping statements about reality and to create calmness and a meditative state. It is more than learning to be creative and contemplative. In tantra, we relate with the details of our everyday life according to our own particular makeup. It is a real and personal experience. But in order to relate to our lives in the tantric fashion, there are certain technical details of tantric experience that we have to understand.

The tantric discipline of relating to life is based on what are known as the five buddha principles, or the five buddha families. These principles are traditionally known as families because they are an extension of ourselves in the same way that our blood relations are an extension of us: we have our daddy, we have our mommy, we have our sisters and brothers, and they are all part of our family. But we could also say that these relatives are principles: our motherness, our fatherness, our sisterness, our brotherness, and our me-ness are experienced as definite principles that have distinct characteristics. In the same way, the tantric tradition speaks of five families: five principles, categories, or possibilities.

Those five principles, or buddha families, are called *vajra, ratna, padma, karma,* and *buddha.* They are quite ordinary. There is nothing divine or extraordinary about them. The basic point is that, at the tantric level, people are divided into particular types: vajra, ratna, padma, karma, and buddha. We constantly come across members of every one of the five families—people who are partially or completely one of those five. We find such people all through life, and every one of them is a fertile person, a workable person who could be related with directly and personally. So, from the tantric point of view, by relating directly with all the different people we encounter, we are actually relating with diffferent styles of enlightenment.

The buddha family, or families, associated with a person describes his or her fundamental style, that person's intrinsic perspective or stance in perceiving the world and working with it. Each family is associated with both a neurotic and an enlightened style. The neurotic expression of any buddha family can be transmuted into its wisdom or enlightened aspect. As well as describing people's styles, the buddha families are also associated with colors, elements, landscapes, directions, seasons—with any aspect of the phenomenal world.

The first buddha family is the *vajra* family, which literally means the family of sharpness, crystallization, and indestructibility. The term *vajra* is superficially translated as "diamond," but that is not quite accurate. Traditionally, vajra is a celestial precious stone that cuts through any other solid object. So it is more than a diamond; it is complete indestructibility. The vajra family is symbolized by the vajra scepter, or *dorje* in Tibetan. This vajra scepter or superdiamond has five prongs, which represent relating to the five emotions: aggression, pride, passion, jealousy, and ignorance. The sharp edges or prongs of the vajra represent cutting through any neurotic emotional tendencies; they also represent the sharp quality of being aware of many possible perspectives. The indestructible vajra is said to be like a heap of razor blades: if we naively try to hold it or touch it, there are all kinds of sharp edges that are both cutting and penetrating. The notion here is that vajra corrects or remedies any neurotic distortion in a precise and sharp way.

In the ordinary world, the experience of vajra is perhaps not as extreme as holding razor blades in our hand, but at the same time, it is penetrating and very personal. It is like a sharp, cutting, biting-cold winter. Each time we expose ourselves to the open air, we get frostbite instantly. Intellectually, vajra is very sharp. All the intellectual traditions belong to this family. A person in the vajra family knows how to evaluate logically the arguments that are used to explain experience. He can tell whether the logic is true or false. Vajra family intellect also has a sense of constant openness and perspective. For instance, a vajra person could view a crystal ball from hundreds of perspectives, according to where it was placed, the way it was perceived, the distance from which he was looking at it, and so forth. The intellect of the vajra family is not just encyclopedic; it is sharpness, directness, and awareness of perspectives. Such indestructibility and sharpness are very personal and very real.

The neurotic expression of vajra is associated with anger and intellectual fixation. If we become fixated on a particular logic, the sharpness of vajra can become rigidity. We become possessive of our insight rather than having a sense of open perspective. The anger of vajra neurosis could be pure aggression or also a sense of uptightness because we are so attached to our sharpness of mind. Vajra is also associated with the element of water. Cloudy, turbulent water symbolizes the defensive and aggressive nature of anger, while clear water suggests the sharp, precise, clear reflectiveness of vajra wisdom. In fact, vajra wisdom is traditionally called the Mirrorlike Wisdom, which evokes this image of a calm pond or reflecting pool.

Incidentally, the use of the word *vajra* in such terms as *vajrayana, vajra master,* and *vajra pride* does not refer to this particular buddha family but simply expresses basic indestructibility.

The next buddha family is *ratna*. Ratna is a personal and real sense of expanding ourselves and enriching our environment. It is expansion, enrichment, plentifulness. Such plentifulness could also have problems and weaknesses. In the neurotic sense, the richness of ratna manifests as being completely fat, or extraordinarily ostentatious, beyond the limits of our sanity. We expand constantly, open heedlessly, and indulge ourselves to the level of insanity. It is like swimming in a dense lake of honey and butter. When we coat ourselves in this mixture of butter and honey, it is very difficult to remove. We cannot just remove it by wiping it off, but we have to apply all kinds of cleaning agents, such as cleanser and soap, to loosen its grasp.

In the positive expression of the ratna family, the principle of richness is extraordinary. We feel very rich and plentiful, and we extend ourselves to our world personally, directly, emotionally, psychologically, even spiritually. We are extending constantly, expanding like a flood or an earthquake. There is a sense of spreading, shaking the earth, and creating more and more cracks in it. That is the powerful expansiveness of ratna.

The enlightened expression of ratna is called the Wisdom of Equanimity, because ratna can include everything in its expansive environment. Thus, ratna is associated with the element of earth. It is like a rotting log that makes itself at home in the country. Such a log does not want to leave its home ground. It would like to stay, but at the same time, it grows all kinds of mushrooms and plants and allows animals to nest in it. That lazy settling down and making ourselves at home, and inviting other people to come in and rest as well, is ratna.

The next family is *padma*, which literally means "lotus flower." The symbol of the enlightened padma family is the lotus, which grows and blooms in the mud yet still comes out pure and clean, virginal and clear. Padma neurosis is connected with passion, a grasping quality, and a desire to possess. We are completely wrapped up in desire and want only to seduce the world, without concern for real communication. We could be a hustler or an advertiser, but basically, we are like a peacock. In fact, Amitabha, the buddha of the padma family, traditionally sits on a peacock, which represents subjugating padma neurosis. A person with padma neurosis speaks gently, fantastically gently, and he or she is seemingly very sexy, kind, magnificent, and completely accommodating: "If you hurt me, that's fine. That is part of our love affair. Come toward me." Such padma seduction sometimes becomes excessive and sometimes becomes compassionate, depending on how we work with it.

Padma is connected with the element of fire. In the confused state, fire does not distinguish among the things it grasps, burns, and destroys. But in the awakened state, the heat of passion is transmuted into the warmth of compassion. When padma neurosis is transmuted, it becomes fantastically precise and aware; it turns into tremendous interest and inquisitiveness. Everything is seen in its own distinct way, with its own particular qualities and characteristics. Thus, the wisdom of padma is called Discriminating Awareness Wisdom.

The genuine character of padma seduction is real openness, a willingness to demonstrate what we have and what we are to the phenomenal world. What we bring to the world is a sense of pleasure, a sense of promise. In whatever we experience, we begin to feel that there is lots of promise. We constantly experience a sense of magnetization of spontaneous hospitality.

This quality of padma is like bathing in perfume or jasmine tea. Each time we bathe, we feel refreshed, fantastic. It feels good to be magnetized. The sweet air is fantastic, and the hospitality of our host is magnificent. We eat the good food provided by our host, which is delicious but not too filling. We live in a world of honey and milk, in a very delicate sense, unlike the rich but heavy experience of the ratna family. Fantastic! Even our bread is scented with all kinds of delicious smells. Our ice cream is colored by beautiful pink lotuslike colors. We cannot wait to eat. Sweet music is playing in the background constantly. When there is no music, we listen to the whistling of the wind around our padma environment, and it becomes beautiful music as well. Even though we are not musicians, we compose all kinds of music. We wish we were a poet or a fantastic lover.

The next family is the *karma* family, which is a different kettle of fish. In this case, we are not talking about karmic debts, or karmic consequences; *karma* in this case simply means "action." The neurotic quality of action or activity is connected with jealousy, comparison, and envy. The enlightened aspect of karma is called the Wisdom of All-Accomplishing Action. It is the transcendental sense of complete fulfillment of action without being hassled or pushed into neurosis. It is natural fulfillment in how we relate with our world. In either case, whether we relate to the karma family on the transcendental level or the neurotic level, karma is the energy of efficiency.

If we have a karma family neurosis, we feel highly irritated if we see a hair on our teacup. First, we think that our cup is broken and that the hair is a crack in the cup. Then there is some relief. Our cup is not broken; it just has a piece of hair on the side. But then, when we begin to look at the hair on our cup of tea, we become angry all over again. We would like to make everything very efficient, pure, and absolutely clean. However, if we do achieve cleanliness, then that cleanliness itself becomes a further problem: we feel insecure because there is nothing to administer, nothing to work on. We constantly try to check every loose end. Being very keen on efficiency, we get hung up on it.

If we meet a person who is not efficient, who does not have his life together, we regard him as a terrible person. We would like to get rid of such inefficient people, and certainly we do not respect them, even if they are talented musicians or scientists or whatever they may be. On the other hand, if someone has immaculate efficiency, we begin to feel that he is a good person to be with. We would like to associate ourselves exclusively with people who are both responsible and clean-cut. However, we find that we are envious and jealous of such efficient people. We want others to be efficient, but not more efficient than we are.

The epitome of karma family neurosis is wanting to create a uniform world. Even though we might have very little philosophy, very little meditation, very little consciousness in terms of developing ourselves, we feel that we can handle our world properly. We have composure, and we relate properly with the whole world, and we are resentful that everybody else does not see things in the same way that we do. Karma is connected with the element of wind. The wind never blows in all directions, but it blows in one direction at a time. This is the one-way view of resentment and envy, which picks on one little fault or virtue and blows it out of proportion. With karma wisdom, the quality of resentment falls away, but the qualities of energy, fulfillment of action, and openness remain. In other words, the active aspect of wind is retained so that our energetic activity touches everything in its path. We see the possibilities inherent in situations and automatically take the appropriate course. Action fulfills its purpose.

The fifth family is called the *buddha* family. It is associated with the element of space. Buddha energy is the foundation or the basic space. It is the environment or oxygen that makes it possible for the other principles to function. It has a sedate, solid quality. Persons in this family have a strong sense of contemplative experience, and they are highly meditative. Buddha neurosis is the quality of being "spaced-out" rather than spacious. It is often associated with an unwillingness to express ourselves. For example, we might see that our neighbors are destroying our picket fence with a sledgehammer. We can hear them and see them; in fact, we have been watching our neighbors at work all day, continuously smashing our picket fence. But instead of reacting, we just observe them and then we return to our snug little home. We eat our breakfast, lunch, and dinner and ignore what they are doing. We are paralyzed, unable to talk to outsiders.

Another quality of buddha neurosis is that we couldn't be bothered. Our dirty laundry is piled up in a corner of our room. Sometimes we use our dirty laundry to wipe up spills on the floor or table, and then we put it back on the same pile. As time goes on, our dirty socks become unbearable, but we just sit there.

If we are embarking on a political career, our colleagues may suggest that we develop a certain project and expand our organization. If we have a buddha neurosis, we will choose to develop the area that needs the least effort. We do not want to deal directly with the details of handling reality. Entertaining friends is also a hassle. We prefer to take our friends to a restaurant rather than cook in our home. And if we want to have a love affair, instead of seducing a partner, talking to him or her and making friends, we just look for somebody who is already keen on us. We cannot be bothered with talking somebody into something.

Sometimes we feel we are sinking into the earth, the solid mud and earth. Sometimes we feel good because we think we are the most stable person in the universe. We slowly begin to grin to ourselves, smile at ourselves, because we are the best person of all. We are the only person who manages to stay stable. But sometimes we feel that we are the loneliest person in the whole universe. We do not particularly like to dance, and when we are asked to dance with somebody, we feel embarrassed and uncomfortable. We want to stay in our own little corner.

When the ignoring quality of buddha neurosis is transmuted into wisdom, it becomes an environment of all-pervasive spaciousness. This enlightened aspect is called the Wisdom of All-Encompassing Space. In itself, it might still have a somewhat desolate and empty quality, but at the same time, it is a quality of completely open potential. It can accommodate anything. It is spacious and vast like the sky.

In tantric iconography, the five buddha families are arrayed in the center and the four cardinal points of a mandala. The mandala of the five buddha families, of course, represents their wisdom or enlightened aspect. Traditionally, the buddha family is in the center. That is to say, in the center there is the basic coordination and basic wisdom of buddha, which is symbolized by a wheel and the color white. Vajra is in the East, because vajra is connected with the dawn. It is also connected with the color blue and is symbolized by the vajra scepter. It is the sharpness of experience, as in the morning when we wake up. We begin to see the dawn, when light is first reflected on the world, as a symbol of awakening reality.

Ratna is in the South. It is connected with richness and is symbolized by a jewel and the color yellow. Ratna is connected with the midday, when we begin to need refreshment, nourishment. Padma is in the West and is symbolized by the lotus and the color red. As our day gets older, we also have to relate with recruiting a lover. It is time to socialize, to make a date with our lover. Or if we have fallen in love with an antique or if we have fallen in love with some clothing, it is time to go out and buy it. The last family is karma, in the North. It is symbolized by a sword and the color green. Finally, we have captured the whole situation: we have everything we need, and there is nothing more to get. We have brought our merchandise back home or our lover back home, and we say, "Let's close the door; let's lock it." So the mandala of the five buddha families represents the progress of a whole day or a whole course of action.

Without understanding the five buddha families, we have no working basis to relate with tantra, and we begin to find ourselves alienated from tantra. Tantra is seen as such an outrageous thing, which seems to have no bearing on us as individuals. We may feel the vajrayana is purely a distant aim, a distant goal. So it is necessary to study the five buddha principles. They provide a bridge between tantric experience and everyday life.

It is necessary to understand and relate with the five buddha principles *before* we begin tantric discipline, so that we can begin to understand what tantra is all about. If tantra is a mystical experience, how can we relate it to our ordinary everyday life at home? There could be a big gap between tantric experience and day-today life. But it is possible, by understanding the five buddha families, to close the gap. Working with the buddha families, we discover that we already have certain qualities. According to the tantric perspective, we cannot ignore them, and we cannot reject them and try to be something else. We have our aggression and our passion and our jealousy and our resentment and our ignorance—or whatever we have. We belong to certain buddha families already, and we cannot reject them. We should work with our neuroses, relate with them, and experience them properly. They are the only potential we have, and when we begin to work with them, we see that we can use them as stepping-stones.

Journey without Goal, Pages 77–84

Mahamudra

MAHAMUDRA IS A Sanskrit word. *Maha* means "big, great," and *mudra* means "symbol." But *maha* doesn't mean "big" in a comparative sense: something bigger compared with something smaller. It is not based on a dichotomy. It is simply that such clarity as this is beyond measure. There is no other clarity like this. It is fullness; it is without association in the sense that this experience is full in itself. And the sense in which *mudra* means "symbol" again has nothing to do with analysis or examples; rather, the thing itself is its own symbol. Everybody represents themselves, and everybody is a caricature of themselves. There is that sense of a humorous aspect, a caricature aspect, as well as everything having its own basic fullness. You represent yourself not by name but by being. So there is a sense of completion.

The mahamudra experience has been compared to the experience of a young child visiting a colorful temple. He sees all kinds of magnificent decorations, displays, rich colors, vividness of all kinds. But this child has no preconception or any concept whatsoever about where to begin to analyze. Everything is overwhelming, quite in its own right. So the child does not become frightened by this vivid scenery and at the same time does not know how to appreciate it. It is quite different from a child walking into a playroom full of toys, where his attention is caught by a particular toy and he runs right over and starts playing with it. A temple, a highly decorated, colorful temple, is so harmonious in its own right that the child has no way of introducing his fascination from one particular standpoint. The experience is all-pervasive. At the same time, it is perhaps somewhat overwhelmingly pleasurable.

So the mahamudra experience is vividness, vividness to such an extent that it does not require a watcher or commentator; or for that matter, it does not require meditative absorption. In the experience of shunyata, or emptiness, there is still a sense of needing a nursing process for that experience; it is not only that the sitting practice of meditation is required, but there is a sense of needing a registrar to record your experience in a memory bank. The very idea of emptiness is an experience, even though you may not have an experiencer as such, since the whole thing is totally open and nondualistic. But even the very sense of nonduality is a faint stain, a very subtle, transparent stain. On the shunyata level, that stain is regarded as an adornment, like putting a varnish over well-finished wood. It is supposed to protect the wood from further stains of dirt or grease, to keep it looking fresh and new, to preserve the newness of this well-finished wood. But in the long run, that clear varnish becomes a factor that ages the new look of this fresh wood. It turns yellow and begins slowly to crumble, and scratches begin to show much more in it than they would in the original wood. So the nonduality becomes a problem in the shunyata experience.

In the experience of mahamudra, even the notion of nonduality is not applied or is not necessary. Therefore, it has been said in the scriptures that the only definition of mahamudra you can use is "unborn" or "unoriginated." Or again, often the mahamudra experience is described in terms of coemergent wisdom—that is, born simultaneously rather than born with the delays of process. This refers to confusion and realization existing simultaneously, as opposed to confusion coming first and then realization taking over and cleaning out the confusion. In the mahamudra, confusion and realization are simultaneous, coemergent.

The eternally youthful quality of the mahamudra experience is one of its outstanding qualities. It is eternally youthful because there is no sense of repetition, no sense of wearing out of interest because of familiarity. Every experience is a new, fresh experience. So it is childlike, innocent and childlike. The child has never even seen its body—such a brand-new world.

Another term for mahamudra, used by Rangjung Dorje and other great teachers, is *ordinary consciousness*. Experience ceases to be extraordinary. It is so ordinary—so clear and precise and obvious. The only thing that confuses us and prevents us from realizing this experience is its ordinariness. The ordinary quality becomes a kind of barrier, because when you look for something, you don't look for the ordinary. Even in the case of losing a pair of glasses that you are completely used to, when you lose them, the glasses become a very interesting object. They immediately become an extraordinary thing, because you lost them. You begin to imagine, "Could they be here? Could they be there?" You shake all the cushions, you move all the chairs and tables, and look underneath the rugs. It becomes an extraordinary case. But the glasses are an ordinary thing.

In that way, mahamudra is self-secret because of its ordinariness. Ordinariness becomes its own camouflage, so to speak. It has also been said that mahamudra cannot be expressed, that even the Buddha's tongue is numb when it comes to describing mahamudra. And it's true. How much can you say about ordinary things? And the more you see that it is very ordinary, the more that becomes an extraordinary case, which creates a further veil.

The experience of mahamudra is also somewhat irritating, or even highly irritating, because of its sharpness and precision. The energies around you—textures, colors, different states of mind, relationships—are very vivid and precise. They are all so naked and so much right in front of you, without any padding, without any walls between you and that. That nakedness is overwhelming. Although it is your own experience, we often find that even when you have only a small glimpse of mahamudra experience, you want to run away from yourself. You look for privacy of some kind— privacy from yourself. The world is so true and naked and sharp and precise and colorful that it's extraordinarily irritating—let alone when other *people* approach you. You think you can avoid them, run away from them physically, put a notice on your door, or take a trip to an unknown corner of the world. You might try to dissociate yourself from the familiar world, run away from your home ground, disconnect your telephone. You can do all kinds of things of that nature, but when the world begins to become *you* and all these perceptions are *yours* and are very precise and very obviously right in front of you, you can't run away from it.

The process of running away creates further sharpness, and if you really try to run away from these phenomena, they begin to mock you, laugh at you. The chairs and tables and rugs and paintings on the wall and your books, the sounds you hear in your head, begin to mock you. Even if you try to tear your body apart, still something follows you. You can't get away from it. That is why it is called the ultimate nakedness. You begin to feel you are just a live brain with no tissue around it, exposed on a winter morning to the cold air. It's *so* penetrating, irritating, and so sharp.

It is a fundamental and very profound irritation. The irritations we discussed before are relatively simple and seem to be ordinary ones. The irritation of the mahamudra experience is very insulting in many ways, disconcerting. That is why the experience of mahamudra is also referred to as "crazy wisdom." It is a crazy experience, but not exactly ego madness. It's wisdom that has gone crazy. The element of wisdom here is its playfulness, humorousness, and its sybaritic quality. Even though you are irritated and naked and completely exposed without your skin, there is a sense of joy or, more likely, bliss.

One of the definite characteristics of the Buddhist tantra, on the mahamudra level at least, is not running away from sense pleasures but rather identifying with them, working with them as part of the working basis. That is an outstanding part of the tantric message. Pleasure in this case includes every kind of pleasure: psychosomatic, physical, psychological, and spiritual. Here it is quite different from the way in which spiritual materialists might seek pleasure—by getting into the other. In this case, it is getting into "this." There is a self-existing pleasurableness that is completely hollow if you look at it from the ordinary point of view of ego's pleasure orientation. Within that, you don't actually experience pleasure at all. All pleasure experiences are hollow. But if you look at it from the point of view of this nakedness, this situation of being completely exposed, any pleasure you experience is full because of its hollowness. On the mahamudra level, pleasure does not take place through the pores of your skin, but pleasure takes place on your very *flesh* without skin. You become the bliss rather than enjoying bliss. You are the embodiment of bliss, and this contains a quality of your being very powerful. You have conquered pleasure, and pleasure is yours. One doesn't even have to go so far as to try to enjoy pleasure, but pleasure becomes self-existing bliss.

In this way, every experience that might occur in our life—communication, visual experience, auditory experience, consciousness: anything that we relate to—becomes completely workable, highly workable. In fact, even the notion of workability does not apply. It's yours. It is *you*, in fact. So things become very immediate.

That is what is often called vajra pride. Pride in this case is not arrogance, but it is being nondualistically self-contained. You are not threatened by your projections or projectors, but you are there, and at the same time everything around you is you and yours.

The experiences of teachers in my lineage, especially the great Indian meditator and teacher Naropa, exemplify this. When Naropa was searching for his guru Tilopa, he had a whole series of powerful but illusory experiences. He had a hard time genuinely encountering Tilopa. He failed over and over again to connect with him. Finally, at the last moment, he thought of killing himself because he couldn't find the guru. He was actually just about to relate with the totality of himself; *finally*, then he experienced that penetrating pain in himself. He thought that maybe if he eliminated his body, he might be able to relieve that pain. At that point, Tilopa finally appeared.

After that, Naropa had many experiences with his guru that led to his ultimate realization of mahamudra. These experiences are often referred to as the twelve trials or tortures of Naropa. Through these twelve subsequent tortures that Naropa went through with the help of Tilopa, sometimes he understood this nakedness—experiencing it fully, totally, completely—and sometimes he didn't understand it and instead tripped out into the highest spiritual mishmash. The perfect example is when Tilopa put sharpened pieces of bamboo between Naropa's nails and his fingers, and then put little flags on the ends of the pieces of bamboo and asked Naropa to hold them into the wind. That exemplifies (through the medium of pain, of course) how real the nakedness could be if it were blissful.

That seems to be a very powerful message for us. Mind you, we are not going to practice that very exercise, but that is an example of what the process is like. How many times can the guru tell a person, "Come out! I know you're there! Be naked!" A student might decide to take off his clothes and say, "OK, I'm naked," but that's not quite it. We have to say: "There's more nakedness. Come on, do more than that. What else can you do?"

Particularly a scholar like Naropa had enormous hang-ups. Receiving instructions from a mahayana teacher requires simple devotion, reducing oneself to an infant and asking the guru to act as the baby-sitter. But on the vajrayana level, the student-teacher relationship demands more than that. It is a process of training the student as a warrior. At first, a warrior teacher does not use a sword on you. He uses a stick and makes you fight with him. Since the student's swordsmanship is not so good, he gets hurt more than he is able to hurt the master. But when the student gains confidence and begins to learn good swordsmanship, he is almost able to defeat his own teacher. Then, instead of a stick, it becomes a sword. Nobody really gets killed or hurt, because all the levels of communication take place within the realm of the rainbow or mirage anyway. But there is a training period. A learning process takes place, which is very immediate and very powerful and very necessary.

On the hinayana level, the teacher is a wise man. On the mahayana level, the teacher is a physician/friend, a spiritual friend. On the vajrayana level, the student-teacher relationship is similar to that in the martial arts. You could get hurt severely if you are too tense. But you could also receive a tremendous—almost physical—message. The message is not verbal or intellectual. It is like a demonstration of putting tables and chairs together. The teachings come out of the world of form, the real world of form. The teachings consist of colors and forms and sounds rather than words or ideas.

This is what Naropa was going through—the physical teachings, which are real and direct and obvious. And they are personal, highly personal. Each time we come closer to tantra in the journey through the yanas, the relationship to the teacher changes and becomes more and more personal. The teacher acts as his own spokesman but also as the spokesman of the vivid and colorful world that you are part of. If you don't have the experience of winter, you have to take off your clothes and lie in the snow at night. That way, you will learn a very good lesson on what winter is all about that doesn't need words. You could read a book about it, but it doesn't mean very much unless you have that very immediate and direct experience—which is frightening, very powerful.

Somehow we are unable to have an experience of this nature without going through the basic learning process that enables you to handle that kind of experience. Therefore, the three-yana principle is very important—the gradual process from hinayana to mahayana to vajrayana. This process makes it all make sense. Without it, tantra does not make any sense; it is just training in masochism.

I heard a story about a certain workshop that took place in this country, I don't remember exactly where. It was supposed to be a workshop in self-exposure, and anybody interested in that workshop could just pay their money and come in, without having the faintest idea what it was all about. They were invited to eat dinner together. There was beautifully prepared food and nice china and a nice tablecloth and candlelight and everything. They ate their food, and they drank their wine. Then at the end of the meal, everybody was supposed to break their plates and glasses and chop up their tables and chairs. That was the workshop. What does it mean? Of course, it might mean a lot if you really knew what it was all about. But on the other hand, if you just saw that advertised in the newspaper and decided to go to it because you thought it was a groovy thing to do—you'd never done *that* before—it wouldn't mean very much. You might feel uncertain how much you should talk to the others about the experience. You might feel slightly awkward and at the same time released or something or other. But on the whole, it would make no sense if there were no training process behind it.

Vajrayana is also very powerful, but you can't just come in and do the workshop of the twelve trials of Naropa. It doesn't mean anything without basic training in mindfulness, awareness, groundlessness, and fearlessness. In that sense, tantra is a very dangerous thing. At the same time, it is very powerful, and every one of us can do it. Other people have done so. Actually, we don't have to be such great scholars as Naropa was. As long as we are interested in using our intellect and our intuition, we can do it. Mahamudra is possible as long as we have some basic training in relating with ourselves. We have to learn fearlessness that is without hesitation but is not based on blind faith. If we have a logical mind, a scientific mind full of suspicion, that is good.

Illusion's Game, Pages 116–124

Working with Negativity

WE ALL EXPERIENCE negativity—the basic aggression of wanting things to be different from how they are. We cling, we defend, we attack, and throughout there is a sense of one's own wretchedness, and so we blame the world for our pain. This is negativity. We experience it as terribly unpleasant, foul-smelling, something we want to get rid of. But if we look into it more deeply, it has a very juicy smell and is very alive. Negativity is not bad per se, but something living and precise, connected with reality.

Negativity breeds tension, friction, gossip, discontentment, but it is also very accurate, deliberate, and profound. Unfortunately, the heavy-handed interpretations and judgments we lay on these experiences obscure this fact. These interpretations and judgments are negative negativity, watching ourselves being negative and then deciding that the negativity is justified in being there. The negativity seems good-natured, with all sorts of good qualities in it, so we pat its back, guard it, and justify it. Or if we are blamed or attacked by others, we interpret their negativity as being good for us. In either case, the watcher—by commenting, interpreting, and judging—is camouflaging and hardening the basic negativity.

Negative negativity refers to the philosophies and rationales we use to justify avoiding our own pain. We would like to pretend that these "evil" and "foul-smelling" aspects of ourselves and our world are not really there, or that they should not be there, or even that they *should* be there. So negative negativity is usually self-justifying, self-contained. It allows nothing to pierce its protective shell—a self-righteous way of trying to pretend that things are what we would like them to be instead off what they are.

This secondary, commenting kind of intelligence of double

negativity is very cautious and cowardly as well as frivolous and emotional. It inhibits identification with the energy and intelligence of basic negativity. So let's forget about justifying ourselves, trying to prove to ourselves how good we are.

The basic honesty and simplicity of negativity can be creative in community as well as in personal relationships. Basic negativity is very revealing, sharp, and accurate. If we leave it as basic negativity rather than overlaying it with conceptualizations, then we see the nature of its intelligence. Negativity breeds a great deal of energy, which, clearly seen, becomes intelligence. When we leave the energies as they are with their natural qualities, they are living rather than conceptualized. They strengthen our everyday lives.

The conceptualized negativity, the negative negativity, must be cut through. It deserves to be murdered on the spot with the sharp blow of basic intelligence—*prajnaparamita*. That is what prajna is for: to cut through intelligence when it changes into intellectual speculation or is based upon a belief of some kind. Beliefs are reinforced endlessly by other beliefs and dogmas, theological or moral or practical or businesslike. That kind of intelligence should be killed on the spot, "uncompassionately." This is when compassion should not be idiot compassion. This intellectual energy should be shot, killed, squashed, razed to dust on the spot with one blow. That one blow of basic intelligence is direct compassion. The way to do this does not evolve out of intellectualizing or trying to find a way to justify yourself, but it just comes as the conclusion of basic intelligence and from a feeling of the texture of the situation.

For instance, if you walk on the snow or ice, you feel the texture of it the minute you put your foot down. You feel whether or not your shoe is going to grip. It is the feeling of texture, the richness of texture that we are talking about. If it is negative negativity, then there will be certain ways to squash or murder it. Somehow the energy to do this comes from the basic negativity itself rather than from some special technique or ability for assassination. There is a time to be philosophical and a time to be soft. There is also a time to be "uncompassionate" and ruthless in dealing with these frivolous situations.

Frivolousness refers to the extra and unnecessary mental and physical acts with which we keep ourselves busy in order not to see what actually is happening in a situation. Whenever there is a frivolous emotional situation and concept growing out of it, then this ground should be completely extinguished with a direct blow—that is, by seeing directly what is not right and wholesome. This is what is called the Sword of Manjushri, which cuts the root of dualistic conceptualization with one blow. Here a person should really be "uncompassionate" and illogical. The real objective is just to squash the frivolousness, the unwillingness to see things as they actually are, which appears rational. Frivolousness does not really get a chance to feel the whole ground. It is preoccupied with reacting to your projections as they bounce back at you. True spontaneity feels the texture of the situation because it is less involved with self-consciousness, the attempt to secure oneself in a given situation.

It is obvious that when you are really squashing frivolousness, you should feel pain, because there is a certain attraction toward the occupation of being frivolous. By squashing it, you are completely taking away the occupation. You begin to feel that you have nothing to hold on to anymore, which is rather frightening as well as painful. What do you do then, after you have extinguished everything? Then you must not live on your heroism, on having achieved something, but just dance with the continuing process of energy that has been liberated by this destruction.

The tantric tradition of Buddhism describes four actions or *karmas*. The first is the action of "pacifying" a situation if it is not right. Pacifying is trying to feel the ground very softly. You feel the situation further and further, not just pacifying superficially but expressing the whole, feeling it altogether. Then you expand your luscious, dignified, and rich quality throughout. This is "enriching," the second karma. If that does not work, then "magnetizing" is the third karma. You bring the elements of the situation together. Having felt them out by pacifying and enriching them, you bring them together. If that is unsuccessful, then there is the action of "destroying" or extinguishing, the fourth karma.

These four karmas are very pertinent to the process of dealing with negativity and so-called problems. First pacify, then enrich, then magnetize, and if that does not work, finally extinguish, destroy altogether. This last is necessary only when the negative negativity uses a strong pseudologic or a pseudophilosophical attitude or conceptualization. It is necessary when there is a notion of some kind that brings a whole succession of other notions, like the layers of an onion, or when one is using logic and ways of justifying oneself so that situations become very heavy and very solid. We know this heaviness is taking place, but simultaneously, we play tricks on ourselves, feeling that we enjoy the heaviness of this logic, feeling that we need to have some occupation. When we begin to play this kind of game, there is no room. Out! It is said in the tantric tradition that if you do not destroy when necessary, you are breaking the vow of compassion, which actually commits you to destroying frivolousness. Therefore, keeping to the path does not necessarily mean only trying to be good and not offending anyone; it does not mean that if someone obstructs our path, we should try to be polite to him or her and say "please" and "thank you." That does not work; that is not the point. If anyone gets abruptly in our path, we just push him or her out because the intrusion was frivolous. The path of dharma is not a good, sane, passive, and "compassionate" path at all. It is a path on which no one should walk blindly. If anyone does—Out! Such persons should be awakened by being excluded.

At the very advanced levels of practice, we can go through the negative negativity and turn it into the original negativity so that we have a very powerful negative force that is pure and un–self-conscious. That is, once having squashed this negative negativity altogether, having gone through the operation without anesthesia, then we reinvite the negativity for the sake of energy. But this could be tricky.

If the pure energy of negativity is involved with any form of ground, then it is always regarded as the property of the secondary, logical energy of negative negativity. This is because of our fascination to relive the basic negativity, to recreate the comfort and occupation of basic negativity. So there should not be any reliving of the occupation at all. Occupations should be completely cleared away. Then the energy that destroys the reliving of occupation turns out to be logical energy transmuted into crazy wisdom—conceptual ideas, let loose. That is to say, there are no more conceptual ideas but only energy run wild. Originally, there were conceptual ideas and then they were cut through altogether, so that you no longer regarded light and dark as light and dark; it becomes the nondualistic state.

Then negativity simply becomes food, pure strength. You no longer relate to negativity as being good or bad, but you continually use the energy that comes out of it as a source of life so that you are never really defeated in a situation. Crazy wisdom cannot be defeated. If someone attacks or if someone praises, crazy wisdom will feed on either equally. As far as crazy wisdom is concerned, both praise and blame are the same thing because there is always some energy occurring . . . a really terrifying thought.

Crazy wisdom could become satanic, but somehow it doesn't. Those who fear crazy wisdom destroy themselves. The negative destruction they throw at it bounces back at them, for crazy wisdom has no notion of good or bad or destruction or creation at all. Crazy wisdom cannot exist without communication, without a situation with which to work: whatever needs to be destroyed, it destroys; whatever needs to be cared for, it cares for. Hostility destroys itself, and openness also opens itself. It depends on the situation. Some people may learn from destruction, and some people may learn from creation. That is what the wrathful and peaceful deities, the *mahakalas* and the buddhas, symbolize.

The four arms of the mahakala (see the illustration on page 184) represent the four karmas. The whole structure of the image is based on energy and complete compassion devoid of idiot compassion. The first left arm represents pacifying. It holds a skull cup of *amrita,* the intoxicating nectar of the gods that is a means of pacification. Another arm holds a hooked knife, which symbolizes enriching, extending your influence over others, feeling the texture of the ground and the richness. The hooked knife is also regarded as the scepter of the gods. The third arm, on the right, holds a sword, which is the tool for gathering energies together. The sword need not strike, but just through its being waved around, energies come together. The fourth arm holds the three-pronged spear, which symbolizes destruction. You do not have to destroy three times, but with one thrust of this spear, you make three

Four-Armed Mahakala, or protector of the teachings. This statue is one of the treasures of the Surmang monasteries, of which Chögyam Trungpa was the supreme abbot, and is one of the few items that Chögyam Trungpa hand-carried with him from Tibet. From the collection of the Shambhala Archives. Photo by Diana Church.

wounds, the ultimate destruction of ignorance, passion, and aggression simultaneously.

The mahakala sits on the corpses of demons, which represents the paralysis of ego. This is very interesting and relates to what we have already discussed. You must not make an impulsive move into any situation. Let the situation come, then look at it, chew it properly, digest it, sit on it. The sudden move is unhealthy, impulsive, and frivolous rather than spontaneous.

Spontaneity sees situations as they are. You see, there is a difference between spontaneity and frivolousness, a very thin line dividing them. Whenever there is an impulse to do something, you should not just do it; you should work with the impulse. If you are working with it, then you will not act frivolously; you want really to see it and taste it properly, devoid of frivolousness. Frivolousness means reacting according to reflex. You throw something, and when it bounces back, you react. Spontaneity is when you throw something and watch it and work with the energy when it bounces back at you. Frivolousness involves too much anxiety. Once you are emotionally worked up, then too much anxiety is put into your action. But when you are spontaneous, there is less anxiety, and you just deal with situations as they are. You do not simply react, but you work with the quality and structure of the reaction. You feel the texture of the situation rather than just acting impulsively.

The mahakala is traditionally surrounded by flames, representing the tremendous unceasing energy of anger without hatred, the energy of compassion. The skull crown symbolizes the negativities or emotions that are not destroyed or abandoned or condemned for being "bad." Rather, they are used by the mahakala for his ornaments and crown.

The Myth of Freedom, Pages 73–80

Crazy Wisdom

PADMASAMBHAVA, or Guru Rinpoche, who brought the Buddhist teachings from India to Tibet, had eight manifestations or aspects. The eighth and final aspect of Padmasambhava is Dorje Trolö, the final and absolute aspect of crazy wisdom. To discuss this eighth aspect of Padmasambhava, we have to have some background knowledge about traditional ways of communicating the teachings. The idea of *lineage* is associated with the transmission of the message of *adhishthana*, which means "energy" or, if you like, "grace." This is transmitted like an electric current from the guru to sentient beings. In other words, crazy wisdom is a continual energy that flows and that, as it flows, regenerates itself. The only way to regenerate this energy is by radiating or communicating it, by putting it into practice or acting it out. It is unlike other energies, which, when you use them, move toward cessation or extinction. The energy of crazy wisdom regenerates itself through the process of our living it. As you live this energy, it regenerates itself; you don't live for death, but you live for birth. Living is a constant birth process rather than a wearing-out process.

The lineage has three styles of transmitting this energy. The first is called the *kangsaknyen-gyü*. Here the energy of the lineage is transmitted by word of mouth using ideas and concepts. In some sense, this is a crude or primitive method, a somewhat dualistic approach. However, in this case, the dualistic approach is functional and worthwhile.

If you sit cross-legged as if you were meditating, the chances are you might actually find yourself meditating after a while. This is like achieving sanity by pushing yourself to imitate it, by behaving as though you were sane already. In the same way, it is possible to use words, terms, images, and ideas—teaching orally or in writing—as though they were an absolutely perfect means of transmission. The procedure is to present an idea, then the refutation of (the opposite of) that idea, and then to associate the idea with an authentic scripture or teaching that has been given in the past.

Believing in the sacredness of certain things on a primitive level is the first step in transmission. Traditionally, scriptures or holy books are not to be trodden upon, sat upon, or otherwise mistreated, because very powerful things are said in them. The idea is that by mistreating the books, you mistreat the messages they contain. This is a way of believing in some kind of entity, or energy, or force—in the living quality of something.

The second style of communicating, or teaching, is the *rigdzin da-gyü*. This is the method of crazy wisdom, but on the relative level, not the absolute level. Here you communicate by creating incidents that seem to happen by themselves. Such incidents are seemingly blameless, but they do have an instigator somewhere. In other words, the guru tunes herself in to the cosmic energy, or whatever you would like to call it. Then, if there is a need to create chaos, she directs her attention toward chaos. And quite appropriately, chaos presents itself, as if it happened by accident or mistake. *Da* in Tibetan means "symbol" or "sign." The sense of this is that the crazy wisdom guru does not speak or teach on the ordinary level, but rather, he or she creates a symbol, or means. A symbol, in this case, is not like something that stands for something else, but it is something that presents the living quality of life and creates a message out of it.

The third one is called *gyalwa gong-gyü*. *Gong-gyü* means "thought lineage" or "mind lineage." From the point of view of the thought lineage, even the method of creating situations is crude, or primitive. Here a mutual understanding takes place that creates a general atmosphere—and the message is understood. If the guru of crazy wisdom is an authentic being, then the authentic communication happens, and the means of communication is neither words nor symbols. Rather, just by being, a sense of precision is communicated. Maybe it takes the form of waiting—for nothing. Maybe it takes pretending to meditate together but not doing anything. For that matter, it might involve having a very casual relationship: discussing the weather and the flavor of tea; how to make curry, chop suey, or macrobiotic cuisine; or talking about history or the history of the neighbors—whatever.

The crazy wisdom of the thought lineage takes a form that is somewhat disappointing to the eager recipient of the teachings. You might go and pay a visit to the guru, which you have especially prepared for, and he isn't even interested in talking to you. He's busy reading the newspaper. Or for that matter, he might create "black air," a certain intensity that makes the whole environment threatening. And there's nothing happening—nothing happening to such an extent that you walk out with a sense of relief, glad you didn't have to be there any longer. But then something happens to you as if everything did happen during those periods of silence or intensity.

The thought lineage is more of a presence than something happening. Also, it has an extraordinarily ordinary quality.

In traditional *abhishekas,* or initiation ceremonies, the energy of the thought lineage is transmitted into your system at the level of the fourth abhisheka. At that point, the guru will ask you suddenly, "What is your name?" or "Where is your mind?" This abrupt question momentarily cuts through your subconscious gossip, creating a bewilderment of a different type [from the type already going on in your mind]. You search for an answer and realize you do have a name and the guru wants to know it. It is as if you were nameless before but have now discovered that you have a name. It is that kind of abrupt moment.

Of course, such ceremonies are subject to corruption. If the teacher is purely following the scriptures and commentaries, and the student is eagerly expecting something powerful, then both the teacher and the student miss the boat simultaneously.

Thought-lineage communication is the teaching of the *dharmakaya;* the communication by signs and symbols—creating situations—is the *sambhogakaya* level of teaching; and the communication by words is the *nirmanakaya* level of teaching.[1] Those are the three styles in which the crazy wisdom guru communicates to the potential crazy wisdom student.

---

1. Please see the discussion of *kaya* in the glossary for a definition of these three terms.

The whole thing is not as outrageous as it may seem. Nevertheless, there is an undercurrent of taking advantage of the mischievousness of reality, and this creates a sense of craziness or a sense that something or other is not too solid. Your sense of security is under attack. So the recipient of crazy wisdom—the ideal crazy wisdom student—should feel extremely insecure, threatened. That way, you manufacture half of the crazy wisdom, and the guru manufactures the other half. Both the guru and the student are alarmed by the situation. Your mind has nothing to work on. A sudden gap has been created—bewilderment.

This kind of bewilderment is quite different from the bewilderment of ignorance. This is the bewilderment that happens between the question and the answer. It is the boundary between the question and the answer. There is a question, and you are just about to answer that question: there is a gap. You have oozed out your question, and the answer hasn't come through yet. There is already a feeling of a sense of the answer, a sense that something positive is happening—but nothing has happened yet. There is that point where the answer is just about to be born and the question has just died.

There is very strange chemistry there; the combination of the death of the question and the birth of the answer creates uncertainty. It is intelligent uncertainty—sharp, inquisitive. This is unlike ego's bewilderment of ignorance, which has totally and completely lost touch with reality because you have given birth to duality and are uncertain about how to handle the next step. You are bewildered because of ego's approach of duality. But in this case, it is not bewilderment in the sense of not knowing what to do but bewilderment because something is just about to happen and hasn't happened yet.

⌒

The crazy wisdom of Dorje Trolö is not reasonable but somewhat heavy-handed, because wisdom does not permit compromise. If you compromise between black and white, you come out with a gray color—not quite white and not quite black. It is a sad medium rather than a happy medium—disappointing. You feel sorry that you've let it be compromised. You feel totally wretched that you have compromised. That is why crazy wisdom does not know any compromise. The style of crazy wisdom is to build you up: build up your ego to the level of absurdity, to the point of comedy, to a point that is bizarre—and then suddenly let you go. So you have a big fall, like Humpty Dumpty: "All the king's horses and all the king's men / Couldn't put Humpty Dumpty together again."

To get back to the story of Padmasambhava as Dorje Trolö, he was asked by a local deity in Tibet, "What frightens you the most?" Padmasambhava said, "I'm frightened of neurotic sin." It so happens that the Tibetan word for sin—*dikpa*—is also the word for scorpion, so the local deity thought he could frighten Padmasambhava by manifesting himself as a giant scorpion. The local deity was reduced to dust—as a scorpion.

Tibet is supposedly ringed by snow-capped mountains, and there are twelve goddesses associated with those mountains who are guardians of the country. When Dorje Trolö came to Tibet, one of those goddesses refused to surrender to him. She ran away from him—she ran all over the place. She ran up a mountain thinking she was running away from Padmasambhava and found him already there ahead of her, dancing on the mountaintop. She ran away down a valley and found Padmasambhava already at the bottom, sitting at the confluence of that valley and the neighboring one. No matter where she ran, she couldn't get away. Finally, she decided to jump into a lake and hide there. Padmasambhava turned the lake into boiling iron, and she emerged as a kind of skeleton being. Finally, she had to surrender, because Padmasambhava was everywhere. It was extremely claustrophic in some way.

One of the expressions of crazy wisdom is that you can't get away from it. It's everywhere (whatever "it" is).

At Taktsang, a cave in Bhutan that is now a sacred shrine to Guru Rinpoche, Padmasambhava manifested as Dorje Trolö.[2] He

---

2. In 1968, Chögyam Trungpa conducted a retreat at Taktsang and received a teaching buried there as a mind treasure by Padmasambhava. (This and other ways that Guru Rinpoche left his teachings to be discovered by future generations are discussed later in this chapter.) The particular text that Chögyam Trungpa discovered at Taktsang is entitled *The Sadhana of Mahamudra*. A portion of it appears in the most recent book of his poetry, *Timely Rain*, pages 169–174.

transformed his consort Yeshe Tsogyal into a pregnant tigress, and he roamed about the Taktsang hills riding on this pregnant tigress. His manifesting this way had to do with subduing the psychic energies of the country, a country that was infested with primitive beliefs concerning ego and God.

Another expression of crazy wisdom is controlling psychic energies. The way to control psychic energies is not to create a greater psychic energy and try to dominate them. That just escalates the war, and it becomes too expensive—like the Vietnam War. You come up with a counterstrategy, and then there is a counter-counterstrategy and then a counter-counter-counterstrategy. So the idea is not to create a superpower. The way to control the psychic energy of primitive beliefs is to instigate chaos. Introduce confusion among those energies, confuse people's logic. Confuse them so that they have to think twice. That is like the moment of the changing of the guards. At that moment when they begin to think twice, the energy of crazy wisdom zaps out.

Dorje Trolö controlled the psychic energies of primitive beliefs by creating confusion. He was half-Indian and half-Tibetan, an Indian-looking person dressed up as a Tibetan madman. He held a vajra and a dagger, flames shot from his body, and he rode a pregnant tigress. It was quite strange. He was not quite a local deity and not quite a conventional guru. He was neither warrior nor king. He was certainly not an ordinary person. Riding on a tiger is regarded as a mistake, but somehow he managed to accomplish it. Was he trying to disguise himself as a Tibetan, or what was he trying to do? He was not particularly teaching anything. You couldn't deal with him as a local priest or a missionary. He wasn't converting anybody; that didn't seem to be his style either. He was just instigating chaos all over the place as he went along. Even the local deities were confused—absolutely upset.

When Padmasambhava went to Tibet, the Indians got very alarmed. They felt they were losing something very precious, since it seemed he had decided to give his teachings of crazy wisdom only to the Tibetans. This was a terrible insult for the Indians. They prided themselves on being the supreme Aryans, the most intelligent race, the ones most receptive to high teachings. And now instead of teaching them, Padmasambhava was going to the savage country of Tibet, beyond the border areas; he had decided to teach the Tibetans instead of them. King Surya Simha of Uttar Pradesh, the central province of India, sent three *acharyas,* or spiritual masters, to the king of Tibet with a polite message saying that this so-called Padmasambhava was a charlatan, a black magician, in fact. The Indian king advised that Padmasambhava was too dangerous for the Tibetans to have in their country and that they should send him back.

The interesting point here is that the teachings of crazy wisdom can only be taught in savage countries, where there is more opportunity to take advantage of chaos, or speed—or whatever you would like to call that factor.

The crazy wisdom character of Padmasambhava as Dorje Trolö is that of a guru who is unwilling to compromise with anything. If you stand in his way, you are asking for destruction. If you have doubts about him, he takes advantage of your doubts. If you are too devotional or too dependent on blind faith, he will shock you. He takes the ironical aspect of the world very seriously. He plays practical jokes on a larger scale—devastating ones.

The symbolism of the tiger is also interesting. It is connected with the idea of flame, with fire and smoke. And a pregnant tigress is supposed to be the most vicious of all tigers. She is hungry, slightly crazy, completely illogical. You cannot read her psychology and work with it reasonably. She is quite likely to eat you up at any time. That is the nature of Dorje Trolö's transport, his vehicle. The crazy wisdom guru rides on dangerous energy, impregnated with all kinds of possibilities. This tigress could be said to represent skillful means, crazy skillful means. And Dorje Trolö, who is crazy wisdom, rides on it. They make an excellent couple.

There is another side to Padmasambhava in Tibet, one that is not part of the eight aspects. For Tibetans, Padmasambhava is a father figure. As such, he is usually referred to as Guru Rinpoche, "*the* guru." He fell in love with the Tibetans and lavished tremendous care on them (not exactly the same way the missionaries fell in love with the Africans). The Tibetans were thought of as stupid. They were too faithful and too practical. Therefore, there was a tremendous opening for introducing the craziness of impracticality: abandon your farm, abandon your livelihood, roam about in the mountains dressed in those funny yogic costumes.

Once the Tibetans began to accept those things as acts of sanity, they made excellent yogis, because their approach to yogic practice was also very practical. As they had farmed faithfully and taken care of their herds faithfully, they followed the yogic calling faithfully as well.

The Tibetans were not artistic like the Japanese. Rather, they were excellent farmers, excellent merchants, excellent magicians. The Pön tradition of Tibet, the indigenous religion, was very earthy. It was purely concerned with the realities of life. Pön ceremonies are also sometimes very practical ones. One of the sacred ceremonies involves making a campfire up in the mountains—which keeps you warm. It seems that the deviousness Tibetans have shown in the course of the political intrigues of the twentieth century is entirely out of character. This kind of corruption and political intrigue came to Tibet from the outside—from the Aryan philosophers of India and from the imperial politicians of China.

Padmasambhava's approach was a very beautiful one, and his prophecies actually foretell everything that happened in Tibet, including the corruption. For example, the prophecies tell us that, in the end, Tibet would be conquered by China; that the Chinese would enter the country in the Year of the Horse; and that they would rush in in the manner of a horse. The Chinese Communists did invade in the Year of the Horse, and they built roads from China to Tibet and all over Tibet and introduced motor vehicles. The prophecies also say something to the effect that in the Year of the Pig, the country would be reduced to the level of a pig, which refers to primitive beliefs, the indoctrination of the Tibetans with foreign ideas.

Another prophecy of Padmasambhava's says that the end of Tibet would occur when the household objects of Tsang, the upper province, would be found in Kongpo, the lower province. In fact, it happened that there was a huge flood in the upper province of Tsang when the top of a glaciated mountain fell into the lake below. The whole of the Brahmaputra River was flooded, and it swept villages and monasteries along in its course. Many of the household articles from these places were found in Kongpo, where the river had carried them. His prophecies also say that another sign of the end of Tibet would be the building of a yellow temple at the foot of the Potala Palace, in Lhasa. In fact, the thirteenth Dalai Lama had a vision that a temple of Kalachakra should be built there, and they painted it yellow. Another of Padmasambhava's prophecies says that at the fourteenth stage, the rainbow of the Potala would disappear. The "fourteenth stage" refers to the time of the present, the fourteenth, Dalai Lama. Of course, the Potala is the winter palace of the Dalai Lama.

When Padmasambhava told these stories, the Tibetan king and his ministers were extremely upset, and they asked Padmasambhava to help them. "What is the best thing we can do to preserve our nation?" they asked him. "There is nothing we can do," he replied, "other than preserve the teachings that are being given now and place them in safekeeping somewhere." Then he introduced the idea of burying treasures, sacred writings.

He had various writings of his put in gold and silver containers like capsules and buried in certain appropriate places in the different parts of Tibet so that people of the future would rediscover them. He also had domestic articles buried: jewelry of his, jewelry belonging to the king and the royal household, and articles from ordinary farming households as well. The idea was that people would become more primitive, human intelligence would regress, and people would no longer be able to work properly with their hands and produce objects on that kind of artistic level.

So these things were buried all over Tibet, making use of scientific knowledge—quite possibly from India—on how best to preserve the parchments and other kinds of objects. The treasures were buried in many protective layers, including layers of charcoal, ground chalk, and other materials with various chemical properties. Also, for security, there was a layer of poison around the outside, so that thieves or other people without the right knowledge would be unable to dig them out. Such treasures have been discovered lately by great teachers who were supposedly *tülkus,* or reincarnations, of Padmasambhava's disciples. They had psychic visions, whatever those are, of certain places where they should dig. Then they set up the unburying process as a ceremony. The devotees would be assembled as well as workmen to do the digging. Sometimes the treasure would have to be dug out of a rock.

This process of rediscovering the treasures has been happening all along, and a lot of sacred teachings have been revealed. One example is *The Tibetan Book of the Dead*.

Another approach to preserving treasures of wisdom is the style of the thought lineage. Teachings have been rediscovered by certain appropriate teachers who have had memories of them and written them down from memory. This is another kind of hidden treasure.

An example of Padmasambhava's acting as a father figure for Tibet was the warning that he gave King Trisong Detsen. The New Year's celebration was about to be held, which traditionally included horse racing and archery, among the other events. Padmasambhava said, "There shouldn't be horse racing or archery this time." But the people around the king found a way to get around Padmasambhava's warning, and the king was killed by the arrow of an unknown assassin at the time of the horse racing and archery.

Padmasambhava loved Tibet and its people dearly, and one might have expected him to stay there. But another interesting part of the story is that, at a certain point, he left. It seems that there is just a certain time to care for and look after situations. Once the country had gotten itself together spiritually and domestically and people had developed *some* sense of sanity, Padmasambhava left Tibet.

Padmasambhava still lives, literally. He is not living in South America but in some remote place—on a continent of vampires, at a place there called *Sangdok Pelri*, "Glorious Copper-Colored Mountain." He still lives. Since he *is* the state of dharmakaya, the fact of physical bodies' dissolving back into nature is not regarded as a big deal. So if we search for him, we might find him. But I'm sure you will be very disappointed when you see him.

Of course, we are no longer talking about his eight aspects alone. I am sure that, since then, he has developed millions of aspects.

Crazy Wisdom, Pages 167–178

Maha Ati

MAHA ATI, OR *ati* yoga, is the final stage of the path. It is both the beginning and the end of the journey. It is not final in the sense that we have finished making a statement and we have nothing more to say, but final in the sense that we feel we have said enough. At this level, if there are any further words, they are the creations of space rather than idle remarks.

The tantric journey is like walking along a winding mountain path. Dangers, obstacles, and problems occur constantly. There are wild animals, earthquakes, landslides, all kinds of things, but still we continue on our journey, and we are able to go beyond the obstacles. When we finally get to the summit of the mountain, we do not celebrate our victory. Instead of planting our national flag on the summit of the mountain, we look down again and see a vast perspective of mountains, rivers, meadows, woods, jungles, and plains. Once we are on the summit of the mountain, we begin to look down, and we feel attracted toward the panoramic quality of what we see. That is ati style. From that point of view, our achievement is not regarded as final but as a reappreciation of what we have already gone through. In fact, we would like to retake the journey we have been through. So maha ati is the beginning of the end and the end of the beginning.

Ati teachings talk of enormous space. In this case, it is not space as opposed to a boundary, but a sense of total openness. Such openness can never be questioned. Ati yana is regarded as the king of all the yanas. In fact, the traditional Tibetan term for this yana, *long gyur thap kyi thekpa (klong gyur thabs kyi theg-pa)*, means "imperial yana." It is imperial rather than regal, for while a king has conquered his own country, in order to become an emperor, he has to conquer a lot of other territories and other continents as well. An emperor has no need for further conquests; his rule is beyond conquering. Likewise, ati is regarded as "imperial" because, from the perspective of ati yoga, hinayana discipline is seen as spaciousness; mahayana discipline is seen as spaciousness; and the tantric yanas, as well, are seen as spaciousness. If you review what we have been discussing throughout this book, you will see that we have been taking that point of view. We have discussed everything from the perspective of ati. Because of that, we have been able to view the characteristics of the various yanas and tantric disciplines in terms of openness and spaciousness and inevitability. That notion of wakefulness we have been discussing constantly is the final wakefulness of ati yoga.

Ati yoga teaching or discipline is sometimes defined as that which transcends coming, that which transcends going, and that which transcends dwelling. This definition is something more than the traditional tantric slogan of *advaita,* or "not two." In this case, we are looking at things from the level of true reality, not from the point of view of slogan or belief. Things are as they are, very simply, extremely simply so. Therefore, things are unchanging, and therefore, things are open as well. The relationship between us and our world is no relationship, because such a relationship is either there or not. We cannot manufacture a concept or an idea of relationship to make us feel better.

From the perspective of ati, the rest of the yanas are trying to comfort us: "If you feel separate, don't worry. There is nonduality as your saving grace. Try to rest your mind on it. Everything is going to be OK. Don't cry." In contrast, the approach of ati is a blunt and vast attitude of total flop, as if the sky had turned into a gigantic pancake and suddenly descended onto our head, which ironically creates enormous space. That is the ati approach, that larger way of thinking, that larger view.

Buddhism has a number of schools, primarily divided into the hinayana, mahayana, and vajrayana traditions, and squabbling goes on among all of them. They all speak the language of totality, and every one of them claims to have the answer. The hinayanists may say that they have the answer because they know reality. The mahayanists may say that the bodhisattva is the best person that we could ever find in the world. Tantric practitioners may say that the most fantastic person is the powerful and crazy yogi who is unconquerable and who has achieved *siddhis* and magical powers of all kinds. Let them believe what they want. It's OK. But what do those things mean to us personally, as students who want to practice and who want to experience the teachings?

The maha ati practitioner sees a completely naked world, at the level of marrow rather than skin or flesh or even bones. In the lower yanas, we develop lots of idioms and terms, and that makes us feel better because we have a lot of things to talk about, such as compassion or emptiness or wisdom. But in fact, that becomes a way of avoiding the actual naked reality of life. Of course, in maha ati, there is warmth, there is openness, there is penetration—all those things are there. But if we begin to divide the dharma, cutting it into little pieces as we would cut a side of beef into sirloin steaks, hamburger, and chuck, with certain cuts of beef more expensive than others, then the dharma is being marketed. In fact, according to Vimalamitra, the reason maha ati is necessary is because, throughout the lower yanas, the dharma has been marketed as a particularly juicy morsel of food. The maha ati level is necessary in order to save the dharma from being parceled and marketed; that is, it is necessary to preserve the wholesomeness of the whole path.

Actually, if we could make an ati yoga remark, all the yanas are purely creating successively more advanced and mechanized toys. At first, when a child is very young, we give him mobiles to look at, rings to suck, and rattles to shake. Then, when the child is more sophisticated, we give him more sophisticated toys, "creative playthings," and brightly colored bricks and sticks to put together. We provide even more sophisticated toys as the child becomes more and more inquisitive and sophisticated, and his mind and body are better coordinated.

Finally, at the level of adulthood, we continue to buy toys for ourselves. When we are old enough, we may buy ourselves a set of *Encyclopaedia Britannica* or a stereo kit that we can put together. We may even build ourselves a house—the ultimate creative plaything. Or we may invent some new gadget: "I designed a new kind of motor car, a new kind of airplane, a new kind of submarine. I built it, and it actually worked. Isn't that fantastic?" We feel that our abilities are becoming much greater because not only can we build fantastic toys and enjoy them ourselves but we learn how to sell them, market them. When we become really sophisticated, we might design a zoo or even an entire city, and be accepted as important people in our society. It feels fantastic, extremely powerful and encouraging. But we are still fascinated by our toys.

According to ati yoga, going through the yanas is similar to that process of collecting more and more toys. The more sophisticated and fascinated we become, the more we are actually reducing ourselves to a childlike level. Somehow, we are not yet at the level of maha ati if we are still fascinated by our toys, our occupations, no matter how extensive or expansive they may be. At the maha ati level, those little tricks that we play to improve ourselves or to entertain ourselves are no longer regarded as anything—but at the same time, they are everything, much vaster than we could have imagined. It is as though we were building a city or a zoo, and suddenly the whole sky turned into a gigantic pancake and dropped on us. There is a new dimension of surprise that we never thought of, we never expected. We never expected the sky to drop on our head.

There is a children's story about the sky falling, but we do not actually believe that such a thing could happen. The sky turns into a blue pancake and drops on our head—nobody believes that. But in maha ati experience, it actually does happen. There is a new dimension of shock, a new dimension of logic. It is as though we were furiously calculating a mathematical problem in our notebook, and suddenly a new approach altogether dawned on us, stopping us in our tracks. Our perspective becomes completely different.

Our ordinary approach to reality and truth is so poverty-stricken that we don't realize that the truth is not one truth but all truth. It could be everywhere, like raindrops, as opposed to water coming out of a faucet that only one person can drink from at a time. Our limited approach is a problem. It may be our cultural training to believe that only one person can get the truth: "You can receive this, but nobody else can." There are all sorts of philosophical, psychological, religious, and emotional tactics that we use to motivate ourselves, which say that we can do something but nobody else can. Since we think we are the only one who can do something, we crank up our machine and we do it. And if it turns out that somebody else has done it already, we begin to feel jealous and resentful. In fact, the dharma has been marketed or auctioned in that way. But from the point of view of ati, there is "all" dharma rather than "the" dharma. The notion of "one and only" does not apply anymore. If the gigantic pancake falls on our head, it falls on everybody's head.

In some sense, it is both a big joke and a big message. You cannot even run to your next-door neighbor saying, "I had a little pancake fall on my head. What can I do? I want to wash my hair." You have nowhere to go. It is a cosmic pancake that falls everywhere on the face of the earth. You cannot escape—that is the basic point. From that point of view, both the problem and the promise are cosmic.

If you are trying to catch what I am saying, quite possibly you cannot capture the idea. In fact, it is quite possible that you do not understand a word of it. You cannot imagine it in even the slightest, faintest way. But it is possible that there are situations that exist beyond your logic, beyond your system of thinking. That is not an impossibility. In fact, it is highly possible.

The earlier yanas talk about the rug being pulled out from under our feet, which is quite understandable. If our landlord kicks us out of our apartment, the rug is pulled out from under our feet, obviously. That is quite workable, and we find that we can still relate with our world. But in ati, we are talking about the sky collapsing onto us. *Nobody* thinks of that possibility. It is an entirely different approach. No one can imagine a landlady or a landlord who could pull that trick on us.

In maha ati, we are not talking about gaining ground or losing ground, or how we settle down and find our way around. Instead, we are talking about how we can develop headroom. Headroom, or the space above us, is the important thing. We are interested in how space could provide us with a relationship to reality, to the world.

I do not think we should go into too much detail about maha ati. I have basically been finger painting, but that is as far as we can go at this point. However, we could discuss another topic that is closely related to ati yana: crazy wisdom.

Using the word *crazy* from the English language to describe tantric experience is very tricky because of the various ideas we have about craziness. In the American Indian tradition, there was a warrior named Crazy Horse. He was a crazy, old, wise eccentric who was a great warrior and had tremendous courage. Being crazy is also associated with the idea of being absurd, on the verge of lunacy. There is also a notion of craziness as being unconventional. And sometimes we talk about somebody's being crazy about music or crazy about honey or sugar. We mean that somebody takes excessive pleasure in something or has an excessive fascination, to the point where he might destroy himself by being so crazy about whatever it is.

We might also say that someone is crazy if he doesn't agree with us. For instance, if we are trying to form a business, we will approach somebody to be our business partner who agrees with our business proposals. We tell him that the two of us can make lots of money. And if we approach this "uncrazy" person properly, he will accept our logic and he will love the idea of going into business with us. Whereas if we approach an intelligent "crazy" person, he will see through us. He will see any holes in our plan or any neurosis that our business might create. So we don't want to approach such a person as a business partner: "I won't talk to him. He's crazy." What we mean is, "He will see through me. He won't buy my simplistic logic, my trip." That description of craziness comes somewhat close to the tantric idea of craziness. Still, such craziness has a sense of basic ground. There is a lot of room, a lot of trust, but there is also a lot of solidity.

We might also view our grandparents' orthodoxy as crazy. They are so soaked in their own culture and their own norms that they don't understand our culture at all. Their crazy ways make them practically unapproachable to us. We cannot shake their faith and their convictions, and we feel frustrated when we have something to say to them and they don't respond as we want. So we might regard them as semicrazy.

I don't think crazy wisdom fits any of the examples above. Instead, crazy wisdom is the basic norm or the basic logic of sanity. It is a transparent view that cuts through conventional norms or conventional emotionalism. It is the notion of relating properly with the world. It is knowing how much heat is needed to boil water to make a cup of tea, or how much pressure you should apply to educate your students. That level of craziness is very wise. It is based on being absolutely wise, knowing exactly what to do. Such a wise person is well versed in the ways of the world, and he has developed and understood basic logic. He knows how to build a campfire, how to pitch a tent, and how to brush his teeth. He knows how to handle himself in relating with the world, from the level of knowing how to make a good fire in the fireplace up to knowing the fine points of philosophy. So there is absolute knowledgeability. And then, on top of that, craziness begins to descend, as an ornament to the basic wisdom that is already there.

In other words, crazy wisdom does not occur unless there is a basic understanding of things, a knowledge of how things function as they are. There has to be trust in the normal functioning of karmic cause and effect. Having been highly and completely trained, then there is enormous room for crazy wisdom. According to that logic, wisdom does not exactly go crazy; but on top of the basic logic or basic norm, craziness as higher sanity, higher power, or higher magic can exist.

One attribute of crazy wisdom is fearlessness. Having already understood the logic of how things work, fearlessness is the further power and energy to do what needs to be done, to destroy what needs to be destroyed, to nurse what should be nursed, to encourage what should be encouraged, or whatever the appropriate action is.

The fearlessness of crazy wisdom is also connected with bluntness. Bluntness here is the notion of openness. It is a sense of improvising, being resourceful, but not in the sense of constantly trying to improvise the nature of the world. There are two approaches to improvising. If we have a convenient accident and we capitalize on that, we improvise as we go along. That is the conventional sense of the word. For instance, we might become a famous comedian, not because of our perceptiveness but purely because we make funny mistakes. We say the wrong things at the wrong time, and people find us hilarious. Therefore, we become a famous comedian. That is approaching things from the back door, or more accurately, it is like hanging out in the backyard.

The other approach to improvising, or bluntness, is seeing things as they are. We might see humor in things; we might see strength or weakness. In any case, we see what is there quite bluntly. A crazy wisdom person has this sense of improvising. If such a person sees that something needs to be destroyed rather than preserved, he strikes on the spot. Or if something needs to be preserved, although it might be decaying or becoming old hat, he will nurse it very gently.

So crazy wisdom is absolute perceptiveness, with fearlessness and bluntness. Fundamentally, it is being wise but not holding to particular doctrines or disciplines or formats. There aren't any books to follow. Rather, there is endless spontaneity taking place. There is room for being blunt, room for being open. That openness is created by the environment itself. In fact, at the level of crazy wisdom, all activity is created by the environment. The crazy wisdom person is just an activator, just one of the conditions that have evolved in the environment.

⁓

Since we are reaching the end of our tantric journey together, so to speak, I would like to say something about how you could relate to all of this information that you have received. You don't have to try to catch the universe in the same way that you would try to catch a grasshopper or a flea. You don't *have* to do something with what you have experienced, particularly. Why don't you let it be as it is? In fact, that might be necessary. If you actually want to use something, you have to let it be. You cannot drink all the water on earth in order to quench your thirst eternally. You might drink a glass of water, but you have to leave the rest of the water, rivers and oceans, so that if you are thirsty again, you can drink more. You have to leave some room somewhere. You don't have to gulp everything down. It's much nicer not to do that; in fact, it is polite.

If you are terribly hungry and thirsty, you want to attack the universe as your prey all at once: "I'll have it for my dinner or my breakfast. I don't care." You don't think about anybody else who might have just a humble request, who might just want to have a sip from your glass of milk or a piece of meat from your plate. If you are told that you should be devotional, you might think that means that you should be even more hungry and try to get every possible blessing into your system. Since you are hungry, you suck up everything, all the systems and resources that exist, including your own. You don't find yourself being a productive human being; instead, you find yourself becoming a monster.

There are a lot of problems with that, unless you have the umbrella notion of maha ati, which says: "It's OK. Everything is OK. Just take a pinch of salt, a spoonful of soy sauce. Just take one shot of whiskey. Don't rush; everything is going to be OK. You can have plenty of room if you want. Just cool it." You don't have to do a complete job, all at once. If you go too far, if you are too hungry, you could become a cosmic monster. That message is very courageous, but very few people have the courage to say that.

I am actually concerned and somewhat worried about how you are going to handle all this material. You could overextend yourselves and get completely zonked or completely bewildered. Or you could use this as just another clever reference point, a new vocabulary or logic to manipulate your friends and your world. What you do with this material is really up to you. I hope that you will feel grateful for this introduction to the tantric world, and I hope that you will realize from this that the world is not all that bad and confused. The world can be explored; it is workable, wherever you go, whatever you do. But I would like to plant one basic seed in your mind: I feel that it is absolutely important to make the practice of meditation your source of strength, your source of basic intelligence. Please think about that. You could sit down and do nothing, just sit and do nothing. Stop acting, stop speeding. Sit and do nothing. You should take pride in the fact that you have learned a very valuable message: you actually can survive beautifully by doing nothing.

Journey without Goal, Pages 133–142

Meteoric Iron Mountain

Meteoric iron mountain piercing to the sky,
With lightning and hailstorm clouds round about it.
There is so much energy where I live
Which feeds me.
There is no romantic mystique,
There is just a village boy
On a cold wet morning
Going to the farm
Fetching milk for the family.
Foolishness and wisdom
Grandeur and simplicity
Are all the same
Because they live on what they are.
There is no application for exotic wisdom.
Wisdom must communicate
To the men of now.
Dharma is the study of what is
And fulfills the understanding of what is here right now.
The ripple expands when you throw the pebble:
It is true, a fact.
That is the point of faith,
Of full conviction,
Which no one can defeat or challenge.

Please, readers,
Read it slowly
So you can feel
That depth of calmness as you read.
Love to you.
I am the Bodhisattva who will not abandon you,
In accordance with my vow.
Compassion to all.

Timely Rain, Pages 27–28

If you enjoyed The Essential Chögyam Trungpa, *you won't want to miss* Chögyam Trungpa's *next book. Here is the first chapter from* Great Eastern Sun: The Wisdom of Shambhala.

The Kingdom, the Cocoon, the Great Eastern Sun

DRIVEN BY SURVIVAL, hassled by the demands of life, we live in a world completely thronged by our holding on to our state of existence, our livelihood, our jobs. People throughout this century and for at least the last few thousand years have been trying to solve our problems right and left. Throughout history, in fact, great prophets, teachers, masters, gurus, yogis, saints of all kinds, have appeared and tried to solve the problems of life. Their message has been quite definite: "Try to be good. Be gentle to yourselves, to your neighbors, your parents, your relatives, your spouse—to the whole world. If you are good to others, you will relieve their anxiety. Then you will have excellent neighbors, excellent relatives, an excellent wife, an excellent husband, an excellent world." That message has been presented a thousand times. Our lives are enriched by many sacred writings, including the ancient traditions of Taoism, Vedic texts, sutras, tantras, and shastras[1]— sacred texts of all kinds. Modern libraries and bookstores are filled with these attempts to reach us. People try so hard to help, even placing the Gideon Bible in hotel rooms.

Many of those teachers and saints belong to a theistic tradition. That is to say, they worship the one God and they are monotheists, or they are presenting sacred messages from the multitheism of other traditions. On the other hand, Buddhism is a nontheistic spiritual discipline, which does not talk in terms of

---

1. Sutras are discourses by the Buddha; tantras are tantric Buddhist texts ascribed to the Buddha in his ultimate or dharmakaya form; and shastras are philosophical commentaries on the sutras.

worship and does not regard the world as somebody's creation. According to the Buddhist teachings, there was no great artificer who fashioned the world. This world is created or produced and happens to be purely through our own existence. We exist; therefore, we have fashioned this particular world. Then, there are entirely different schools of thought, supported by scientific discoveries, which say that everything is an evolutionary process. We have Darwinian theories of how, from a monkey or a fish, human beings came to exist.

There are many conflicting notions about the origins of existence. But whether it is according to theism, nontheism, or a scientific approach, there *is* this particular world—which is created and which we have. To theologians or scientists, it may be terribly important to figure out why we are here or how we came to be here. But from the point of view of Shambhala vision, the main concern is not *why* I am here or *why* you are here. *Why* you happen to have a white shirt, a red shirt, long hair, or short hair is not the question. The real question is: since we're here, how are we going to live from now onward? We may or may not have a long time to live. Impermanence is always there. Right now, you may cease to live. As you walk out of the room you're in right now, something may happen to you. You may face death. There are many eventualities of life or death. You may face physical problems, sicknesses of all kinds. You may be subject to cancer. Nonetheless, you have to live from now onward.

The basic point of the Shambhala teachings is to realize that there is no outside help to save you from the terror and the horror of life. The best doctor of the doctors and the best medicine of the medicines and the best technology of the technologies cannot save you from your life. The best consultants, the best bank loans, and the best insurance policies cannot save you. Eventually you must realize that *you* have to do something, rather than depending on technology, financial help, your smartness or good thinking of any kind—none of which will save you. That may seem like the black truth, but it is the real truth. Often, in the Buddhist tradition, it is called the vajra truth, the diamond truth, the truth you cannot avoid or destroy. We cannot avoid our lives at all. We have to face our lives, young or old, rich or poor. Whatever happens, we cannot save ourselves from our lives at all. We have to face the eventual truth—not even the eventual truth but the *real* truth of our lives. We are here; therefore, we have to learn how to go forward with our lives.

This truth is what we call the wisdom of Shambhala. The introduction of such wisdom into North American culture is an historical landmark. However, my purpose is not to convert you to what I have to say. Rather, the more you understand, the more you will realize your own responsibility. So I am speaking to you not only from the point of view of the trumpeter, but also from the point of view of the trumpetees. Rather than watching the trumpeter, what is important is to hear the trumpet music.

The Kingdom

According to tradition, the Kingdom of Shambhala was a kingdom in Central Asia where this wisdom was taught and an excellent society was created. In that society, the citizens' conduct and their behavior were based on having less anxiety. Essentially, anxiety comes from not facing the current situation you are in. The Kingdom of Shambhala and the citizens, the subjects, of Shambhala were able to face their reality. The Kingdom of Shambhala could be said to be a mythical kingdom or a real kingdom—to the extent that you believe in Atlantis or in heaven. It has been said that the kingdom was technologically advanced and that the citizens had tremendous intelligence. Spirituality was secularized, meaning that day-to-day living situations were handled properly. Life was not based on the worship of a deity or on vigorous religious practice, as such. Rather, that wonderful world of Shambhala was based on actually relating with your life, your body, your food, your household, your marital situations, your breath, your environment, your atmosphere.

According to the legends, the vision and the teachings of Shambhala were embodied in that Central Asian kingdom. If we go deeper, we could say that such a situation of sanity comes about because you connect with your own intelligence. Therefore, the Kingdom of Shambhala exists in your own heart right at this moment. You are a citizen of Shambhala and part of the Kingdom of Shambhala, without doubt. We are not trying to bring a myth into reality, which would be the wrong thing to do. Actually, I have even written a book to that effect, entitled *The Myth of Freedom*. On the other hand, as human beings we do possess the sense faculties: we can see, we can hear, we can feel, we can think. Because of that, we can do something to bring about the Kingdom of Shambhala once again.

This time it doesn't have to be a Central Asian kingdom. We aren't talking about going over there and digging up graves, digging up ruins, to find the remains of the truth of Shambhala. We are not talking about conducting an archaeological survey. On the other hand, we *might* be talking about some kind of archaeological survey, which is digging up our minds and our lives, which have been buried and covered with layers and layers of dirt. We have to rediscover something in our lives. Is it possible? It is very possible, extremely possible. How should we go about it? From the very day of your birth, you have never really looked at yourself, your life, and your experiences in life. You have never really felt that you could create a good, decent world. Of course, you may have tried all sorts of things. You may have marched in the street in the name of the happiness of humanity, complained about the existing political system, written up new ideas and manifestos to prevent this and that: that pain, this pain, this confusion, that confusion. You may have been somewhat heroic, and you could say that you've tried your best. Nonetheless, have you found any real peace or rest? A real, dignified world has not been created.

Often, we complain because of our aggression. We are so angry and resentful. Instead of short hair, we want long hair. Instead of long hair, we cut our hair short. Instead of a coat and tie, we want to wear jeans and a T-shirt. Instead of this, we do that. Instead of that, we do this. We try to find some easy way to gain the freedom and the vision of human society. Instead of eating peanut butter, we try eating brown rice. Instead of that, we try this; instead of this, we try that. That, this, this, that. We have tried so many things. Particularly in the United States, people have tried *so* hard to reestablish a good world. I appreciate that integrity, which is quite relentless, in some sense, and pretty good.

However, the principle of the Shambhala training is that, instead of trying so hard to remove problems, you should reestablish or plant something positive. The point is that you don't have to take so many showers to remove the dirt. The real question is what clothes you put on after your shower and how you perfume and beautify your body. One shower is good enough; it makes you clean. Then, after that, if you continue to take showers, you become stark, too clean. There is certainly an absence of dirt, but what comes after that? There's no warmth, no dignity. Can't we do something more to bring reality and goodness into society?

The Cocoon

The point of Shambhala training is to get out of the cocoon, which is the shyness and aggression in which we have wrapped ourselves. When we have more aggression, we feel more fortified. We feel good, because we have more to talk about. We feel that we are the greatest author of the complaint. We write poetry about it. We express ourselves through it. Instead of constantly complaining, can't we do something positive to help this world? The more we complain, the more concrete slabs will be put on the earth. The less we complain, the more possibilities there will be of tilling the land and sowing seeds. We should feel that we can do something positive for the world, instead of covering it with our aggression and complaints.

The approach of the Shambhala training is to do something very concrete, very basic, very definite, and to begin at the beginning. In the Shambhala tradition, we talk about being a warrior. I would like to make it clear that a warrior, in this case, is not someone who wages war. A Shambhala warrior is someone who is brave enough not to give in to the aggression and contradictions that exist in society. A warrior, or *pawo* in Tibetan, is a brave person, a genuine person who is able to step out of the cocoon—that very comfortable cocoon that he or she is trying to sleep in.

If you are in your cocoon, occasionally you shout your complaints, such as: "Leave me alone!" "Bug off." "I want to be who I am." Your cocoon is fabricated out of tremendous aggression, which comes from fighting against your environment, your parental upbringing, your educational upbringing, your upbringing of all kinds. You don't really have to fight with your cocoon. You can raise your head and just take a *little* peek out of the cocoon. Sometimes, when you first peek your head out, you find the air a bit too fresh and cold. But still, it is good. It is the best fresh air of spring or autumn or, for that matter, the best fresh air of winter or summer. So when you stick your neck out of the cocoon for the first time, you like it in spite of the discomfort of the environment. You find that it's delightful. Then, having peeked out, you become brave enough to climb out of the cocoon. You sit on your cocoon and look around at your world. You stretch your arms and you begin to develop your head and shoulders. The environment is friendly. It is called "planet Earth." Or it is called "Boston," or "New York City." It is your world.

Your neck and your hips are not all that stiff, so you can turn and look around. The environment is not as bad as you thought. Still sitting on the cocoon, you raise yourself up a little farther. Then you kneel and finally you stand up on your cocoon. As you look around, you begin to realize that the cocoon is no longer useful. You don't have to buy the advertisers' logic that if you don't have insulation in your house, you're going to die. You don't really need the insulation of your cocoon. It's just a little cast that's been put on you by your own collective imaginary paranoia and confusion, which didn't want to relate with the world outside.

Then, you extend one leg, rather tentatively, to touch the ground around the cocoon. Traditionally, the right leg goes first. You wonder where your foot is going to land. You've never touched the soles of your feet before on the soil of this planet Earth. When you first touch the Earth, you find it's very rough. It's made out of earth, dirt. But soon you discover the intelligence that will allow you to *walk* on the Earth, and you begin to think the process might be workable. You realize that you inherited this family heirloom, called "planet Earth," a long time ago.

You sigh with relief, maybe a medium sigh, extend your left foot and touch the ground on the other side of the cocoon. The second time you touch the ground, to your surprise you find that the Earth is kind and gentle and much less rough. You begin to feel gentleness and affection and softness. You feel that you might even fall in love on your planet Earth. You *can* fall in love. You feel real passion, which is very positive.

At that point, you decide to leave your old beloved cocoon behind and to stand up without touching the cocoon at all. So you stand on your two feet, and you take a walk outside of the cocoon. Each step is rough and soft, rough and soft: rough because the exploration is still a challenge, and soft because you don't find anything trying to kill you or eat you up at all. You don't have to defend yourself or fight any unexpected attackers or wild beasts. The world around you is so fine and beautiful that you know that you can raise yourself up as a warrior, a powerful person. You begin to feel that the world is absolutely workable, not even workable alone, but *wonderful*. To your surprise you find that lots of others around you are also leaving their cocoons. You find hosts of ex-cocooners all over the place.

As ex-cocooners, we feel that we can be dignified and wonderful people. We do not have to reject anything at all. As we step out of our cocoons, we find goodness and gratefulness taking place in us all the time. As we stand on the Earth, we find that the world is not particularly depressed. On the other hand, there is need for tremendous hard work. As we stand up and walk around, having finally got out of our own cocoons, we see that there are hundreds of thousands of others who are still half breathing in their cocoons. So we feel very touched and sad, extremely sad.

From the dictionary's point of view, *sadness* has negative connotations. If you feel sad, you feel unfortunate or bad. Or you are sad because you don't have enough money or you don't have any security. But from the Shambhala point of view, sadness is also inspiring. You feel sad and empty-hearted, but you also feel something positive, because this sadness involves appreciation of others. You would like to tell those who are still stuck in their cocoons that if they got out of the cocoon, they would also feel that genuine sadness. That empty-heartedness is the principle of the broken-hearted warrior. As an ex-cocooner, you feel it is wonderful that people of the past have gotten out of their cocoons. You wish that you could tell the cocooners the story of the warriors of the Great Eastern Sun and the story of the Kingdom of Shambhala. All the warriors of the past had to leave their cocoons. You wish you could let the cocooners know that. You would like to tell them that they are not alone. There are hundreds of thousands of others who have made this journey.

Once you develop this quality of sadness, you also develop a quality of dignity or positive arrogance within yourself, which is quite different from the usual negative arrogance. You manifest yourself with dignity to show the degraded world that trying to avoid death by sleeping in a cocoon is not the way. The degraded world, in which people are sleeping in their cocoons trying to avoid the pain of death, is called the setting-sun world. In that world, people are looking for the sunset as a sign that there will be a peaceful night ahead. But that night is never peaceful: it is always pitch-dark. Those who arise from the cocoon are called the people of the Great Eastern Sun. They are not blinded by opening their eyes, and they are not embarrassed about developing head and shoulders and stepping out of their cocoons. Such people begin to breathe the fresh morning air. They experience brilliance, which is constant and beautiful.

In the sitting practice of meditation, which is part of the Shambhala training, we stress the importance of good posture. Posture is important, not just in sitting practice, but in whatever you do. Whether you are talking to a client or talking to your mate, whether you're talking to your pets or talking to yourself—which does sometimes happen—having a good posture of head and shoulders is an expression that you've stepped out of your co-coon. One of the reasons that people sing in the shower is that the water showering down on you forces you to stand up and have good head and shoulders. You begin to feel cleaned out, so you begin to sing or hum. This is not a myth; it's true. When you have water falling on your shoulders, your head, and your face, there's a sense that you're relating with heaven.

Helping Others

The Shambhala training is based on developing gentleness and genuineness so that we can help ourselves and develop tenderness in our hearts. We no longer wrap ourselves in the sleeping bag of our cocoon. We feel responsible for ourselves, and we feel good taking responsibility. We also feel grateful that, as human beings, we can actually work for others. It is about time that we did something to help the world. It is the right time, the right moment, for this training to be introduced.

The fixation of ego is manifested in the words "I am." Then there is the conclusion: "I am . . . happy." Or "I am sad." There is the first thought (I) and the second thought (am), and finally the third thought is the conclusion. "I am *happy*," "I am *sad*," "I feel *miserable*," "I feel *good*"—whatever the thought may be. The Shambhala idea of responsibility is to drop "am." Just say, "I happy." "I sad." I know there's a bit of a linguistic problem here, but I hope that you can understand what I'm saying. The point is to be responsible to others, without self-confirmation.

To put it slightly differently, suppose your name is Sandy. There is "Sandy," and there is the "world." You don't need a verb between them as confirmation. Just be kind to others. Sandy should be genuine. When she is the real, genuine Sandy, she can help others a lot. She may not have any training in first aid, but Sandy can put a Band-Aid on someone's finger. Sandy is no longer afraid to help, and she is very kind and on-the-spot. When you begin to help others, you have raised your head and shoulders, and you're stepping out of your cocoon. The point of the Shambhala training is not to produce fake people. The point is to become a real person who can help others.

Being in the cocoon is almost like being a child in the womb, a child who doesn't particularly want to come out. Even after you're born, you aren't happy about being toilet trained. You would prefer to stay in your nappies, your diapers. You like to have something wrapped around your bottom all the time. But eventually your diapers are taken away. You have no choice. You have been born and you've been toilet trained; you can't stay forever in your diapers. In fact, you might feel quite free, no longer having a diaper wrapped around your bum. You can move around quite freely. You might eventually feel quite good about being free from the tyranny that parenthood and home life impose.

Still, we don't *really* want to develop discipline. So we begin to create this little thing, this little cocoon. We get wrapped up in all sorts of things. When we're in the cocoon, we don't want to sit upright and eat with good table manners. We don't really want to dress elegantly, and we don't want to conform to any discipline that requires even three minutes of silence. That's partly because of being raised in North America, where everything is built for children to entertain themselves. Entertainment is even the basis for education. If you can raise your own children outside of the cocoon, you will raise lots of bodhisattva children, children who are real and face facts and are actually able to relate with reality properly. I have done that myself with my own children, and it seems to have worked out.

As decent human beings we face the facts of reality. Whether we are in the middle of a snowstorm or a rainstorm, whether there is family chaos, whatever problems there may be, we are willing to work them out. Looking into those situations is no longer regarded as a hassle, but it is regarded as our duty. Although helping others has been preached quite a lot, we don't really believe we can do it. The traditional American expression, as I've heard it, is that we don't want to get our hands or our fingers dirty. That, in a nutshell, is why we want to stay in the cocoon: we don't want to get our fingers dirty. But we must do something about this world, so that the world can develop into a nonaggressive society where people can wake themselves up. Helping others is one of the biggest challenges.

I appreciate your inquisitiveness, your sense of humor, and your relaxation. Please try to elegantize yourself and step out of the cocoon. The basic point is to become very genuine within yourselves. This means being free from the plastic world, if such a thing is possible. Also, please don't hurt others. If you can't do that, at least treat yourself better and don't punish yourself by sleeping in your cocoon. Finally, please try to work with people and be helpful to them. A fantastically large number of people need help. *Please* try to help them, for goodness' sake, for heaven and earth. Don't just collect Oriental wisdoms one after the other. Don't just sit on an empty *zafu*, an empty meditation cushion. But go out and try to help others, if you can. That is the main point.

We have to do something. We've *got* to do something. As we

read in the newspapers and see on television, the world is deteriorating, one thing after the other, every hour, every minute, and nobody is helping very much. Your help doesn't have to be a big deal. To begin with, just work with your friends and work with yourself at the same time. It is about time that we became responsible for this world. It will pay for itself.

Glossary

The definitions in this glossary are particular to the use of the terms in the text and are often taken from the glossary of the book(s) in which the term appeared. Unless otherwise indicated, foreign terms in the glossary are Sanskrit.

abhisheka Ceremony or formal experience of vajrayana transmission.

adhishthana Blessings or grace that one receives as a product of practice and devotion in the vajrayana.

alaya Fundamental unbiased ground of mind.

amrita Blessed liquor used in vajrayana meditation practices. More generally, spiritual intoxication.

Asanga Fourth-century Buddhist teacher, one of the founders of the Yogachara, or "mind only," school of Buddhism.

asura Jealous god in the six realms of existence.

bodhi Enlightenment, wakefulness, or awakened mind.

bodhichitta Awakened mind or heart. Ultimate or absolute bodhichitta is the union of emptiness and compassion, the essential nature of awakened mind. Relative bodhichitta is the tenderness arising from a glimpse of ultimate bodhichitta that inspires one to work for the benefit of others.

bodhisattva Awake being. One who has committed himself or herself to practicing the six paramitas, or the transcendent virtues, of generosity, discipline, patience, exertion, meditation, and knowledge. The bodhisattva takes a vow to postpone enlightenment in order to work for the benefit of beings.

bodhi tree Tree under which the Buddha attained enlightenment.

Brahma In early Hinduism, one of three main gods: Brahma the creator, Vishnu the preserver, and Shiva the destroyer. The god Brahma is also associated with the quality of brahma: supreme, eternal, or absolute existence.

buddha Awakened or enlightened. It may refer either to the principle of enlightenment or to an enlightened being, especially to Shakyamuni Buddha, the historical buddha.

buddhadharma   Teaching of the Buddha. See also *dharma.*

buddha nature   Enlightened basic nature of all beings. See also *tathaga-tagarbha.*

cakra   Circle or wheel. Often used in the vajrayana to refer to centers in the head, throat, heart, and navel of the illusory body, or the body that one visualizes in vajrayana practice.

Chökyi Gyatso (Sanskrit *Dharma Sagara*)   Expanded form of *Chögyam,* the author's dharma name, which means "Dharma Ocean" or "Ocean of Teachings."

Dawa Sangpo   Tibetan name of the first king of Shambhala.

dharma   Truth, norm, or law. Often used to refer to the teachings of the Buddha, which are also called the buddhadharma.

dharma art   Term coined by the author to refer to art that is based on nonaggression and that expresses the basic dharma, or truth, of things as they are.

dharmakaya   One of the three bodies of enlightenment. See *kaya.*

dohā   Verse or song spontaneously composed by vajrayana practitioners as an expression of realization.

Dorje Trolö   Eighth and final manifestation of Guru Rinpoche, or Padmasambhava, the founder of Buddhism in Tibet.

drala   In the Shambhala teachings, the manifestation, strength, or bravery that transcends or conquers aggression. Sometimes translated as "war gods," *drala* means to be above or beyond war.

five buddha families   The mandala of the five buddha families represents five basic styles of energy, which can manifest as either confusion or enlightenment, as discussed in "The Five Buddha Families" in this volume.

Gampopa   Founder of the monastic order of the Kagyü lineage, Gampopa was the chief disciple of Milarepa and the author of *The Jewel Ornament of Liberation.*

Gesar of Ling   Mythical hero who inspired the greatest epic of Tibetan Buddhism. Legend has it that Gesar will reappear, being reborn in Shambhala.

guru   Sanskrit for *lama.* A master or teacher, especially in the tantric or vajrayana tradition of Buddhism.

Guru Rinpoche   "Precious Teacher," the name by which Padmasambhava, the founder of Buddhism in Tibet, is often referred to by the Tibetan people.

hatha yoga   School of Indian philosophy that stresses mastery of the body as a way of attaining spiritual perfection.

hinayana   Narrow way or path. The first of the three yanas of Tibetan

Buddhism, the hinayana focuses on meditation practice and discipline, individual salvation, and not causing harm to others. See also *yana.*

Kadam The Kadam lineage was founded by Dromtönpa, the main disciple of Atisha, who came to Tibet in the eleventh century. These teachings emphasize mind training and the development of compassion.

Kagyü Tibetan for "ear-whispered" or "command lineage." *Ka* refers to the oral instructions of the teacher.

Kalacakra Wheel of time. The last and most complex Buddhist Tantra, said to have been taught by the Buddha in Shambhala.

karma Deed or action. The universal law of cause and effect.

kaya Body. According to tradition, the *trikaya,* or the three bodies of enlightenment, refers to three modes of existence of the Buddha, or enlightenment itself. These correspond to mind, speech, and body. The *dharmakaya* (dharma body) is unoriginated, primordial mind, devoid of concept. The *sambhogakaya* (enjoyment body) is its environment of compassion and communication. The *nirmanakaya* (emanation body) is the buddha that takes human form. In the mahayana, this usually refers to Shakyamuni, the historical buddha; in the vajrayana, it may refer to the body, speech, and mind of the guru.

Kukuripa One of the Indian gurus of Marpa the Translator.

kusha grass The Buddha attained enlightenment while seated on kusha grass, which he was given by a farmer.

Lankavatara Sutra Famous mahayana sutra, or discourse by the Buddha, that expounds on the realization of buddha nature.

lohan Chinese for the Sanskrit *arhat,* the ideal of a saint or realized one in the hinayana school of Buddhism.

maha ati (also *ati;* Tibetan *dzogchen*) Great perfection. The ultimate teaching of the Nyingma school of Tibetan Buddhism, maha ati is considered the final fruition of the vajrayana path. It teaches the indivisibility of space and wisdom.

mahakalas Chief dharmapalas, or protectors of the dharma. They are wrathful and usually depicted as either black or dark blue.

mahamudra "Great seal, symbol, or gesture." The central meditative transmission of the Kagyü lineage.

Maharishi Occasionally used as an epithet of the Buddha, *Maharishi* literally means "the great sage." The seers who revealed the Vedas were rishis. *Rishi,* especially in Tibetan translation, has the connotation of someone who always speaks the truth and whose righteous speech leads to realization.

mahayana   Great vehicle, or the open path. One of the three major schools of Buddhism, which emphasizes the emptiness of phenomena, the development of compassion, and the acknowledgment of universal buddha nature.

Manjushri   Bodhisattva of knowledge and learning. Often shown holding a book and the sword of prajna, or discriminating awareness. The sword of Manjushri represents intellectual sharpness and cutting through ignorance and delusion.

Marpa   The chief disciple of Naropa, Marpa of Lhotrak brought the Kagyü teachings from India to Tibet in the eleventh century. He is often called "Marpa the Translator." A farmer with a large family, he was known not only for his meditative realization of mahamudra but for his attainment of spiritual realization within a secular lifestyle.

Milarepa   The chief disciple of Marpa, Jetsun Milarepa is the most famous of all Tibetan poets and one of Tibet's greatest saints. After studying with Marpa, Milarepa became a wandering yogi who spent many years in solitary retreat, practicing asceticism and undergoing great deprivation.

Naropa   The chief disciple of Tilopa, Naropa was a great Indian scholar. Realizing that he understood the words but not the inner meaning of the teachings, he left Nalanda University to find his teacher. Naropa endured many trials in order to attain mahamudra, and he is renowned as a great mahasiddha, or tantric master, of the Kagyü lineage.

nirmanakaya   One of the three bodies of enlightenment. See *kaya*.

nirvana   Enlightenment or realization.

Padmasambhava   Also referred to as Guru Rinpoche, or the precious teacher, Padmasambhava introduced Buddhism to Tibet in the eighth century.

paramita   Literally, "gone to the other shore." The paramitas are the transcendent actions or virtues practiced by a bodhisattva. The six paramitas are generosity, discipline, patience, exertion, meditation, and knowledge (prajna). The paramitas differ from ordinary activities or virtues in that they are all based on realization free from ego-clinging.

pawo   Tibetan for "warrior." *Pawo* literally means "one who is brave" and is used in the Shambhala teachings to mean one who conquers aggression rather than one who wages war.

prajna   Knowledge as well as the natural sharpness of awareness that sees, discriminates, and also cuts through the veils of ignorance.

prajnaparamita   The sixth paramita, considered to be the eye without which the other five transcendent actions of a bodhisattva would be blind. Prajnaparamita is called the mother of all the buddhas and is sometimes depicted as a youthful, smiling deity.

pranayama   Form of vajrayana yogic practice that involves controlling mind, body, and breath.

preta   Hungry ghost in the six realms of being.

Rangjung Dorje   Third Karmapa, the supreme head of the Karma Kagyü lineage, who lived in the fourteenth century.

Rigden kings   Kings of Shambhala, who are said to watch over worldly affairs from their celestial kingdom. Symbolically, the Rigdens represent the complete attainment of bravery and compassion in the Shambhala teachings.

samadhi   Meditative absorption, which refers to a state of total involvement in which the mind rests unwaveringly and the content of the meditation and the meditator's mind are one.

Samadhiraja Sutra   Important mahayana sutra, or discourse by the Buddha.

sambhogakaya   One of the three bodies of enlightenment. See *kaya.*

samsara   Vicious cycle of existence, arising from ignorance and characterized by suffering.

samyaksambuddha   Sanskrit epithet for the Buddha that means "the completely perfect awakened one."

sangha   The community of Buddhist practitioners.

shamatha   Basic sitting practice of meditation, which emphasizes mindfulness and taming the mind. See also *vipashyana.*

shunyata   Emptiness or openness, the experience of which is central to the development of compassion and skillful means in the mahayana. A completely open and unbounded clarity of mind.

skandha   Group, aggregate, or heap. The five skandhas are the five aggregates or psychophysical factors that make up what we generally understand as personality or ego.

sutra   One of the texts on the dharma attributed to the Buddha. A sutra generally takes the form of a discourse by the Buddha and a dialogue with students.

Sword of Manjushri   See *Manjushri.*

tantra   Synonym for vajrayana, one of the three great vehicles of Tibetan Buddhism. *Tantra* literally means "continuity." It may refer to vajrayana texts as well as to the systems of meditation they describe.

tathagatagarbha Buddha nature, the enlightened basic nature of all beings, is a central theme of the Mahayana. *Tathagata* is an epithet of the Buddha that means "he who has gone beyond." *Garbha* means "womb" or "essence."

thangka Form of Tibetan religious painting that depicts the gurus, mandalas, deities, and other iconographical aspects of the vajrayana.

Trisong Detsen Eighth-century Tibetan king who was a famous proponent of Buddhism and established Samye, the first monastery in Tibet.

tulku Tibetan for *nirmanakaya, tulku* often refers to the incarnation of a previously enlightened teacher. See also *kaya*.

vajra (Tibetan *dorje*) Adamantine or having the qualities of a diamond. In the vajrayana, *vajra* refers to the basic indestructible nature of wisdom and enlightenment. A vajra is also a tantric ritual scepter representing a thunderbolt, the scepter of the king of the gods, Indra.

vajrayana Diamond way or the indestructible vehicle, vajrayana is the third of the three great yanas of Tibetan Buddhism. It is synonymous with tantra and is sometimes subdivided into four or six subsidiary yanas.

vidyadhara Title for a vajrayana teacher, signifying a holder of wisdom or a crazy wisdom lineage holder.

Vimalamitra Indian teacher who, along with Guru Rinpoche, brought the teachings of maha ati, or dzogchen, to Tibet in the eighth century.

vipashyana Awareness practice. Shamatha and vipashyana together constitute the basic practice of meditation. Vipashyana also refers to the development of insight and discriminating awareness in meditation practice. It is the hallmark of the development of egolessness in the hinayana.

visual dharma Term for visual arts that embody the principles of egolessness and nonaggression. See also *dharma art*.

yana Vehicle in which, symbolically, the practitioner travels on the road to enlightenment. The different vehicles, or yanas, correspond to different views of the journey, and each yana comprises a body of knowledge and practice. The three great yanas in Tibetan Buddhism are the hinayana, mahayana, and vajrayana.

Acknowledgments

THE PUBLICATION OF *The Essential Chögyam Trungpa* provides an opportunity to thank many of the people who have helped in the creation of Chögyam Trungpa's books. Certainly, the audiences he spoke to and the community of his students should receive a general acknowledgment, for most of his books were based on his lectures. These teachings were not given in a vacuum; the richness and diversity of the audiences helped to color the talks. Thanks also to all those who have made and preserved the recordings and transcriptions of Chögyam Trungpa's lectures.

Enormous thanks are due to the author's dedicated editors: Esme Cramer Roberts (now deceased), Richard Arthure, John Baker, Marvin Casper, Sherab Chödzin, Judith Lief, David I. Rome, and Sarah Coleman—and to the other editors who worked on Chögyam Trungpa's books and articles. These editors have played a major role in shaping the author's books, and often their individual inspiration has led to the decision to publish a particular manuscript.

Larry Mermelstein, Scott Wellenbach, and other members of the Nalanda Translation Committee have translated many of Chögyam Trungpa's writings from Tibetan, reviewed the translation of Sanskrit and Tibetan terms in many of Trungpa Rinpoche's books, and contributed in many other ways. A thank-you to all of the translators who worked on the author's books over the years. This certainly extends to those who worked so hard to translate his books into other languages, especially Richard Gravel.

Samuel Bercholz, the editor in chief and founder of Shambhala Publications, has supported the publication of works by Chögyam Trungpa both during the author's lifetime and posthumously. Mr. Bercholz has published both the popular and the more scholarly works and has shown a commitment to the entire canon of Chögyam Trungpa's teachings. Emily Hilburn Sell, editor at Shambhala Publications, has worked on more than a dozen of Chögyam Trungpa's titles and works with several of his editors. Thanks are due to many other staff at Shambhala Publications, especially Hazel Bercholz, Jonathan Green, and Jacquie Giorgi.

Mrs. Diana J. Mukpo, the author's widow, continues to support the publication of his dharma teachings. Her dedication to seeing her husband's teachings made available has been inspiring. A debt of thanks is owed to her and to the Mukpo family.

For help in preparing the manuscript of *The Essential Chögyam Trungpa*, I would like to thank Samuel Bercholz, Emily Sell, Judith Lief, David Rome, Sherab Chödzin, and Scott Wellenbach for editorial suggestions. In addition, I would like to thank my editor at Shambhala Publications, Emily Sell, for insight, inspiration, and the occasional glass of white wine; Helen Berliner for the index; Scott Wellenbach and Larry Mermelstein for reviewing parts of the manuscript and the glossary; and James Gimian for patience and a keen eye.

About the Author

THE VENERABLE CHÖGYAM TRUNGPA was born in the province of Kham in eastern Tibet in 1940. When he was just thirteen months old, Chögyam Trungpa was recognized as a major *tulku*, or incarnate teacher. According to Tibetan tradition, an enlightened teacher is capable, based on his or her vow of compassion, of reincarnating in human form over a succession of generations. Before dying, such a teacher leaves a letter or other clues to the whereabouts of the next incarnation. Later, students and other realized teachers look through these clues and, based on careful examination of dreams and visions, conduct searches to discover and recognize the successor. Thus, particular lines of teaching are formed, in some cases extending over several centuries. Chögyam Trungpa was the eleventh in the teaching lineage known as the Trungpa Tulkus.

Once young tulkus are recognized, they enter a period of intensive training in the theory and practice of the Buddhist teachings. Trungpa Rinpoche (*Rinpoche* is an honorific title meaning "precious one"), after being enthroned as supreme abbot of Surmang monastery and governor of Surmang District, began a period of training that would last eighteen years, until his departure from Tibet in 1959. As a Kagyü tulku, his training was based on the systematic practice of meditation and on refined theoretical understanding of Buddhist philosophy. One of the four great lineages of Tibet, the Kagyü is known as the "practice lineage."

At the age of eight, Trungpa Rinpoche received ordination as a novice monk. After his ordination, he engaged in intensive study and practice of the traditional monastic disciplines as well as in the arts of calligraphy, thangka painting, and monastic dance. His primary teachers were Jamgön Kongtrül of Sechen and Khenpo Kangshar—leading teachers in the Nyingma and Kagyü lineages. In 1958, at the age of eighteen, Trungpa Rinpoche completed his studies, receiving the degrees of *kyorpön* (doctor of divinity) and *khenpo* (master of studies). He also received full monastic ordination.

The late fifties were a time of great upheaval in Tibet. As it became clear that the Chinese Communists intended to take over the country by force, many people, both monastic and lay, fled the country. Trungpa Rinpoche spent many harrowing months trekking over the Himalayas (described in his book *Born in Tibet*). After narrowly escaping capture by the Chinese, he at last reached India in 1959. While in India, Trungpa Rinpoche was appointed to serve as spiritual adviser to the Young Lamas Home School in Dalhousie, India. He served in this capacity from 1959 to 1963.

Trungpa Rinpoche's first opportunity to encounter the West came when he received a Spaulding sponsorship to attend Oxford University. At Oxford, he studied comparative religion, philosophy, and fine arts. He also studied Japanese flower arranging, receiving a degree from the Sogetsu School. While in England, Trungpa Rinpoche began to instruct Western students in the dharma (the teachings of the Buddha), and in 1968, he cofounded the Samye Ling Meditation Centre in Dumfriesshire, Scotland. During this period, he also published his first two books, both in English: *Born in Tibet* and *Meditation in Action*.

In 1969, Trungpa Rinpoche traveled to Bhutan, where he entered into a solitary meditation retreat. This retreat marked a pivotal change in his approach to teaching. Immediately upon returning, he became a layperson, putting aside his monastic robes and dressing in ordinary Western attire. He also married a young Englishwoman, Diana Pybus, and together they left Scotland and moved to North America. Many of his early students found these changes shocking and upsetting. However, he expressed a conviction that, in order to take root in the West, the dharma needed to be taught free from cultural trappings and religious fascination.

During the seventies, America was in a period of political and cultural ferment. It was a time of fascination with the East. Trungpa Rinpoche criticized the materialistic and commercialized approach to spirituality he encountered, describing it as a "spiritual supermarket." In his lectures, and in his books *Cutting Through Spiritual Materialism* and *The Myth of Freedom*, he pointed to the simplicity and directness of the practice of sitting meditation as the way to cut through such distortions of the spiritual journey.

During his seventeen years of teaching in North America, Trungpa Rinpoche developed a reputation as a dynamic and controversial teacher. Fluent in the English language, he was one of the first lamas who could speak to Western students directly, without the aid of a translator. Traveling extensively throughout North America and Europe, Trungpa Rinpoche gave hundreds of talks and seminars. He established major centers in Vermont, Colorado, and Nova Scotia, as well as many smaller meditation and study centers in cities throughout North America and Europe. Vajradhatu was formed in 1973 as the central administrative body of this network.

In 1974, Trungpa Rinpoche founded the Naropa Institute, which became the only accredited Buddhist-inspired university in North America. He lectured extensively at the institute, and his book *Journey without Goal* is based on a course he taught there. In 1976, he established the Shambhala Training program, a series of weekend programs and seminars that provides instruction in meditation practice within a secular setting. His book *Shambhala: The Sacred Path of the Warrior* gives an overview of the Shambhala teachings.

In 1976, Trungpa Rinpoche appointed Ösel Tendzin (Thomas F. Rich) as his Vajra Regent, or dharma heir. Ösel Tendzin worked closely with Trungpa Rinpoche in the administration of Vajradhatu and Shambhala Training. He taught extensively from 1976 until his death in 1990 and is the author of *Buddha in the Palm of Your Hand*.

Trungpa Rinpoche was also active in the field of translation. Working with Francesca Fremantle, he rendered a new translation of *The Tibetan Book of the Dead*, which was published in 1975. Later he formed the Nalanda Translation Committee, in order to translate texts and liturgies for his own students as well as to make important texts available publicly.

In 1978, Trungpa Rinpoche conducted a ceremony empowering his son Ösel Rangdröl Mukpo as his successor in the Shambhala lineage. At that time, he gave him the title of Sawang, or "earth lord."

Trungpa Rinpoche was also known for his interest in the arts and particularly for his insights into the relationship between contemplative discipline and the artistic process. Two books published since his death—*The Art of Calligraphy* (1994) and *Dharma Art* (1996)—present this aspect of his work. His own artwork included calligraphy, painting, flower arranging, poetry, playwriting, and environmental installations. In addition, at the Naropa Institute, he created an educational atmosphere that attracted many leading artists and poets. The exploration of the creative process in light of contemplative training continues there as a provocative dialogue. Trungpa Rinpoche also published two books of poetry: *Mudra* and *First Thought Best Thought*. In 1998, a retrospective compilation of his poetry, *Timely Rain,* was published.

In a meeting with the president of Shambhala Publications, Samuel Bercholz, shortly before his death, Chögyam Trungpa expressed his interest in publishing a series of 108 volumes of his teachings, to be called the Dharma Ocean Series. "Dharma Ocean" is the translation of Chögyam Trungpa's Tibetan teaching name, Chökyi Gyatso. The Dharma Ocean Series was to consist primarily of edited transcripts of lectures and seminars, allowing readers to encounter this rich array of teachings simply and directly rather than in an overly systematized or condensed form. In 1991, the first posthumous volume in the series, *Crazy Wisdom*, was published, and since then another half dozen volumes have appeared.

Trungpa Rinpoche's published books represent only a fraction of the rich legacy of his teachings. During his seventeen years of teaching in North America, he crafted the structures necessary to provide his students with thorough, systematic training in the dharma. From introductory talks and courses to advanced group retreat practices, these programs emphasize a balance of study and practice, of intellect and intuition. Students at all levels can pursue their interest in meditation and the Buddhist path through these many forms of training. Senior students of Trungpa Rinpoche continue to be involved in both teaching and meditation instruction in such programs.

In addition to his extensive teachings in the Buddhist tradition, Trungpa Rinpoche also placed great emphasis on the Shambhala teachings, which stress the importance of mind training, as distinct from religious practice; community involvement and the creation of an enlightened society; and appreciation of one's day-to-day life. A second volume of these teachings, entitled *Great Eastern Sun,* will be published in November 1999.

Trungpa Rinpoche passed away in 1987, at the age of forty-seven. He is survived by his wife, Diana, and five sons. His eldest son, the Sawang Ösel Rangdröl Mukpo, succeeds him as president and spiritual head of Vajradhatu. Acknowledging the importance of the Shambhala teachings to his father's work, the Sawang changed the name of the umbrella organization to Shambhala, with Vajradhatu remaining one of its major divisions. In 1995, the Sawang received the title of Sakyong and was also confirmed as an incarnation of the great ecumenical teacher Mipham Rinpoche.

By the time of his death, Trungpa Rinpoche had become known as a pivotal figure in introducing dharma to the Western world. The joining of his great appreciation for Western culture and his deep understanding of his own tradition led to a revolutionary approach to teaching the dharma, in which the most ancient and profound teachings were presented in a thoroughly contemporary way. Trungpa Rinpoche was known for his fearless proclamation of the dharma: free from hesitation, true to the purity of the tradition, and utterly fresh. May these teachings take root and flourish for the benefit of all sentient beings.

Books by Chögyam Trungpa

Books in print are in italic type.[1] An asterisk indicates that material from this title was included in *The Essential Chögyam Trungpa*.

1966   ***Born in Tibet***

Chögyam Trungpa's account of his upbringing and education as an incarnate lama in Tibet and the powerful story of his escape to India. An epilogue added in 1976 details Trungpa Rinpoche's time in England in the 1960s and his early years in North America.

*1969   ***Meditation in Action***

Using the life of the Buddha as a starting point, this classic on meditation and the practice of compassion explores the six paramitas, or enlightened actions on the Buddhist path. Its simplicity and directness make this an appealing book for beginners and seasoned meditators alike. "The Manure of Experience and the Field of Bodhi" is taken from this volume.

*1972   ***Mudra***

This collection of poems mostly written in the 1960s in England also includes two short translations of Buddhist texts (one of which, "Listen, Abushri," is included in *The Essential Chögyam Trungpa*) and a commentary on the ox-herding pictures, well-known metaphors for the journey on the Buddhist path.

*1973   ***Cutting Through Spiritual Materialism***

The first volume of Chögyam Trungpa's teaching in America is still fresh, outrageous, and up-to-date. It describes landmarks on the Buddhist path and focuses on the pitfalls of materialism that plague the modern age. Both "The True Spiritual Path" and "The Spiritual Friend" were drawn from this title.

---

1. This list includes all books by Chögyam Trungpa published by Shambhala Publications. It does not include books by other publishers, nor does it include articles, interviews, and so forth.

1975   *The Dawn of Tantra*

Jointly authored by Chögyam Trungpa and Buddhist scholar Herbert Guenther, this volume presents an introduction to the Buddhist teachings of tantra.

1975   *Glimpses of Abhidharma*

An exploration of the five skandhas, or stages in the development of ego, based on an early seminar given by Chögyam Trungpa. The final chapter on auspicious coincidence is a penetrating explanation of karma and the true experience of spiritual freedom.

1975   *The Tibetan Book of the Dead: The Great Liberation through Hearing in the Bardo*

Chögyam Trungpa and Francesca Fremantle collaborated on the translation and are coauthors of this title. Trungpa Rinpoche provides a powerful commentary on death and dying and on the text itself, which allows modern readers to find the relevance of this ancient guide to the passage from life to death and back to life again.

*1976   *The Myth of Freedom: And the Way of Meditation*

In short, pithy chapters that exemplify Chögyam Trungpa's hard-hitting and compelling teaching style, this book explores the meaning of freedom and genuine spirituality in the context of traveling the Buddhist path. The "Styles of Imprisonment" section that appears in *The Essential Chögyam Trungpa*, as well as the chapters "Cool Boredom," "The Way of the Buddha," "The Bodhisattva Vow," "The Lion's Roar," and "Working with Negativity" are all taken from *The Myth of Freedom*.

*1980   *The Rain of Wisdom*

An extraordinary collection of the poetry, or songs, of the teachers of the Kagyü lineage of Tibetan Buddhism, to which Chögyam Trungpa belonged. The text was translated by the Nalanda Translation Committee under the direction of Chögyam Trungpa. The volume includes an extensive glossary of Buddhist terms. The piercing incantation that opens *The Essential Chögyam Trungpa*, "The Dohā of Confidence: Sad Song of the Four Remembrances," was originally written by Trungpa Rinpoche in Tibetan and included in *The Rain of Wisdom*.

*1981   *Journey without Goal: The Tantric Wisdom of the Buddha*

Based on an early seminar at the Naropa Institute, this guide to the tantric teachings of Buddhism is provocative and profound, emphasizing both the dangers and the wisdom of the vajrayana, the diamond path of Buddhism. *The Essential Chögyam Trungpa* includes three chapters from this volume: "Vajra Nature," "The Five Buddha Families," and "Maha Ati."

1982 *The Life of Marpa the Translator*

A renowned saint of the Tibetan Buddhist tradition who combined scholarship and meditative realization, Marpa made three arduous journeys to India to collect the teachings of the Kagyü lineage and bring them to Tibet. Chögyam Trungpa and the Nalanda Translation Committee have produced an inspiring translation of his life's story.

1983 *First Thought Best Thought: 108 Poems*

This collection emphasized Chögyam Trungpa's poetry from his first ten years in North America, showing his command of the American idiom, his understanding of American culture, as well as his playfulness and his passion. Some poems from earlier years were also included. Many of the poems from *First Thought Best Thought* have been reprinted in the newly released *Timely Rain*.

*1984 *Shambhala: The Sacred Path of the Warrior*

An attitude of fearlessness and open heart provide us with the courage to meet the challenges of modern life. Chögyam Trungpa's classic on warriorship still offers timely advice. "Creating an Enlightened Society," "Discovering Basic Goodness," "The Genuine Heart of Sadness," "Discovering Magic," and "The Universal Monarch" are all taken from this volume.

*1991 *Crazy Wisdom*

Two seminars from the 1970s were edited for this volume on the life and teachings of Guru Rinpoche, or Padmasambhava, the founder of Buddhism in Tibet. "Padmasambhava and Spiritual Materialism" and "Crazy Wisdom" were both excerpted from this title.

*1991 *The Heart of the Buddha*

A collection of essays by Chögyam Trungpa. "Meditation and Mind" and "Acknowledging Death" appear in *The Essential Chögyam Trungpa*.

1991 *Orderly Chaos: The Mandala Principle*

The mandala is often thought of as a Buddhist drawing representing tantric iconography. However, Chögyam Trungpa explores how both confusion and enlightenment are made up of patterns of orderly chaos that are the basis for the principle of mandala. A difficult but rewarding discussion of the topic of chaos and its underlying structure.

*1992   *Transcending Madness: The Experience of the Six Bardos*

The editor of this volume, Judith Lief, calls it "a practical guide to Buddhist psychology." The book is based on two early seminars on the intertwined ideas of *bardo* (or the gap in experience and the gap between death and birth) and the six realms of being. "The Lonely Journey" is excerpted from this book.

*1993   *Training the Mind: And Cultivating Loving-Kindness*

An original translation and a commentary on fifty-nine slogans that show a practical path to making friends with oneself and developing compassion for others, through the practice of sacrificing self-centeredness for the welfare of others. The chapter "Compassion" is drawn from this volume.

1994   *The Art of Calligraphy: Joining Heaven and Earth*

Chögyam Trungpa's extensive love affair with brush and ink is showcased in this book, which also includes an introduction to dharma art and a discussion of the Oriental principles of heaven, earth, and man as applied to the creative process. The beautiful reproductions of fifty-four calligraphies are accompanied by inspirational quotations by the author.

*1994   *Illusion's Game: The Life and Teaching of Naropa*

The great Indian teacher Naropa was a renowned master of the teachings of mahamudra, an advanced stage of realization in Tibetan Buddhism. This book presents Chögyam Trungpa's teachings on Naropa's life and his arduous search for enlightenment. The chapter "Mahamudra" was taken from this book.

*1995   *The Path Is the Goal: A Basic Handbook of Buddhist Meditation*

A simple and practical manual for the practice of meditation that evokes the author's penetrating insight and colorful language. "Mindfulness and Awareness" was based on a chapter in this book.

*1996   *Dharma Art*

Chögyam Trungpa was a calligrapher, painter, poet, designer, and photographer—as well as a master of Buddhist meditation. Drawn from his many seminars and talks on the artistic process, this volume presents his insights into art and the artist. "The Art of the Great Eastern Sun" and "Art in Everyday Life" were taken from this book.

*1998   *Timely Rain: Selected Poetry of Chögyam Trungpa*

With a foreword by Allen Ginsberg, this volume of Chögyam Trungpa's poetry was organized thematically by editor David I. Rome to show the breadth of the poet's work. Core poems from *Mudra* and *First Thought Best Thought* are reoffered here, along with many poems and "sacred songs" newly published by Shambhala Publications (although some have appeared in small-press publications). "Afterthought," "Looking into the World," and "Meteoric Iron Mountain" were taken from *Timely Rain*.

*1999   *The Great Eastern Sun: The Wisdom of Shambhala*

The sequel and complement to *Shambhala: The Sacred Path of the Warrior*, to be published in November 1999, brings more heartfelt wisdom from this master of Shambhala warriorship. The first chapter, "The Kingdom, the Cocoon, the Great Eastern Sun," appears in *The Essential Chögyam Trungpa*.

Resources

For further information regarding meditation or inquiries about a meditation center near you, please contact:

Shambhala International
1084 Tower Road
Halifax, Nova Scotia
Canada B3H 2Y5
Telephone: (902) 425-4275, extension 10
E-mail: shambint@shambhala.org
Web site: www.shambhala.org. The Web site contains information about the more than one hundred centers affiliated with Shambhala.

For Europe, please contact:

Shambhala Europe
Wilhelmstrasse 20
D35037 Marburg, Germany
Telephone: 49 6421 17020
E-mail: europe@shambhala.org

For publications from Shambhala International, please contact:

Vajradhatu Publications
1084 Tower Road
Halifax, Nova Scotia
Canada B3H 2Y5
Telephone: (902) 420-1118, extension 18
E-mail: vajrapub@shambhala.org

For audiotape and videotape recordings, please contact:

Kalapa Recordings
1084 Tower Road
Halifax, Nova Scotia
Canada B3H 2Y5
Telephone: (902) 420-1118, extension 19
E-mail: recordings@shambhala.org
Web site: www.shambhala.org/recordings

For information about Buddhist postsecondary education, call or write:

The Naropa Institute
2130 Arapahoe Avenue
Boulder, Colorado 80302
U.S.A.
Telephone: (303) 444-0202

For information about the archive of the author's work—which includes more than 5,000 audio recordings, 1,000 video recordings, original Tibetan manuscripts, correspondence, and more than 30,000 photographs—please contact:

The Shambhala Archives
1084 Tower Road
Halifax, Nova Scotia
Canada B3H 2Y5
Telephone: (902) 425-4275, extension 21
Web site: www.shambhala.org/archives

INDEX

Body, mindfulness and, 129–130
Boredom, 87–91
  cool, 87, 91
  in filmmaking, 89
  in meditation practice, 89
  styles of, 90
Born in Tibet (Trungpa), ix
Brahma, 110–111
Bravery, 5–6, 29
  essence of, 10
Breath (in meditation), 91, 92
Buddha, Shakyamuni, 3, 12, 104–107
  Brahma and, 110–111
  enlightenment of, 92
  as grain of sand, 93
  on meditation, 44–46, 78, 82–83,
    91–93
Buddha (buddha family), 162, 167–
    168, 169
Buddhadharma, 82
  without credentials, 88, 125
  in Tibet, 48, 54
Buddhahood, attainment of, 46–47
Buddha nature, 105, 120, 146
  Great Eastern Sun and, 30
  identifying with, 115
Buddhism
  lexicon of, in West, xii
  meditation as way of, 76–77
  mind in, 77
  schools of, 197
  Shambhala kingdom and, 3

Casualness, 21
Chaos, 11, 114–116, 187
  as good news, 123
  psychic energies and, 181
Charlatanism, 126
A Child's Garden of Verses (Steven-
    son), 25
Chödzin, Sherab, x
Clear light, 160
  vs. mahayana luminosity, 160
  vs. vajrayana brilliance/clarity, 160
Clear seeing. *See* Awareness
Co-emergent wisdom, 172
Compassion, 93, 117–122
  absolute bodhichitta and, 121–122
  destroying karma/action and, 182
  with ego, 107
  in healer-patient relationship,
    131–132
  idiot, 180

as soft spot/open wound, 118–120
as total openness, 93
Competitiveness, 63, 66
Compromise, 189–190
Concentration (in meditation),
  83–84
  vs. mindfulness, 83, 88
Concepts/theories
  crazy wisdom and, 182–183
  fourth skandha and, 57
  imagination and, 112
  as starting point to wisdom, 104,
    106–112
  transmission through, 186
  transparency of, 46
  as way to solidify world, 46
Conditionality, 22, 36
Confusion
  acknowledging, 114–116
  bodhisattva vow and, 114–116
  as Godhead, 52
  heart of, 41
  Lord of Mind and, 43
  samsara as ocean of, 62
  simultaneous realization and, 172
  spirituality and, 50, 53
  styles of, 59
Consciousness
  alaya (8th), 118, 121–122
  fantasy worlds of, 58
  fifth skandha and, 58
  "ordinary," 172–173
  perception and, 23
Contemplation, 12
Continuity, meditation and, 80
Cool boredom, 87–91
  as "anticredential," 89
  in hinayana, 89–90
Cosmic elegance, 29
Cosmic joke, 55–58
Cosmic mirror, 22
  wisdom of, 24, 27
Cosmic monster, 119
Cosmic wound, 120
Cowardice, 28, 29
  space and, 36
Crazy Horse (Native American war-
    rior), 201
Crazy wisdom, 53–54, 182–183, 186–
    195, 201–203
  chaos and, 191–192
  as characteristic of "saint," 54
  definition of, 201–202

Exhibitionistic art, 94–95, 98
Expectation(s), 111
  cutting through, 54
  in meditation, 84
Experience, manure of, 103–113

Fear
  of death, 111, 127, 132
  of emotions, 124
  of foreignness, 82
  of loss, 127
  setting sun world and, 29
Fearlessness, 5, 28, 178
  birth of, 20
  crazy wisdom, 202–203
  generosity as gift of, 117
  lion's roar as proclamation of, 124, 125
Fifth skandha (consciousness), 58
Filmmaking, boredom in, 89
Fire element, 165
First skandha (basic ignorance/ form), 56
First thought–best thought, 30–31
  gap and, 31
Five buddha families, 162–170
  as bridge between tantra/everyday life, 169–170
  mandala of, 168–169
Five skandhas, 56–58
  as shield from insubstantiality, 58
Fixation
  dualistic, 55
  intellectual, of vajra family, 164
  as stronghold of ego, 76–77
Flower arranging, 26, 32
Food, 71
Foreignness, fear of, 82
Four-armed mahakala, 183–185
Four aspects of mindfulness, 83–84
Four foundations of mindfulness, 85
Four karmas/actions, 181–182
Four noble truths, 92
Four stages of meeting spiritual friend, 143
Fourth abhisheka, 188
Fourth skandha (intellect/concept), 57–58
Four wheels of chariot. See Four aspects
  of mindfulness
Freedom, 9
  as absence of struggle, 46

Freemantle, Francesca, ix
Frivolousness, 180–182
  vs. spontaneity, 181, 185

Gampopa
  Milarepa and, 149
  on mixing mind with space, 84
Gap(s), 31, 106, 119, 189
  mishandling of, 129
  nowness and, 106
  in self-consciousness, 42
Generosity (Tib. *jinpa*), 117–118
  vs. poverty mentality, 116
  three types of, 117
  as wish-fulfilling jewel, 117
Gesar of Ling (warrior king), 4
Glorious Copper-Colored Mountain (Tib. *Sangdok Pelri*), 195
God realm, 59–62
  as bondage of silkworm, 61
Great (principle), 28
Great Commentary on Kalacakra (Mipham), 3–4
Great Eastern Sun, 28–33
  art of, 28–33
  Occidental, 33
  vs. rising sun, 30
  vs. setting sun, 30
  three attributes of, 30
  three principles of, 28–29
  vision, 29–33
Great Eastern Sun: The Wisdom of Shambhala (Trungpa/ed. Gimian), x
Guru, 134, 140
  relationship with, 149
  universality of, 145–146
  See also Spiritual friend
Guru Rinpoche, 192–195
  See also Padmasambhava

Habitual patterns, 59
Headroom, developing, 200
Healer, role of, 128–129
  See also Health practitioners
Healer-patient relationship, 128–133
  common ground in, 131–132
Healing process, 127–133
  attitude to death and, 127–132
  meditation and, 130
  openness as key to, 128
Health practitioner(s), 127–133
Heaven/earth, 17, 31

Ratna (buddha family), 162, 164–165, 169
Realization
   point of, 110
   simultaneous confusion and, 172
Reference point(s), 158–159
   as conditions of life, 35–37
   as credentials, 125
   indestructibility as being without, 158
   spirituality without, 53
Relative bodhichitta, 121–122
Relaxation, 22, 27
   vs. flopping, 22
Richness (principle), 164–165
Rigden kings, 4
Rome, David I., x

Sacredness, 187
Sacred world, 29, 31, 34
Sadness, genuine heart of, 17–20
Saint Exupéry, Antione de, 25–26
Saint(s)
   in Buddhist tradition, 49
   in Christian tradition, 49
Samadhiraja Sutra (on meditation technique), 83–84
Sambhogakaya, 188
Samsara, 55–56, 62
   as entrance/vehicle for nirvana, 106
   meditation and, 106
   nonparticipation in vs. boycotting, 159
Samurai tradition, 5
Satipatthana (resting in intelligence), 85
Second skandha (feeling), 56–57
Secret doctrine, no such thing as, 105
Secular enlightenment, ix, 5
Seeing things as they are, 53
Self, sense of, 41–42
   as heart of confusion, 41
   perception and, 77–78
Self-absorption, 59–62
Self-consciousness
   gaps in, 42
   Lord of Mind and, 43
Selflessness, discovery of, 56
Sense perception(s), 23–27
   discovering drala through, 24–27
   sacredness of, 23
Sense pleasures (in mahamudra), 174

Setting sun style
   art, 29
   fear and, 29
   in Japanese tradition, 32
   space and, 36
   world, 29
Shamatha practice, 80–84
   combing vipashyana and, 84, 121–122
   mindfulness in, 81–83
   peace of, 80–81
Shambhala kingdom, 3–5
   Buddhism and, 3
Shambhala path/teachings, x
   essence of, xi
Shambhala vision, 5–10
   humor as basis of, 9
   premise of, 6–7
Shambhala: The Sacred Path of the Warrior (Trungpa), ix
Shunyata (emptiness), 172
   compassion and, 118
   definition of, 118
   problem of nonduality in, 172
Sickness. See Illness/disease
Sign/symbol lineage (Tib. rigdzin da-gyü), 187
Simplicity, 21
   nowness and, 21
   vastness in, 25
Six realms, 58, 59–74
   making friends with, 148
Smriti-upasthana (resting in intelligence), 85
Society, 5
   See also Enlightened society
Soft spot, 118–120
   as embryonic compassion, 119
Solidity
   basic myth of, 44–45
   concepts and, 46
   development of ego and, 56
   as hoax, 55–56
Space, 35–36
   in ati yana, 196
   buddha family and, 167
   freezing, 56
   matter and, 93
   mixing mind with, 84
   putting cosmetics on, 35
   setting sun world and, 36
Spiritual friend, 134–146
   four stages of meeting, 143–146

Vajra (Tib. *dorje*), definition of, 159–160
Vajra (buddha family), 162, 163–164, 169
Vajra clarity, 160–161
Vajradhatu Publications, x
Vajra-hardheadedness, 159
Vajra nature, 157–161
Vajra pride, 175
Vajra scepter, 163
Vajrayana, xi, 157
    dangers of, 157–158
    teacher, 176
    See also Tantra
Vastness
    of perceptions, 23–25
    of simplicity, 25
Victory over three worlds, 31
Vimalamitra (on maha ati), 198
Vipashyana/awareness practice, 84–86, 92–100
    appreciation/artfulness in, 94–99
    combining shamatha and, 84, 121–122
    implications of art in, 98–99
    as ultimate nonviolence, 93

"Waiting at the Window" (Milne), 25
Wakefulness, 28
    of ati yoga, 197
    See also Bodhichitta
Walking meditation, 83–85
Warrior (Tib. *pawo*), 5
    path of, 34–35
    space and, 36
Warriorship, enlightened, 5–6
    challenge of, 37
    essence of, 10
    fruition of, 37
    goal of, 21
    key to, 6
    principles of, 35

Watcher, 88
    artist's, 96
    in awareness practice, 97
    mahamudra and, 172
Water element (in vajra family), 164
Wind element
    jealous god realm and, 63
    karma family and, 167
Wisdom, 189–190
    of All-Accomplishing Action, 166
    of All-Encompassing Space, 168
    coemergent, 172
    concepts/theories and, 104, 106–112, 182–183
    of cosmic mirror, 24, 27
    Discriminating Awareness, 30, 165
    as drala, 24
    of Equanimity, 165
    lineage, 95
    Mirrorlike, 164
    sense perceptions as source of, 23–24
    See also Crazy wisdom
Witness, earth as, 92
Workability, 123–125
Working
    with karmic pattern of America, 147
    with negativity, 179–185
    with oneself, 147–150
    with others, 117, 121, 127
World
    helping the, 16
    sacred, 29, 31, 34

Yeshe Tsogyal, 191–192
    as pregnant tigress, 191–192

Zazen, 90
Zen tradition
    art in, 96
    boredom in, 90
Zhang-zhung (Central Asian kingdom), 4